The Story UNFOLDS

A Personal Journey Through the Word of God

January 2014

Bob Highlands III

The Story Unfolds

A Personal Journey Through the Word of God

ISBN-13:

978-1490530512

ISBN-10:

1490530517

BobHighlands.com

Printed in the United States of America

To

Bob & Beulah Smith

In each of our lives we are privileged to meet certain people who by their very nature enrich us with their presence. Bob and Beulah are such people. They touched my life as a young ministerial student and have been my friends ever since. Their open home and warm hearts are forever part of my story.

Contents

Preface

We all are faced with daily choices and decisions that impact our time and ultimately our lives. It is the small decisions we make day in and day out that determine who we really are. The large decisions may scream for attention, yet they are just the result of all the small decisions we have made, or avoided making, that brought us to that point in life.

The decision to make the study of the Bible a part of a person's life is in many ways one of the small choices we make every day. It takes a few minutes of our time. It takes a small amount of commitment. It requires very little real effort and yet it seems so difficult for so many people to include the Word of God in their daily lives.

There was a time when it was taught in school. It was looked on as the foundation of any good education to know the moral codes contained in the book we know as the Bible. Many would like us to believe that those days are past and the book has somehow lost its value. This is as far from the truth as the east is from the west. The Bible has been banned from many school libraries, and people who once handed it out freely now find their path blocked by laws, and those who want "to protect" our children from religious materials, but that does not reduce its value. In fact it may show how important it is to the enemy, to try and keep the influence of the Bible from our children.

The worth of this book has not diminished. It is needed more today than ever. Each person should make a commitment to hide the Word of God in their heart. They need to know that the truth found within the pages of the Bible can change lives, revive nations and make a difference for eternity.

INSTRUCTIONS

The Story[i] was published in 2010 and 2011 by Zondervan. It is the Bible written as one continuous story. It has removed tedious details and put the events into chronological order. It makes the Bible easier to read and understand. It is designed to be a starter Bible for those who are new to the Word of God or want a fresh approach.

This book is designed to be a companion to The Story. Each chapter of *The Story* is lined up with the chapters in *The Story Unfolds. The Story Unfolds* is designed to add additional information and to allow the reader to go deeper in their personal experience.

Read the corresponding chapter in *the Story* and then read the same chapter number in *the Story Unfolds.* This will allow you to get the maximum use out of both books.

The materials contained in *The Story Unfolds* are from the preaching, teaching and ministerial experiences of the author, Bob Highlands.

Bible quotes in *The Story Unfolds* are from the New International Version 1984 edition unless otherwise noted.

The study notes at the end of each chapter include the page number in *The Story* (TS) so you can look up and find the information to answer the questions.

The ultimate goal is to read *The Story* and understand that it is not only about those whose lives are contained within the pages, but it is also about you.

Throughout the book there are Bible references to the full unabridged Bible. Some of these references are not included in *The Story.* Remember that *The Story* is a special version of the Bible, but it is not the complete

Bible. *The Story* is good place to start reading the Bible to get a complete overview of scriptures but it should not replace or be the only scriptures you use.

Finally let me encourage you to make sure you are practicing the five basic disciplines of the Christian life. I learned these from an old pastor on the day I gave my life to the Lord and surrendered to the ministry. That was over forty years ago now but they are just as true today as they were then.

These five are:

1) Pray every day: You need this contact with God more than you will ever know.
2) Read your Bible everyday: There is more there than you can learn in a lifetime.
3) Attend church: Find a church that is preaching the Word of God and start learning.
4) Support the church: This means giving Time, Talents, and Tithe as a part of the fellowship of local believers.
5) Share what God is doing in your life: If you don't share with your family, friends and people you meet, who will? They need to know about Jesus and you are the one God has placed in their lives.

Now, forty years later, I am the *Old Pastor* sharing this with you. So get in the Word of God, read the Story, and discover its great riches and strength.

The One Thing That Matters Most
The Story Unfolds Introduction

With all the modern gadgets we have to communicate it is remarkable that people know so little about the Bible. This is especially true when we see how available the scriptures are to anyone and everyone. It is the most printed book in history. It is free to download on any smart phone, tablet or computer. Yet the only way it can make any difference in a person's life is if they actually read it and apply the principles found there personally.

THE BIBLE:

The Bible is actually 66 books written over many thousands of years. It comes in two sections. The first section is the Old Testament which was written in Hebrew and Aramaic. These trace the acts of God from the creation of the world, to his developing a close relationship with a special group of people known to us as the Jews. God directs and corrects His people. The Old Testament ends with 400 years of silence as God moves all the pieces into place for a grand plan he has been working on since Adam and Eve sinned in the garden.

The second section is the New Testament. It was written in *Koine* Greek which was the common language of the day. It opens with the four gospels telling the life and sacrifice of Jesus and then moves through Acts and the history of the early church, then through the letters and theology of the Church to finish up in the Book of Revelation. Many do not understand this final book of the Bible, but it really is simple. The message of Revelation says, 'God wins and everyone on God's side wins.' In fact, that message is repeated seven times in the last book of the Bible.

The Bible was not compiled in chronological order. It overlaps and when read through can be very confusing. This, along with all the names, details of sacrifices, tabernacle and temple construction make it, at times, a bog that is almost impossible to get through.

The Bible has a remarkable and storied history. It was translated into Latin early in the life of the church (which was the common language of the time), but as less and less of the general population spoke Latin the Bible became obscured from the general public. It would remain so for the next 1,000 years until 1380 when John Wycliffe tried translating it into common language from Latin. He was persecuted by the established church for this. After his death they found where he had been buried, dug up his body, burned it and declared him a heretic. The next big event for the Bible was when it was published on the Gutenberg press around 1455. This was a great advancement. More people could have it than ever before, the only problem was it was still in Latin. Then, in 1525, William Tyndale started to translate the Bible into common language. He wanted to translate it from Greek and Hebrew text to make sure it was accurate. He worked on this, against the wishes of the church, until 1536 when he was arrested and burned at the stake. Friends finished this translation in 1537. It was the first Bible in common language in over 1,100 years that had been translated from the Greek and Hebrew text.

This was followed by a series of Bible translations to meet the needs of Protestants, Catholics, and various rulers. The Great Bible was the next successful translation. This was followed in England with the Bishop's Bible translation. Then, in 1611, King James ordered a new translation of the Bible. In reality it was just the Bishop's Bible reworked to make the king happy. This became the authorized King James Bible, which remained the leading English Bible translation for over 300 years.

The next great breakthrough came with the uncovering of the Dead Sea Scrolls in 1947. These opened the door to modern translators returning to some of the earliest text available. The most remarkable part of this is that after 1800 years of the Bible being translated and hand copied over and over, the texts were almost exact. The biggest problem was translators' notes that had been included and needed to be removed from the text. Yet, for some Protestants, the King James Bible had become what the Latin Vulgate Bible was to the Catholic Church when Tyndall and Wycliffe worked to translate it. Even though it is in English that was used over 400 years ago they hold to it with a devotion that overlooks its weaknesses and use of inferior text from which it was translated.

Today there are dozens of translations of the Bible in English. I counted 27 versions that I have access to on my smart phone. It is available on the internet in 100s of languages for free. YET if people do not read it and apply it to their lives, what good is it?

THE STORY

The Story is the Bible as one continuous narration. It has 31 chapters that cover the main themes and people in the Bible. The stories are placed in chronological order for better understanding. Transitions have been added, but are clearly marked so as not to be confused with the Bible text. The Bible translation used is the New International Version published in 1978. When you read The Story you are reading The Bible. The key differences are the order it is in and the many details that are skipped or jumped over to keep the Story from bogging down the average reader.

The story comes in two parts. There is the story from God's point of view. This is the large picture without time restraints or human limitations. This is the story we see in the first chapter of Genesis as we watch God create everything. There is also the story from the viewpoint of humanity. It is confined to the perspective and the time of individuals. It is defined by the moment and current events. This limited story is seen when we look, not at all of creation, but at Adam and Eve and their personal life struggles against temptation and sin. It is this Story in two parts: through God's eyes and through the eyes of everyday people we will look at, and see if we can understand over the next 31 chapters.

GETTING THE MOST OUT OF THE WORD

"Emperor Menelik II was an African ruler who defeated the Italian army at Adwa in 1896 and established the nation of Ethiopia. He believed the Bible had power to cure illness, and he would eat a few pages of it any time he felt sick. He suffered a stroke in 1913, after which he ate the entire Book of Kings. As a result, his bowels became obstructed and he died of related complications."[2]

This is not a way to get the best and most out of your Bible. Now it does need to get on the inside of you, but not into your stomach. You need the word in your heart and mind. When tempted by Satan it was Jesus who said, "*It is written; 'Man does not live on bread alone, but, on every word that comes from the mouth of God.'*" Matthew 4.4 The Bible is intended to be part of our protection from doing evil, and missing the mark, or coming up short of what God has set for each of our lives. The psalmist put it well when he wrote, "*I have hidden your word in my heart that I might not sin against you.*" Psalm 119.12 When everything is whittled down to its core it really is only a matter of directions and there are only two directions to from which to choose.

All Scripture is inspired by God and profitable for teaching, for reproof, for correction, for training in righteousness; so that the man of God may be adequate, equipped for every good work. 2 Timothy 3.16-17

This scripture shows us one of the two directions life can take and what it takes to keep going the right way. The teaching of scripture gets us pointed in the right direction, but sometimes we make a wrong choice and stray from where we should be. That is when the scriptures rebuke or show us we are going the wrong way. If we listen, then we will follow the correction and get back on the right path. If we fail to do this, and continue away from the teachings of scripture as inspired by the Holy Spirit, we move from needing correcting to needing to repent because we have sinned.

Our Goal is to stay on the path of righteousness or the path of making correct decisions each day. This is the direction the believer's life is to take. Those who reject scripture and the teachings of God have chosen to take the other path. They are choosing a life of unrighteousness. They are being disobedient to God by ignoring the teachings, rebukes, correction, and path of righteousness. We each must choose which path we will take, but we always need to be aware that God is watching the decisions we are making.

WHAT YOU NEED TO DO?

When I was a small boy, four or five years old, I would visit my grandmother at her country house. Now she was not rich, just the opposite was true. It was not only their country house, it was their only house. It had no running water and limited electrical connections. There was a hand pump at the kitchen sink and there was one in the front yard. If you wanted water you had to pump the handle to get it. My brother and I loved to play on the pump in the front yard. We could just reach the handle, but boy could we pump. We would start pumping and listen, as with each stroke, we could hear the water rising in the pump. Then, suddenly, the water would come gushing out. The water was always waiting, but we had to pump the handle to get it. We also had to keep pumping the handle to keep the water flowing. That is what Jesus was talking about when he said:

"*Give, and it will be given to you. They will pour into your lap a good measure—pressed down, shaken together, and running over. For by your standard of measure it will be measured to you in return.*" Luke 6.38

If you are going to succeed spiritually you have to do your part. The living water is waiting to come into your life, but you need to pump the handle. That includes prayer, Bible reading, giving, sharing your faith, and finding a personal ministry. You need to stretch, evaluate, and devote if it is going to work. You have to stretch and do things you have not done before. You have to evaluate your life decisions and make changes where they are needed. You will have to decide what to keep doing, what to stop, and what new things you need to do. You have to devote yourself; that means you will sacrifice, surrender and spend the time necessary to keep on the path of righteousness.

In the end, it comes down to you and your commitment to getting to know God through the Story. You will see things from God's point of view and from man's point of view, and you will see how God has prepared the whole story so it unfolds just for you.

INTRODUCTION Review

How many books in the Bible?

How many parts is the Bible divided into?

What is different in the way The Story was put together?

According to 2 Timothy 3.16-17 what are four reasons we should study scripture? Why is each one important to the believer?

1.

2.

3.

4.

Three Questions
The Story Unfolds Chapter 1

Genesis 3.1-14

The garden went from paradise to chaos in a very short period of time. The transition was seamless and almost predictable when we look at it from our point of view. Yet, in the original setting it was anything but preordained. We have the appearance of a completely new set of characters interacting with each other at the beginning of the story.

UNANSWERED QUESTION

First, there is the man and woman. They are innocent to the dangers that are real and which they have never faced before. They are like small children who are being watched over by their parents who know the danger and want to protect them as long as possible. Then, there is the serpent that we later learn is also known as Satan and the Devil. This evil being will remain the protagonist of humanity and God until the end of time. Now I want to start with a fact that the Bible DOES NOT tell us. This may seem to be a contradiction of terms to speak of a fact and then say we do not have the information. The popular belief or fact is that the serpent was once a beautiful angel in heaven who rebelled against God and was thrown out of heaven with his followers. This is not true. Wait, let me explain. It is the common belief held by many, based in most part, not on scripture, but on the work of John Milton called Paradise Lost. In this epic poem Milton mixes scripture, conjuncture and pure imagination to create a story that is no more Biblically true than an Archie comic book. Here is what you need to know. There never has been sin in heaven. There never will be sin in heaven. Heaven is a perfect place. If there had been sin in heaven it would not be a perfect place, and it would be a place where sin could invade again. That is just not the case. So where does the serpent come from? The Bible just does not tell us. The only way you get what Milton wrote about is to glue verses from Isaiah, Ezekiel, Matthew,

Thessalonians, and Revelation together that have nothing to do with each other. The Bible does not tell us everything, but it does tell us what God wants us to know. There are some things that we just don't have the answer to.

THE 'S' WORD

Questions that have answers are easier to deal with. Like the question, "what is the definition of SIN?" Now, here is a question the Bible DOES give us the answer to. In fact even before Eve sinned she knew the answer to this question. When the serpent first approached Eve to eat she said, "*but God did say.*" She had directions from God.

First we learn that SIN IS WHAT GOD SAYS SIN IS!

Eve knew what God had said and she now had to choose whether she would obey or disobey. God is the creator, the beginning and the end. We may see ourselves as someplace in the middle but we all will get to the end and then we have to face God. God is the adult in the room. (more on this in a moment)

Second we learn that SIN IS LAWLESSNESS. **1 John 3.4**

That means sin is breaking the rules. Now let me illustrate this using my grandson. When he comes over to our house he knows the rules. He has always had rules. When he was one and a half he would come over to play. He loved to go into grandma's kitchen and get into the pots and pans cabinet. He would drag them all out on the floor and beat on them, smack them together, and when he was done he would crawl into the cabinet and play there. There is a second half to this. When in the kitchen, he was not allowed to get into the drawer containing the sharp knives. He was not to even touch the handle of that drawer. He did not understand the danger, but he knew that was a NO TOUCH item. Grandpa, grandma, mommy and daddy could touch it but not the little grandson. It came with a repeated DANGER warning. Now the tree in the garden came with a NO TOUCH warning. It could hurt them, and they would die, whatever that meant. It was for God only because he was the adult in the room, or in this case, the garden. Why was the tree in the garden where Adam and Eve could touch it? Well, why are there knives in a kitchen? They belong there, and though we do not understand it, the tree of the knowledge of Good and Evil belonged in the Garden. It was supposed to be there and we will just have to accept it. Let's go back to my grandson for a second. There were more items in the kitchen he could touch than those he was not to touch. Eve and Adam had more positive choices than negative choices but when they touched and ate they learned the third truth about sin.

Third we learn that SIN HAS CONSEQUENCES.

Fewer and fewer people today believe in sin and that they will pay for the wrong choices. They are denying the creator and his rules for the Garden and the world in which we live. The truth of the matter is that sinning leads to death. Death is being separated from God. Death is temporary as long as we are alive and can still change our course, but it becomes permanent when we die physically and have not changed course.

WELL, EXCUSE ME!

There are plenty of people who want to say that sin is excusable, or that they are not responsible for their actions. You will not find this in the story that God laid out for us. It is what people say who want to convince themselves and others sin is not sin but acceptable behavior. They are wrong. Sin is still sin, even in our modern world.

WHO IS RESPONSIBLE THEN?

Was it the woman who touched first? Was it the serpent that put her up to it? Was it the man who just stood there and watched not saying anything? Was it God's fault for putting the tree there in the first place? God held Eve and Adam responsible for their actions, and he holds us responsible for our actions. I read about a study done on twins. One set was raised in a home where both parents were alcoholics. The one twin was an alcoholic. When they asked him why he was an alcoholic he blamed his parents. They had been his example. The other twin was a teetotaler. That means he did not drink any alcoholic beverages under any circumstances. When asked why, he cited his parents' drinking. Here we have two identical twins in the same environment and exactly the opposite results. They made their choices and they would each have to live with the results. The garden was the perfect environment, and both of the first two children of God sinned while living there, and God held them responsible for their actions. "*The soul who sins is the one who will die.*" Ezekiel 18.4 That was true in the garden, it was true in the time of Ezekiel, and it is still true today. You are responsible for your choices.

IS IT SOCIALLY ACCEPTABLE?

Today we are being told that standards have changed, and what was a sin in times gone by is no longer a sin. People have progressed and everyone is doing it. Well everyone in the garden had progressed to the point of eating from the tree of knowledge of good and evil. Literally, everyone was doing it. That did not change the results that God had said would happen if they touched or ate of the tree. We need to remember who sets the standards of what is and is not sin. In the kitchen at our house, the grandchildren do not set the standards. In the garden and in the world, we do not get to set the standards. Remember, God is the adult here when it comes to what is considered right and wrong.

IS IT A PRIVATE MATTER?

What happens in a person's home or between consenting adults is different according to the new standards. That means if we hide it then it is ok. Well, not according to

God. Adam and Eve were hiding, and they were consenting adults, and they had to pay the price for disobeying God. That has not changed. Everyone who sins in public or private has to deal with it before God.

TEMPTATION EYES **1 John 2.16**

When Eve looked at the fruit of the tree she saw "*that the fruit of the tree was good for food and pleasing to the eye, and also desirable for gaining wisdom.*" Genesis 3.6 Now she had her excuses lined up for eating. It was all beneficial and for her good. The truth is "*everything in the world—the cravings of sinful man, the lust of his eyes and the boasting of what he has and does—comes not from the Father but from the world.*"1 John 2.16 We have to choose between the physical world or the spiritual world. We choose between listening to God, or listening to the serpent. He is still whispers into people's hearts what they need to touch and eat. He wants people to listen to him and not to God.

Eve saw it was GOOD FOR FOOD.

These are the CRAVINGS of sinful man justified as needs. This is calling gluttony, eating. This is calling the lust of the flesh, natural desires that should not be denied. This is giving in to the base desires and saying they are necessary and proper.

Eve saw it was PLEASING TO THE EYE.

Greed is the need to own and to control, it is desire to have more than anyone else. The LUST OF THE EYES is to be controlled by the amount of things you own or the amount of money you have in the bank. This is about power and control. It makes the person important by what they have. Often, the opposite is true. It not the person who has the possessions, but the person who is possessed by everything they have.

Eve saw it was DESIRABLE FOR GAINING WISDOM.

People with worldly wisdom have the ability to think on a higher plane, to be smarter than other people, even being smarter than God. This is BOASTING that comes through knowledge. This is the modern man who knows so much about creation that he or she denies the creator. The person who is so smart that they refute the wisdom of thousands of years because they have progressed so far in learning they can change God's rules and directions. Eve was the first one to say this, but she was far from the last. Every generation has those who say exactly the same things as they deny God's word and authority as creator to set the rules for his garden, world, and kitchen. God is the adult in the room, but so few are listening to Him.

THREE QUESTIONS?

There are three questions we need to be able to answer. They were first asked of Eve and Adam in the garden but they are just as relevant today as they were then. God called out to them in the garden and wanted to know where they were. Then He wanted to know who they had been talking to and told them that they were naked. Finally He wanted to know what they had done. He already knew the answer to the questions He was asking. He wanted them to realize what they had done. They could not hide. They had to know that they had taken bad directions and that their actions were the reason they were in their current predicament.

Question ONE - WHERE ARE YOU?

God came looking for Eve and Adam. He is looking for everyone and is calling to each person to respond. Are you hiding from God, living in the trees where you feel safe, and hoping that he does not notice you are not around? You might want to make a personal evaluation of your life. Take stock of where you are in your spiritual relationship with God. Do you have a spiritual life plan, or are you just hoping you make it through without being noticed by the creator? He cares and is looking for you.

Question TWO - WHO ARE YOU LISTENING TO?

God asked them, *who told you were naked*? Who have you been talking to? We are either listening on the human, physical level where we do not take into account the final outcome of our actions, or we are listening on the spiritual level where we know God is aware and sees all, and where we trust his judgment. The physical level is about feelings, and the spiritual level is about faith. The physical level is where the serpent operates, and the spiritual level is where God guides and protects.

Question THREE - WHAT HAVE YOU DONE?

We will all give an accounting for our lives someday. Getting ready for that moment the believer needs to first acknowledge some things that he/she needs to stop doing. Actions or attitudes that need to be corrected should be corrected. The believer should also look at the things in life that need to be repeated. Things that need to become life habits. These actions and attitudes are the way a person should live his/her life. There are things you need to stop doing and things you need to start doing. Here is the challenge. You need to answer these three questions honestly. You need to know that excuses or hiding out will not get you past God. You have choices to make, and, if you are reading this, it is not too late.

Where are you?
God wants to know.
Who are you listening to?
God wants it to be Him.
What have you done?
God wants you to make changes.

God will ask you these questions face to face sooner than you think, and you need to be ready when He does. You will have another opportunity to respond to these three questions at the end of this book.

Review Chapter 1 From The Story

Can you identify the following People or Places?

Adam

Eve

Cain

Abel

Noah

Shem, Ham, Jepheth

What happened on Each Day of Creation?

1.

2.

3.

4.

5.

6.

7.

Page numbers are from The Story

1. How would you describe God's feelings during the creation process? Pages 1-3

2. Describe how and why God made woman. Page 4

3. What caused the Woman to decide she wanted to try some of the forbidden fruit? Page 5 (list at least three reasons)

4. How did Cain's response to God lead to his actions against his brother? Page 7

5. How does God change as he watches humanity grow and develop? Page 8

6. What challenges did Noah face, that are similar to challenges we face in modern times? Page 8

7. How many people were on the ark to start over? List them here. Page 9

8. What covenant (contract) did God establish with Noah, and what did he use as the sign so everyone would remember? Page 11

9. Give at least four examples of God's judgment in chapter one.

10. Give at least four examples of God's love in chapter one.

11. What one thing in this chapter did you learn that can help you on your personal faith journey?

Faith for Daily Living
The Story Unfolds Chapter 2

Do you know what faith is? Many people think faith is what God does for them; that it is about receiving blessings and physical benefits in return for believing. Faith is almost exactly the opposite of that. The first thing you need to know for sure is that FAITH IS NOT ABOUT YOU! Faith is about you and your relationship with God. When you leave God out of your faith equation, you end up sinning.

WHAT FAITH IS NOT.......

It may seem like a strange place to start, but if we can know what faith is not, then we can prepare ourselves for what faith is. When the Devil approached Jesus in the wilderness he tried to get Jesus to use his relationship with God for selfish reasons. The word faith does not appear here but the remarkable part of the exchange between Jesus and the Devil is that everything Jesus is tempted to do is what many today think faith really is. Jesus was hungry after a forty day fast. The Devil wanted Him to turn some stones into bread. This is about a selfish desire to take care of yourself and use your relationship with God for personal needs and gains. There are a lot of believers today who would see nothing wrong with this. Jesus knew it was wrong and said that the spiritual trumps the physical. "*Man does not live on bread alone but on every word that comes out of the mouth of God.*" Wow, extreme hunger does not allow a person to use their relationship with God for personal gain. You can pray for healing, or jobs or physical needs, but you cannot demand or even force God to take care of these. He has a plan for your life and the tough times may be necessary to get you where He needs or wants you to be. (The next chapter deals with this in detail when we look at the life of Joseph and his ultimate understanding of why God allowed him to face such a tough life.) FAITH is not about getting my physical needs taken care of.

Then the Devil wanted Jesus to show how powerful He was by throwing himself down from the top of the temple. Because He was God's only son, the Devil told him, the angels would be sent to catch Him. At least that is how the Devil saw it. The Devil wants you to believe you can do things others cannot do because you are a believer. Jesus knew it was wrong "*to put God to the test.*" He knew that God's laws apply to everyone equally and to misuse the relationship with God for personal or stupid reasons was not acceptable. The kings of Israel, without exception, fell prey to this lie. They thought they could do anything as God's representatives here on earth, and in every case, they were punished by God for stepping over this line. When we ignore God's laws we will pay the price. Jesus knew that, and it is a lesson we need to remember. FAITH is not about being protected by God when we do something stupid.

The Devil was not done yet. How rich did Jesus want to be? This one is really popular today. All you have to do is bow down and worship the Devil and he will give you riches beyond your imagination. This is exactly what happened to Esau when he gave up his birthright for a bowl of stew. That seems really stupid to me. One passing meal for a lifetime's birthright that would buy you more stew than anyone could imagine. Hey, how much money or gold or land or stocks will you accept in return for submitting to the lies of the Devil? Jesus knew we must "*worship and serve God only.*" To put a price on it was not part of the covenant or contract. How many today are following preachers who tell them that their faith is evident in how richly God rewards them? Nothing could be further from the truth. FAITH is not about how richly God rewards me with earthly treasures.

WHAT FAITH REALLY IS....

If we want to know what faith is, we need to remember the four rules of interpreting scripture: 1. Scripture interprets scripture. 2. The easy explains the difficult. 3. Nothing taken out of context. 4. Jesus is Boss! We learn the story about Abraham and his faith connection in the book of Genesis but we have to go to the New Testament book of Hebrews to learn what faith is. Here is the New Testament interpreting the Old Testament. The eleventh chapter of Hebrews is the faith chapter. Here we learn what faith really is. The greatest problem is most people lift a verse or two out of this chapter to prove what they believe instead of learning what the scripture says faith is. So let us take a look and learn what faith really is. There are five things we can learn for sure about faith from this chapter, and most of them are directly connected to Abraham and his life of faith.

First faith is always about the FUTURE

"*Now faith is being sure of what we hope for and certain of what we do not see.*" Hebrews 11.1 Faith is not about what I have or where I am. Faith is about the future. (We will define the future very shortly.) Faith uses words like hope, and says it is what we cannot and do not see. Now some want you to believe this is about that shiny new car you are hoping for, or it is about what you want from God. It could not be further from the truth. This is very important, and the scripture will bear this up shortly, but remember, faith is about the future.

Second faith is always about OBEDIENCE

"*By faith Abraham, when called to go to a place he would later receive as his inheritance, obeyed and went, even though he did not know where he was going.*" Hebrews 11.8 When God is directing our lives; we need to remember He can see more of it than we can. He is looking at the whole life and where He wants us to end up, while we are looking at the immediate circumstances. Abraham had no idea where he was going to end up. He just knew that, in order to live a life of faith, he had to obey. A life of faith believes God has plans that are for the better no matter what is happening right now. Faith is always about obedience to God.

<u>Third</u> faith is always about PROMISES

"*By faith he made his home in the promised land like a stranger in a foreign country; he lived in tents, as did Isaac and Jacob, who were heirs with him of the same promise. For he was looking forward to the city with foundations, whose architect and builder is God.*" Hebrews 11.9-10 God has made promises to those who believe and obey. The scriptures are full of them. The greatest promise is not for health, or wealth or even our personal happiness. The greatest promise is the one God gives to every believer. Abraham was looking for a city; not an earthly city but an eternal heavenly one. Every believer is promised an eternity with God. The reason Abraham did not mind living in tents is he had a promise of a city built by God where he would live forever. This is the same city we read about in Revelation chapter 22. Remember that faith is about the future and it is in the future, we will enter that great city. You might even get to live next door to Abraham.

<u>Fourth</u> faith is always about OPTIMISM

"*By faith Abraham, even though he was past age—and Sarah herself was barren—was enabled to become a father because he considered him faithful who had made the promise. And so from this one man, and he as good as dead, came descendants as numerous as the stars in the sky and as countless as the sand on the seashore.*" Hebrews 11.11-12 If we are going to have faith we need to be optimistic. I do not know how much more optimistic a person can be than an eighty-five year old man with a seventy-five year old wife believing they are going to be parents. He would have to wait until he was ninety-nine or another fourteen years until he had a son. Abraham was the most optimistic person who ever lived. He is not even called by God to follow Him until he was already seventy-five years old.

Fifth faith is always about RISKS

"*By faith Abraham, when God tested him, offered Isaac as a sacrifice. He who had received the promises was about to sacrifice his one and only son, even though God had said to him, "It is through Isaac that your offspring will be reckoned." Abraham reasoned that God could raise the dead, and figuratively speaking, he did receive Isaac back from death.*" Hebrews 11.17-19 We have to be willing to put it all on the line if we are really living a life of faith. We may not be called on to sacrifice (kill) our oldest child, but we are called to sacrifice, to make choices that go against the average non-believer's lifestyle. Faith is about risks. It is about putting it all on the line.

EXAMPLES OF FAITH FROM HEBREWS 11

Faith is about the FUTURE "*By faith Isaac blessed Jacob and Esau in regard to their future.*" Hebrews 11.20

Faith is about OBEDIENCE: "*By faith Noah, when warned about things not yet seen, in holy fear built an ark to save his family.*" Hebrews 11.7

Faith is about PROMISES. "*By faith Jacob, when he was dying, blessed each of Joseph's sons, and worshiped as he leaned on the top of his staff.*" Hebrews 11.21

Faith is about OPTIMISM: "*By faith Moses, when he had grown up, refused to be known as the son of Pharaoh's daughter. He chose to be mistreated along with the people of God rather than to enjoy the pleasures of sin for a short time.*" Hebrews 11.24-25

Faith is about RISKS: "*By faith Moses' parents hid him for three months after he was born...*" Hebrews 11.23

ONE MORE FAITH FACT

Faith is ALWAYS NECESSARY. "*And without faith it is impossible to please God, because anyone who comes to Him must believe that He exists and that He rewards those who earnestly seek Him.*" Hebrews 11.6 As believers we are called to live a life of faith. We are to focus on the future and God's long term plans. We are to be obedient and follow the directions given us by God. We are to focus on the promises and know God rewards those who live in faith. We are to be optimistic and keep a positive attitude even when everything seems to be going against us. God has a master plan, and we all win in the end. We also need to remember that living a life of faith comes with risks. The safe road is not the faith road.

DEFINING PERSONAL FAITH

There is so much to learn about faith in the eleventh chapter of Hebrews. Yet, there is one verse that expresses faith that is almost always overlooked. Speaking about the ultimate faith and defining faith as clearly as it can be the writer says, "*Women received back their dead, raised to life again. Others were tortured and refused to be released, so that they might gain a better resurrection.*" Hebrews 11.35 They were, "*commended for their faith.*" Hebrews 11.39 Faith is about life and death. It is about the future and the resurrection of the dead. Let me paraphrase this verse. What it says is '**Whether I live or die I believe God is my God and Jesus is my savior**.' That is a perfect definition of faith. Every person who has ever lived his/her life in faith dies. Along the way there are blessings and opportunities to discover what God has planned for his/her life. In the end, it is not about what we get in this life or how we leave this life, but about what we get in the next life. To live a life of faith you have to be able to say... **Whether I live or die I believe God is my God and Jesus is my savior.**

There is a picture that I use as a screen saver on my office computer. It is a field of wild sunflowers. It is just a little before dawn, and you can see the mist on the ground and a slight pink to the sky where the sun will be coming up shortly. All the flowers have their faces turned toward the horizon where the sun will be coming up. Their heads are slightly facing downward. Every time I look at the picture, I think about what it means to be a Christian believer and to live a life of faith. We wait the returning Son as the flowers wait the coming morning sun. We watch the eastern sky with our heads bowed low in prayer. As the flowers anticipate the coming morning sun we anticipate the returning Lord. The flowers know that the sun is coming, and wait its warmth and strength. As Christian believers we wait for the coming Son of God and His eternal kingdom. Faith says, though I cannot see Him now I know He is coming.

Review Chapter 2

Can you identify the following People or Places?

1. Abram/Abraham

2. Hagar

3. Isaac

4. Ishmael

5. Jacob

6. Leah

7. Melchizedek

8. Rachel

9. Rebekah

10. Sarai/Sarah

11. Harran

12. Canaan

God entered into a contract or covenant with Abraham. Page 17 As part of this covenant he required every male be circumcised. Why does God say this is necessary?

Page numbers are from The Story

1. How much was Abram asked to do just to start to follow God's plan for his life? TS Page 13

2. What does God promise to do for Abram? TS Page 14

3. Contrast the way Abram lived with what he was expecting to receive from God in the future.TS Page 14

4. When things did not seem to be going according to plan, how does Abram try to make the promises of God happen? TS Page 16

5. How much longer did Abram have to wait for the birth of Isaac after he tried to force God's plan with the birth of Ishmael? TS Pages 16-17

6. Why do you think God ask Abraham to sacrifice Isaac? TS Pages 19-20

7. What do we know about the two sons of Isaac: Esau and Jacob? TS Pages 21-22

8. How did the brothers, Jacob and Esau, change after all the years apart?

9. How would you describe Jacob's response to his fears as he was returning back home?

10. What one thing in this chapter did you learn that can help you on your personal faith journey?

Defining Moments
The Story Unfolds Chapter 3

What is a defining Moment?

I wonder if I asked you what the defining moment in the life of George Washington was, what you would say? Would you choose when they tried to make him king and he refused? Or would you choose when he refused to run for a third term because he did not believe in career politicians? You might choose when he orchestrated the compromise that allowed the constitution to replace the failing articles of confederation by helping set up the Senate and House of Representatives as we now have them. You could choose the little known confrontation between Washington and his officers at what is known as the Newburgh Conspiracy. The army had not been properly paid for their service. The British were leaving and some in the new government felt that they could skip any final payments to the army. The officers were planning to act against their own government and use force if necessary. The only person standing in their way was George Washington. He stood in the gap between the army and the elected officials and saved the struggling revolution and the new nation at a most critical moment. Yet, in my opinion, none of these was the defining moment in the life of George Washington. The defining moment came, not during the revolutionary war or in his service as an officer in the British army when he fought against the French and Indians, the defining moment came on June 12, 1747.[3]

George Washington was fifteen years old and had received a royal midshipman's warrant from the British navy. This was before we decided to break away and form a new country, and they were still our friends. This would fulfill his lifelong dream. He would escape the drudgery of the family farm and his responsibilities as the oldest male child helping his widowed mother. He arrived at the dock side that day and had passed his bag along to be put on the ship, and then he waited to say goodbye to his mother, Mary Ball Washington. He told his mother goodbye and turned to board the ship when she spoke to him. It was a plea for him to stay. She said they would not make it without him. Imagine, ready to leave, friends have been told goodbye, and his bag was on the ship. What he must have felt as a fifteen year old is beyond imagining. He turned and started up the plank toward the ship. His mother called to him, "George, did you hear me? George, where are you going?" He looked back and said he had to get his bags that had already been put on the ship. That was the defining moment. Without it, there would have been no great general to lead a ragtag army against the greatest military force on the planet at that time. There would have been no one to stand in the gap between the army and the foolish civilians that thought they could skip paying the soldiers that had won the war. There would not have been the leader who refused to be made king or serve a third term. What if someone else had been there? A Fidel Castro or Hugo Chavez or Stalin or any number of men who, when faced with power, grabbed it and abused it. Washington was a committed man at fifteen and served his mother and his country as a servant of all. Defining moments are usually not great victories or defeats, but they are turning points that shape our lives and our destinies.

What does it mean when scripture says, "in all things God works for the good of those who love him?" (Romans 8.28) When we think of all things that covers a lot of ground. It covers good times and some really bad times. What we need to remember is that it says God works. Sometimes we think it is what we do that makes the difference, it is finally and always in God's hands to determine what He considers good. God does this on His time schedule no matter what we may think. He does it for those who love Him and who are called according to His purpose. He does not do this for everyone. So two people may have the exact same thing happen to them and the one who is a believer can know that God will be using all things for good. While the non-believer will have just gone through an event that carries only personal pain or joy and has no long term use or significance when put in the light of God's eternal plans. This is about God's purpose for our lives and not about our wants or desires. It is about God who sees in both directions forever, working in and through our lives.

Are You Ready For IT?

"*Everything that we do in life - every battle that we fight and every mountain that we climb, no matter how many times that we may fall - may be for no other purpose than to prepare us for that moment when we are called upon to make a difference.*

In fact, every decision that we make, even those that seem small and perhaps irrelevant - may be moving us toward that moment when we can change a life for the better.

We may only get one chance to make a difference. But there is no doubt that such a moment in each of our lives is going to come. The only question that really matters is, Will we be ready for it?" Glenn Beck in being George Washington (c) 2011

This is not reserved for great people or famous people or just a selected few. The truth is we all are challenged to make decisions and life choices that make a difference, a difference for us, and a difference for others. George Washington made his first such decision at fifteen and made them over and over the rest of his life. This was also true of Joseph, the eleventh son of Jacob. He had to make decisions over and over, and each decision could have ruined his life and the lives of so many others. Yet, when we look at Joseph's life, we see the moment when everything comes to a climax. His brothers are in front of him, tears of fear in their eyes. Joseph has the power to destroy them and he says to them, "*You intended to harm me, but God intended it for Good to accomplish what is now being done, the saving of many lives.*" Genesis 50.20 What brought him to this moment? When was Joseph's defining moment?

Joseph's Timeline

When we look at an overview of Joseph's life it gives us a glimpse of the man, but it does not reflect the defining moments clearly. (We will look at them shortly.)

- Born the 11th Son of Jacob and Rachel
- Age 17 receives the coat of many colors from father, beaten up and sold as a slave by his brothers.
- Serve Potiphar and spends time in pharaoh's prison (13 years total)
- Age 30 heads up Pharaoh's Save Egypt policy
- Age 37+ his brothers show up to buy food.
- Age 39 Family moves to Egypt to live under his care
- Age 56 his father Jacob dies
- Age 110 Joseph dies

It's Tebow Time

The 2012 Superbowl will be played this coming weekend and Tim Tebow will not be there. He was world famous for a short time, you could not turn on the news or sports without hearing his name. In 2011 he started twelve games for the Denver Broncos. Ten of these were in the regular season. He won eight of these and lost two. People began to discuss his miracle wins and his relationship with God. He moved on to the playoffs and was expected to lose but he beat the Pittsburgh Steelers 29 to 23 in one of the most dramatic overtime wins in football history.

Yet, why is he world famous? Is it because of his football abilities? I wonder. I live in Olympia WA just 50 miles south of Seattle WA and the home of the Seattle Seahawks. I quit paying attention to them early in the season because of their propensity to lose games and only mildly paid any attention to them. I could not even name the quarterback for the team. He was that impressive, yet when I compared him to Tim Tebow it sheds some light on the question of how good a quarterback Tebow is. I looked it up and Travaris Jackson was the Seattle QB for the 2011 season. During this past season Tebow had QB rating of 72.9%, Jackson had a QB rating of 79.2%. Tebow threw for just over 1,700 yards; Jackson threw for over 3,000 yards. Tebow completed 46.5% of his passes; Jackson completed 60.2% of his passes. The record said Jackson was a better quarterback, but no one knew who he was, not even a lot of the Seattle fans.

Again why is Tebow so famous? It could be because he is a committed Christian believer. He was a committed believer in high school. Then, in college, he got in trouble for wearing John 3.16 stickers on those dark strips players put under their eyes. When he started winning games this year he gave God the credit. The week after he beat the Steelers a survey was taken that showed that 43% of the people thought that God was helping him win games. I wondered if God was helping him win, why had he lost any games at all? Now I want to give Tim Tebow credit, he gave God credit as the guiding force in his life but he does not think God helps him win or lose football games.

This brings me to what I think was a defining moment for Tim Tebow. The Broncos were playing the New England Patriots with Tom Brady. Brady has a QB rating of 105.6 and threw for over 5200 yards so far this season. It was the third quarter and the Pats were leading Denver by 42 to 3. It was hard to watch. Then it happened, Tebow fell back to pass and he was hit hard and knocked to the ground. The backup QB for Denver put on his helmet and was ready to go in but Tebow went back to the huddle and called the next play. He finished the game with a final score of Patriots 45 Denver 10. 43% of the people must have been shocked that God could not have helped Tebow win the big game.

The following week a medical report was released on the injury suffered by Tebow in the third quarter. Tebow tore cartilage on his first rib where it attaches to his sternum, bruised his lung and had fluid buildup in his pleural cavity. When he was asked why he stayed in a game he was losing so badly with his injury he said,

> *"I just wanted to show character. You just continue to fight and it doesn't change who you are, how you play, how you go out there,* ***you should be the same at all times****... It does not matter if it was the first play or the last play or if you were down by 42."* (Emphasis added)

That made this a defining moment for Tim Tebow. It was about being consistent in his approach to life no matter what was happening. Anyone can get hurt and play, but who plays because "***you should be the same at all times***." That is the attitude a believer should have about life. Whether Tebow becomes a great QB will be determined in the future, but he has had a defining moment and the world was watching.

Joseph Time (defining moments)

When we look at Joseph we see moments that defined him and his relationship with God. Each time he has had to determine if he continues with God or quit and become bitter.

- There is the day he is thrown into the well. This is not a good day by anyone's standards, but it is one of those "*all things work for good*" moments. There is no record what happened at the bottom of the well, but the next time we see Joseph he has not stopped serving God. So when he shows up at Potiphar's house he is under the purpose and plans of God. "*When his master saw that the Lord was with him and that the Lord gave him success in everything he did, Joseph found favor in his eyes and became his attendant.*"

- There is the day he left Potiphar's house on the way to prison. He had to make the decision that no matter what was coming next he would not compromise or give in to evil. Things were bad but he still had God even though he (Joseph) couldn't see what was coming.

- There is the day he arrives in prison. That morning he was living large and in charge and that night he was in chains completely without any hope. How did he respond? Did he give up, quit? Why should he continue? Talk about getting dealt a bad hand. Where was God anyway? Then again this could have been one of those "all things work for good" days. "*But while Joseph was there in prison, the Lord was with him; he showed him kindness and granted him favor in the eyes of the prison warden.*" One thing about Joseph he depended on God and God used him. Things were bad but God was still God and Joseph was going to serve him no matter what happened.

- There is the day his father Jacob dies. (the story page 41) To understand this let me take you to a scene in a famous movie trilogy about the Godfather. It is a mafia family that is run by Don Corleone. His son Michael has become second in command and wants to deal with people who hurt him or the family but his dad, the Godfather, will not let him. Then the Don dies and Michael becomes the Godfather. He agrees to become the godfather to his sister's son. While he

> is in church he has everyone killed who has ever crossed him. Mobsters, politicians, police, even some family members. Right after the baby's baptism he has the baby's father go on an errand. Now remember, this is his brother-in-law. This is his sister's husband. This is the baby's father. The errand he goes on is a one way trip that ends in his being killed. Now I don't know if Joseph's brothers ever saw the Godfather, but I think they knew what could happen now that their father was dead. Would Joseph get even for the well, the slavery, the time in prison? Would he strike with hate in vengeance? So his brothers send him a message asking for forgiveness. They even use the name of their dead father to touch the heart of Joseph. (the story page 41)

"*When their message came to him, Joseph wept.*" This was no small moment. In the book of John there is the account about Jesus going to see Lazarus, who was very sick. When he arrived he knew that Lazarus was dead. He talked with his sisters and then asked, "*Where have you laid him?... Come and see, Lord,*" they replied. Then it says "*Jesus Wept.*" (John 11.35) He cried his eyes out. His sorrow was so great He weeps. This was no small event. This was not two tears and let's go raise the guy from the dead.

Last year I got a call from my father. My younger brother was in the hospital, but it looked like everything was going to be all right. They would run some tests in the morning and find out why he was feeling so badly. He was in intensive care just as a precaution. I decided it was late and would call him in the morning. Then two hours later, my dad called back. He could barely talk. He was weeping. My brother had died. Even as I write this, I have tears in my eyes and a lump in my throat. I sat down in my chair and I wept. No words, just weeping. No one could comfort me. It hurt too deeply. So when Jesus wept, it was an intense moment. When Joseph wept, it was intense. No words, just a man weeping. This was the moment when the last 39 years came to a climax. This was Joseph's Godfather moment. This was the moment when everything that had been done to him, could be dealt with. His father was dead, and there was no one to stop him. So how did he respond? He called his brothers, who showed up and threw themselves down on the floor. Joseph said, "*You intended to harm me.*" His brothers must have thought, "Here it comes." Joseph continued "*but God intended it for good to accomplish what is now being done the saving of many lives.*" Joseph understood the all things principle. He would not have chosen this path himself, but he knew that God had chosen it. He would have liked things to have gone differently but now he could see that the bottom of the well was used by God for a greater purpose. God's purpose and God's plan were all that really mattered to him in the end.

Jesus understood the all things principle. "*When they came to the place called the skull, there they crucified him....*" They intended to harm him. But "*Jesus said, "Father, forgive them, For they do not know what they are doing.*"" (Luke 23.33-34) Jesus knew that God intended to use this for good to accomplish his purpose and to make his plans come to fulfillment.

"*And we know that in all things God works for the good of those who love him, who have been called according to his purpose.*" (Romans 8.28)

Joseph did not allow his circumstances to make him bitter. He used them to make him better. George Washington did not become bitter over his early experience and change of direction. He became a better man and leader because of it. Tim Tebow was not bitter at losing the big game or even in being injured, it appears he is better for the experience and his testimony has not suffered because of it, except for the 43% of the people who think God is fixing football games.

Are you allowing life and circumstances to define who you are? Or, are you defining your life by the standards and principles of God's word? No matter what happens, that means all things; God has a purpose and plan that includes you. God has defining moments scheduled for your life. These are not usually reported in the news or observed by the majority of the world. Washington defeats British at Trenton is NOT a defining moment. George goes home with his mother and passes up British navy opportunity, that is a defining moment. Tebow wins game is NOT a defining moment. Tebow staying in game while injured and losing is a defining moment. Joseph saves Egypt is not a defining moment. "*Joseph's master took him and put him in prison,*" (The Story page 32) is a defining moment. Not by what is happening but by the way Joseph responds to that moment. Our response is crucial. Will we live for God no matter what is happening, or will we give up and grow bitter and angry?

Remember, the definition of faith says, "Whether I live or die, God is my God and Jesus is my savior." It is impossible to please God without faith, and it is impossible to make it through defining moments without faith in God. God knows what others intend for evil, and He knows how He will use their evil plans for His perfect purpose.

Review Chapter 3

Can you identify the following People or Places and tell how they are important to this week's lesson?

1. Joseph
2. Reuben
3. Potiphar
4. Pharaoh
5. Benjamin
6. Israel/Jacob
7. Egypt

How can tough times be a positive in the life of a person?

When something bad happens to a believer, does it mean that they are outside of God's will?

How is forgiveness an important part of the story of Joseph and his family? (See also Matthew 18.21-35 on forgiveness and its importance to the Christian believer.)

Page numbers are from The Story

1. What part do dreams play in The Story this week?

2. Were the dreams Joseph had about his family a positive or a negative influence on his life? (pages 26-27, 29-30, 34)

3. How were the actions of Joseph's brothers (pages 29-30) used by God ?

4. What can we learn about Joseph's character in the incident with Potiphar's wife? (pages 31-32)

5. How was God caring for Joseph even in the toughest of times? (page 32)

6. What personal lesson should we learn from the way God watched over Joseph?

7. Why do you think Joseph did not reveal himself to his brothers when they first arrived in Egypt? (page 34)

8. Did Joseph's brothers deserve the way he treated them?

9. How can you apply the attitude of Joseph toward everything that had happened to him to your life? (page 42) (see also Romans 8.28)

10. What one thing in this chapter did you learn that can help you on your personal faith journey?

The Real Meaning of Communion
The Story Unfolds – Chapter 4

Christianity grew out of the Jewish religion. To understand the Christian beliefs you have to know their Jewish and Old Testament foundations. In Christian churches we celebrate communion by using a small cup of grape juice and a cracker-like wafer. Communion has evolved to this within the church, but it is far from the Passover Seder meal that Jesus took part in the night before he died. To understand the meal that Jesus was taking part in, you need to go back to Moses and the Hebrew People living as slaves in Egypt.

God had sent Moses to lead the Hebrew people out of Egypt after 430 years of slavery. They had gone from honored guest, when Joseph was second in command to Pharaoh, to slaves struggling to survive. Moses confronted Pharaoh and with the directions from God brought the first nine plagues upon Egypt. These included the waters of Egypt being turned into blood, plagues of frogs, gnats, flies, livestock dying, boils, locust, and then darkness over the whole land. Still Pharaoh was unwilling to let the Hebrews leave. God set up one last plague. The firstborn of each family and the firstborn of all the livestock were to die when the death angel passed over Egypt during the night. The only way to avoid this was given to the Hebrew families. They were given a fourfold directive to follow.

1. They were to obtain a one year old lamb without spot or blemish. This lamb was to be killed. The lamb was to be cooked and would be eaten at the proper time as part of a special meal. Exodus 12.5

2. The blood of the sacrificial lamb was to be put on the doorpost with a hyssop branch as a marker to the death angel to pass over that home and not to kill anyone in that house. "*On that same night I will pass through Egypt and strike down every firstborn—both*

men and animals—and I will bring judgment on all the gods of Egypt. I am the LORD. The blood will be a sign for you on the houses where you are; and when I see the blood, I will pass over you. No destructive plague will touch you when I strike Egypt. Exodus 12.12-13

3. They were to eat a special meal. This included the lamb, bitter herbs and unleavened bread or cracker wafers. Exodus 12.8-9

4. They were to be dressed and prepared to leave as soon as the command came that Pharaoh had let them go. Exodus 12.11

They killed the lamb, put the blood on the doorpost, ate the meal and left rapidly when they got the word to leave. God gave them directions to celebrate this leaving as a festival of remembrance every year. This is done today by Jewish families around the world. The festival of Passover is an eight day festival that commemorates the Hebrews being released by Pharaoh from Egypt. The focal point of the festival is the eating of the Seder meal. This meal is also about the future and the promise of the coming Messiah for the Jewish people. There are four elements used in the meal which we will look at one at a time and put them in their place within the meal.

1. The unleavened bread or Matzah. There are three pieces of unleavened bread or crackers on the table. The father takes the center cracker, breaks it into two pieces. One piece he sets aside for the end of the meal and the other part he wraps or hides it in a napkin and sets it aside for later in the meal just before the third cup of wine. The family has prepared for this during the preceding two weeks by removing all yeast products from their home.

2. There are bitter herbs that are prepared to be eaten as part of the meal. These are eaten to remind them of

the bitterness of the slavery and all the suffering under the Egyptians.

3. They will drink four cups of wine during the meal. Wine is considered a royal drink and is symbolic of their freedom from slavery. Each cup has a special meaning. (These will be covered shortly.)

4. The reciting of the Haggadah or the telling of the exodus story in detail. This story is told every year so that the Hebrew (Jewish) people do not forget God's deliverance. This meal is also about the promise of a coming messiah. The Jewish people believe that Elijah will come before the messiah comes to set them completely free. Malachi 3:1 and 4:5-6 Jesus spoke about this in reference to John the Baptist. Matthew 11.12-14 The Jewish people do not accept this as having happened and are still waiting for the coming of Elijah. Each year at the end of the meal they send the youngest child who can open the door to check and see if Elijah has come. When the child returns and says that Elijah was not there the father says, "Next year in Jerusalem," and everyone replies "Next year in Jerusalem." Their hope is by next year Elijah will have come, and the messiah will be ruling in Jerusalem.

These four parts or elements of the meal have been the same throughout history. It is basically the same today as it was in the time of Jesus. This is how the early church celebrated communion. Well, it is how they were supposed to celebrate communion. The church at Corinth was a church full of problems. Ten of them are listed in the book of 1st Corinthians.

1. They were fighting over their favorite pastor.
2. They had allowed sexually immoral people to remain in the church (a man was living with his father's wife.)

3. They were suing each other in court.
4. They were confused whether Christians should get married or stay single.
5. They argued about what foods they could eat or not eat.
6. They did not want to pay their pastor for his services to the church (now that one hits close to home for me).
7. They were confused about the place of women in the church. (When we take Paul's directions out of context we make a bigger mess of it than they did.)
8. Their sharing of communion was an embarrassing display of hedonistic selfishness.
9. They could not agree on what language to hold their services in, so they all spoke in their own language even if others did not understand.
10. They thought if a person died before Jesus returned they would not go to heaven. They thought when the body died the soul died too.

Their approach to communion or the Seder meal was not anything like the Jews did or what Jesus took part in. Paul describes what happened when they came together for the Passover or Seder meal in 1st Corinthians 11.17-22. Here is a church that Paul describes as "*full of divisions.*" I would have said they had CDS or *church dysfunctional syndrome* (this exists in some churches even to this day). The families would arrive at the church with their Seder meals; their cooked lamb, bitter herbs and bottles of wine. Well, the better off families would show up with these. The poor families would just come with nothing to eat or drink. They called it the Lord's Supper in remembrance of the meaning that Jesus had given it, but Paul said it was nothing like that. The rich families would sit down and start eating their meals right in front of the poor families who had nothing. They would not share with them. So here were the poor members of the church standing around the walls watching the rich people eat this meal. Then, to make matter worse, some of them were drinking a lot more than the four cups of wine. Paul says some of the church members were getting drunk at the meal in the church. Paul said they were humiliating those who had nothing. I cannot imagine how they even functioned or called themselves a church. Yet, from the description Paul gave of them, we can determine seven qualities that a church should have by seeing what they were doing wrong.

Seven questions every church should ask to see if they are on the right track:

1. **What benefit comes from being together?** Paul said that their "*meetings do more harm than good.*" We should not be selfish or self-centered when we meet as a church, but the results of our coming together should be positive and not negative.

2. **Is the church united or divided?** At Corinth Paul said "*I hear that when you come together as a church, there are divisions among you.*" The church will and should be made up of a variety of people, and they should be united in the Lord and serving Him together. Look at the list of the problems in this church and you see that they were badly divided going so far as to sue each other in the local courts.

3. **Are there both believers and non-believers in the church?** Paul knew that "*there have to be differences among you to show which of you have God's approval.*" Paul was trying to tell them that they were outside of God's approval with the way they were living. We need to know that a church is made up of both believers and non-believers. The believers should be setting an example of the right way to live. That would include sharing meals and not getting drunk at church or anywhere else.

4. **Are you there for the Lord?** At the church at Corinth they would eat "*without waiting on anyone else.*" They

were flaunting what they had in front of those who had nothing. They were showing off. This was not about fellowship or brothers and sisters in the Lord coming together. It was about every person or family for themselves.

5. **Is there compassion and caring?** How could they eat knowing that even "*one remains hungry*?" The church needs to be a place where people are cared for and needs are taken care of. (This is not about a social gospel that forgets Jesus or gives without considering the receiver. see Matthew 7.6)

6. **Are lives being changed?** At Corinth that does not seem to be what was happening. They were getting "*drunk*" during the Lord's Supper or Seder meal. Nothing had changed except instead of getting drunk at home now they could get drunk at the church too. The church and a relationship with Jesus should change a person's life. They should not be the same. Sinners or non-believers should not feel so comfortable in the church that they openly sin without feeling it is wrong. Getting drunk and living with your father's wife should not ever be the norm for believers.

7. **Is there respect for God's Church?** Paul asked what had to be a rhetorical question, "*Do you despise the church of God and humiliate those who have nothing? What shall I say to you? Shall I praise you for this? Certainly not!*" Your actions as a believer reflect upon the local church you attend, and also reflect on God. If you are living as the Corinthians church was, it cannot reflect the grace and forgiveness of God. They were one messed up bunch of people.

The right way to do communion 1st Corinthians 11.23-26

Then Paul reminds the church at Corinth the right reason for communion. It was "*the Lord Jesus, on the night He was betrayed.*" These directions are not from thousands of years in the past or from a rabbi. They were given by Jesus himself. It is Jesus who breaks the bread, or the center cracker of the Seder meal. It is Jesus, who at the right time, retrieves the hidden piece wrapped in a napkin and says, "*This is my body, which is for you; do this in remembrance of me.*"

This is not a meal to fill the stomachs as much as it is a meal to remember the body of Jesus stripped and pierced for our sins. Then Jesus reaches for the third cup of wine that has been poured and says, "*This cup is the new covenant in my blood; do this, whenever you drink it, in remembrance of me.*" The third cup of wine is forever changed or clarified in its meaning. Then Paul reminds the Corinthians the two things we are always to remember when we share in communion or the Passover meal. This meal "*proclaims the Lord's death.*" It is a reminder of what He has done for us. It is to be done "*until he comes.*" This meal is a reminder that Jesus will return and gather all living believers to join those who have already died and ascended to live with Him. This coming return is to be as much of our lives as his death for our sins.

REMEMBER ME!

The Seder meal Jesus shared with his disciples, was about Him. He was the sacrificial lamb without blemish or sin, who shed his blood that God would pass over our sins and forgive us. He is the center piece of bread who was pierced and whipped or stripped in our place. He is the center piece of bread who died between two sinners. He was hidden in the grave as the bread is hidden in the napkin to be discovered and to bring life to us by the sacrifice of His body. He is to be shared even as the center piece of bread is shared and eaten. He is the third cup of wine. It is through his death the old covenant of laws and ceremonial regulations are replaced with the New Covenant of grace and forgiveness.

Four Cups of Wine

At the beginning of the Seder meal the first cup of wine is **the cup of Sanctification**. It is based on the statement, "*I will bring you out from under the burdens of the Egyptians.*" The word sanctification means 'to set apart' or 'to free for use'. God freed the Hebrews to serve Him without the cruel Egyptians. Today, through the sacrifice of Jesus, we are freed from the power and will of Satan so we can serve God openly and without conflict.

The second cup of wine at the Seder meal is **the cup of Deliverance**. It is based on the statement, "*I will deliver you from slavery to them.*" They were set free from being slaves and taking orders from the Egyptians. We are set free from the sinful habits that have controlled and held us captive.

The third cup of wine at the Seder meal is **the cup of Redemption.** It is based on the statement, "*I will redeem you with an outstretched arm.*" God completely set them free from Pharaoh. The word "redeem" means to 'pay the full price.' Jesus paid the full price for our sins. "*For the wages of sin is death, but the gift of God is eternal life in Christ Jesus our Lord.*" Romans 6.23 This gift is only possible because Jesus died for us. Nothing else is possible or acceptable.

The fourth cup of wine at the Seder meal is **the cup of Praise**. It is based on the statement, "*I will take you to be my people, and I will be your God.*" This is the new covenant in His blood. It is why we rejoice, and what we have to look forward to. We wait for Jesus' return, but even if we die before He comes back, we will live with Him forever. This is something the church at Corinth did not understand.

It is when we become the body of Christ that the church comes alive. It is when those people covered by the blood live their lives as His followers, servants, disciples, and friends. It is when they become Christ like in their lives. "*The disciples were called Christians first at Antioch.*" Acts 11.26 Someone saw how they were living their lives, and they said they were just like Jesus. They were Christ like, they were Christians. That others could look at any of us and say we are just like Jesus. We are Christ like, we are Christians. This should be our goal as followers of our Lord. Either we will be like the church at Corinth, divided, despised, and doomed, or we strive to be like the church at Antioch and be Christ like Christians following our Lord, waiting for his return.[4]

When we share communion we need to ***Remember Him*** and set our lives in order. Corinth or Antioch, which church shall we be?

Communion has its roots in the Old Testament when the death angel passed over the blood of the lamb on the doorpost. It took on a deep spiritual meaning because Jesus said it was His body and blood represented by the bread and wine. It is to be celebrated as our reminder that, as believers, our sins are forgiven and covered by the blood of Jesus.

Finally, as we take communion, we can ask ourselves which cup we need to drink, the cup of Sanctification showing us the way out of an evil life? Is it the cup of Deliverance, freeing us from our habits and sins? It is it the cup of Redemption, accepting the price Jesus has paid for sins? Is it the cup of Praise, declaring personal commitment and excitement about His imminent return? The next time you share in communion remember He is the center piece of bread. It is His blood we commemorate. He is the Lamb of God without blemish that sets us free. We wait for His return as His Church.

Review Chapter 4

Can you identify the following People or Places and tell how they are important to this week's lesson?

1. Moses

2. Aaron

3. Zipporah

4. Miriam

5. Reuel (Jethro)

What do we learn about God from the name He gives Moses? (the Story Page 46)

Do you know what happened to Moses when he was 40 years old?

When he was 80 years old?

When he was 120 years old?

Which of the plagues would have bothered you the most and why? (Exploring the story page 30)

Page numbers are from The Story

1. How does God prepare Moses to lead the people of Israel out of Egypt?

2. What mistakes did Moses make, and how could they have slowed down God's plan? (Did God know in advance Moses would make these mistakes? Hint: The prophecy of the number of years until they would be set free)

3. How does Moses' helping the daughters of Reuel foreshadow his work with the Hebrew people? (page 45)

4. How does Pharaoh's attitude and treatment of the Hebrews reflect his personal inner being? (Page 50)

5. How many years did the Hebrews have to wait to be freed by God from their Egyptian masters?

6. How did the Hebrew people respond when they were free and had to face tough times in the desert? (pages 55-56)

7. What personal lessons should we learn from the life of Moses? The Hebrew People? The way Pharaoh responded to God?

8. What symbolism does the lamb and the blood on the doorpost carry for Christian believers? Page 50-51 What other ways can you see parallels in Christian beliefs?

9. What one thing in this chapter did you learn that can help you on your personal faith journey?

Removing the Veil
The Story Unfolds Chapter 5

God's Disclaimer

Have you ever read God's disclaimer? There are some really good ones written by lawyers in our time. A child's Batman costume that carried the disclaimer, "Wearing of this garment does not enable wearer to fly." There is a clothes iron that has a warning disclaimer, "Warning, never iron clothes while wearing them." The slushy cup that warns, "Ice may be cold." There is the 500 piece puzzle box that says, "Some assembly required." The night time sleep aid that says, "Use of this product may cause drowsiness." These may seem obvious, but they are there to cover the bases from the most outrageous lawsuits.

God puts disclaimers or Conditional Promises through his word. He put one in the book of Exodus. The people of Israel had been delivered from the Egyptians and were about to receive directions from God on how to live their lives, but before that, He gave them a disclaimer. "*Now IF you obey me fully and keep my covenant, THEN out of all nations you will be my treasured possession. Although the whole earth is mine, you will be for me a kingdom of priests and a holy nation.*" Exodus 19.5-6 The Story page 59 emphasis added

We need to know that every promise of God is CONDITIONAL. IF is about our actions and attitudes. Those attitudes and actions must be in line with the concept of OBEY ME FULLY. This is not based upon what we want to do, but on what God has told us to do. It is based on the condition that it is fully done or completed. We do not get to choose or change the directions. We do not get to set the conditions. They are directions given to us by God. People who think that they can vote to change the rules set up by God are only temporarily fooling themselves. When they stand before God they will not get to argue that they had the majority vote in their favor. God's vote is the only one that will ultimately matter.

We also need to know that every promise of God is GUARANTEED. IF we do our part and meet the conditions set up by God, THEN we can take God's promises to the bank. It is not that God does not want to do what He has promised. It is that we, more often than not, refuse to do our part. That is when the disclaimer kicks in. It says IF you do, THEN God will. The opposite is also true, IF you don't, THEN He won't. Expecting God to reward disobedience is foolishness to the max.

The OLD Standards or Rules

God gave Moses the Ten Commandments on stone tablets. Remember that God gave his disclaimer to the Hebrews before He gave them the 10 commandments. This was not an afterthought or an 'Oh, by the way,' on God's part. The Ten Commandments were not suggestions to the Hebrews. The problem with them was that they were only about external actions and easily corrupted the person who thought by following them made a person right with God. That was not ever God's intent or purpose for them. (I will explain this shortly.)

The NEW Higher Standards

When interpreting scripture we need to remember four simple rules: 1. Scripture interprets scripture. 2. The easy interprets the difficult. 3. Nothing taken out of context . 4. Jesus is Boss! The last one is important to us here. Jesus is the Son of God. Jesus is God. When He speaks it is the final authoritative word on any matter. Jesus even spoke about upgrading the Ten Commandments to a higher standard. You may not remember reading that. Well, you may not have been paying attention because it is there. In Matthew the 5th chapter Jesus says, "*You have heard that it was said to the people long ago, 'Do not murder, and anyone who murders will be subject to judgment.' But I tell you that anyone who is angry with his brother will be subject to judgment."* Matthew 5.21-22 He quotes one of the Ten Commandments as something they may have heard about, and then He used one of the most powerful words in the whole world. He said 'but.' Anything that comes after the 'but' in a sentence is the most important part of the sentence. A husband says he loves his wife's cooking and then says 'but.' Well she will be paying more attention to what comes next. Jesus says, "but I tell you." What is really important is next. Jesus is about to raise the standards. Murder is an outward action, but Jesus says if you get angry with your brother, you are subject to judgment. This is about the inner person. It is about thoughts and attitude. At least five more times in this chapter Jesus raised the standards above those of the Old Testament.

The Veil Exodus 34.33-35

Moses speaks to God and his face glows. Then he comes out and talks to the Hebrew people and they can see that his face is glowing. Moses puts on a full face veil so they cannot see his face anymore. The glow of Moses' face is about external holiness. It represents the old standards and rules. These change you on the outside but they do not change you on the inside. Jesus knew that was true. He knew that was what was wrong with the Pharisees that he had to deal with every day. He even confronted them about it. *"Woe to you, teachers of the law and Pharisees, you hypocrites! You clean the OUTSIDE of the cup and dish, but INSIDE they are full of greed and self-indulgence. Blind Pharisee! First clean the INSIDE of the cup and dish, and then the OUTSIDE also will be clean."* Matthew 23.25.26 The Pharisees were masters at following the Old Testament law. They worked to be perfect on the outside, but inside it was just the opposite. Jesus called them on it when he said, *"Woe to you, teachers of the law and Pharisees, you hypocrites! You are like whitewashed tombs, which look beautiful on the OUTSIDE but on the INSIDE are full of dead men's bones and everything unclean. In the same way, on the OUTSIDE you appear to people as righteous but on the*

INSIDE you are full of hypocrisy and wickedness." Exodus 23.27-28 No one has ever been set free by meeting all the conditions of the old standards. That is why Jesus knew it was necessary to raise the standards. We know that "*through the law we become conscious of sin.*" Romans 3.20 The law does not make you right with God. The law is about external standards. By following the law the Pharisees were clean or proper on the outside, but on the inside they were dirty, dead and sinful. The Pharisees were mad at Jesus. The old standards were the foundation of their lives and Jesus was saying it was not enough.

The Power of the New Standards 2 Corinthians 3.12-18

Paul wrote to the church at Corinth about the choice between the Old and the New standards. He focused on helping them understand the benefits or superior position of those who accepted Jesus' higher standards. "*Therefore, since we have such a hope, we are very bold.*" Paul was sure that believers in Christ as their personal savior could know that, when they approached God, it was not as beggars, but as His children. The problem with the old standards and the law is that it causes you to live by external standards that fade or do not last. He wanted the believer to know that "*We are not like Moses, who would put a veil over his face to keep the Israelites from gazing at it while the radiance was fading away.*" The problem with those who remain under the old law standards is "*their minds were made dull, for to this day the same veil remains when the old covenant is read.*" This is the veil that separates them from God. They have no way of getting through to God. For them the veil "*has not been removed, because only in Christ is it taken away*" and they have not accepted Jesus who could and would remove it. The only way to really deal with the OUTSIDE is to get Jesus on the INSIDE. "*Even to this day when Moses is read, a veil covers their hearts.*" The law does not set them free. It only shows them how far from God they really are. The veil separates people from God, just like the veil in the tabernacle separated God and the people. There is good news. "*Whenever anyone turns to the Lord, the veil is taken away.*" They have direct contact with God. They now have unveiled faces because of this direct communication and the Spirit being part of their lives. "*Now the Lord is Spirit, and where the Spirit of the Lord is, there is freedom.*" This means a person has been changed on the INSIDE and that it will show on the OUTSIDE. In the end, all believers are different because "*we, who with unveiled faces all reflect the Lord's glory, are being transformed into his likeness with ever-increasing glory, which comes from the Lord, who is Spirit.*" The change comes from the INSIDE and shows on the OUTSIDE.

New Disclaimer New Covenant John 14.5-6

Thomas was having a discussion with Jesus. In the discussion Jesus wants them to take comfort in knowing who He is, and what He is about to do for them. Thomas is confused about where Jesus is going and wants to know why this is all happening. Jesus comforts him by saying "*I am the way and the truth and the life. No one comes to the Father except through me.*" Now the disclaimer words are not written down, but they are here just the same. IF you accept Jesus as the WAY.... IF you accept Jesus as the TRUTH... IF you accept Jesus as the LIFE... THEN you can make direct contact with the FATHER. The opposite is also true. IF you do NOT accept Jesus as the WAY... IF you do NOT accept Jesus as the TRUTH.... IF you do NOT accept Jesus as the LIFE... THEN you CANNOT make contact with the FATHER. The NEW STANDARDS set by Jesus are not without conditional clauses. IF you do your part or meet the conditions, THEN God will do His part that is GUARANTEED.

Removing the Veil Matthew 27.50-51, John 19.30

The curtain that was erected in the tabernacle that separated God from everyone else was not how He wanted it to be. It was necessary because of the sins of humanity. As Jesus was dying on the cross he cried out and declared "*It is finished*!" Most people miss the significance of this.

They just see Jesus' dying as the sacrifice for our sins. It was much more than that. Jesus died and "*at that moment the veil of the temple was torn in two from the top to the bottom.*" This veil or curtain had grown from a thin layer to over two feet thick. It showed that God and humanity had been growing further and further apart. This veil was forty feet high and twenty feet wide. At the moment of Jesus' death, the veil, that symbolized how far apart we were from God, was removed. It was as if God reached down into the temple, grabbed this veil and ripped it apart. Jesus declared that the separation between God and humanity was finished, and to show it, God tore the curtain apart. Now for those who would accept Jesus and his disclaimer or his conditional clause, it was now possible to have full communion with God. No one or nothing, including a veil, is between you and God.

The Temple of God 1 Corinthians 6.19-20

It was never God's plan to be separated from humanity. When He entered the tabernacle behind the veil it was a temporary arrangement until He could take care of the sin problem. God moved from the tent tabernacle to the stone temple but that is not how He wanted it to remain. The death of Jesus was God moving from the stone temple to a new temple. "*Do you not know that your body is a temple of the Holy Spirit, who is in you, whom you have received from God? You are not your own; you were bought at a price. Therefore honor God with your body.*" God moved from tent to stone temple, and finally to you. That is, if you meet the conditions that he has guaranteed to follow.

God has removed the veil and wants to know you on a one-on-one basis.

Review Chapter 5

Can you identify the following People or Places and tell how they are important to this week's lesson?

1. Moses
2. Aaron
3. Joshua
4. Tabernacle

List the Ten Commandments: The Story Pages 61-62

1.
2.
3.
4.
5.
6.
7.
8.
9.
10.

Page numbers are from The Story

1. How did God appear to the Hebrew people during their time in the wilderness? Why was this necessary? Pages 60-61

2. How should the modern believer view the Ten Commandments?

3. How does Aaron's attitude before the people and later before Moses reflect his commitment and character? Pages 64 & 65-66

4. How does God react to the people worshipping the Golden Calf (the idol)? Pages 64-65

5. How is Moses' reaction different while on the Mountain, and when he comes down and actually sees what they are doing? Pages 64-67

6. What symbolism is there in the glow on Moses' face? Page 69

7. How did the presence of God determine the direction the lives of the Hebrew people took? Page 70 What can we learn from this?

8. Why do you think the Hebrews were so easily swayed in their on and off relationship with God?

9. What do we learn about the character of God in this chapter?

10. Which of the Ten Commandments do you think is the most important? Why?

11. What one thing in this chapter did you learn that can help you on your personal faith journey?

Why so Downcast? The Story Unfolds – Chapter 6

Do You Talk to Yourself?

Do you talk to yourself? When I ask this question most people say 'yes'. Then I want to know, do you answer yourself? People are a little slower to answer, but most people admit to answering themselves. Now, I did not ask if you hear voices. That is very different and, if you do you may need to seek professional help. Talking to yourself is nothing new. In fact, the psalmist in chapter 42 of the book of Psalms talks to himself and answers.

He asks himself, "*Why are you downcast, O my soul? Why so disturbed within me?*" Sounds like this is not what you would call a good day. Things aren't going right, and it has gotten to the core of his being, to his very soul. But he does not allow it to overcome or dominate who he is. He answers himself with a challenge. "*Put your hope in God, for I will yet praise Him, my Savior and my God.*" He is down, but not out. He knows where to turn his focus if he is going to make it through his current problems.

Always Downcast, Always Disturbed

The Hebrews following Moses seemed to maintain constant negative attitudes in their lives. They were always downcast and disturbed. It did not matter what was happening.

"The *whole community grumbled.... Egypt is where we sat around pots of meat and ate all we wanted.*" God was right in front of them every day. He showed himself as a pillar of smoke during the day and a pillar of fire at night. But they did not see God and what He was doing. They just grumbled and complained and thought about how great it was in Egypt. So what did God do for them? "*I will rain down bread from heaven.*" They grumbled some more and God gave them quail to eat. They ate from the miraculous provision given them by God for 40 years and they always did the same thing the moment things did not go their way. They grumbled. (see Exodus 16-1-36)

On several occasions they were in dry places where there did not appear to be any water. So what did the people do? *They quarreled with Moses and said, "Give us water to drink*." Moses wanted to know why they were turning on him and God. The people were not through. They continued their attack on Moses by asking him, "*Why did you bring us up out of Egypt to make us and our children and livestock die of thirst?*" They were always negative, downcast, and everything disturbed them. God had Moses strike the rock and water gushed out. The people drank, and there was not one word of thanks, or praise or anything positive. It was if they were thinking, 'Well it's about time.' (see Exodus 17.1-6)

"*The people grumbled against Moses...*" (Exodus 15.24) It got so bad that "*In the desert the whole community grumbled against Moses...*" (Exodus 16.2) When they had nothing else to do "*The people... grumbled against Moses.*" (Exodus 17.3) Poor Moses, he led them, protected them from God, helped get them out of Egypt, pleaded for water, food, and their lives and what did he get for it? In the end, he grew into an angry old man who ended up slamming his staff against the rock twice instead of following directions. (Numbers 20.8, 11) They helped cost him the Promised Land. Downcast and tired, he crossed the line, but not the finish line, and lost the Promised Land he had been headed toward, for forty years.

WHY? WHY? WHY? (Deuteronomy 8.1-5)

Why did it take the Hebrews so long to get across the wilderness to the Promised Land? The obvious answer is they did a poor job of spying, and God punished them one year for each day they spied, and they did not trust God to give them the victory. Yet there was more. God wanted those forty years to help prepare them and to change them from negative downcast people into a people ready to conquer their enemies with His help.

Moses has lost the Promised Land and is making final preparations to hand over the leadership. As he does this he gives directions to the Hebrews. He wants to be sure they are on the right path, especially since he will not be there to watch out for them. He starts by telling them to "*Be careful to follow every command I am giving you today.*" Following directions was never their strong point. They had trouble seeing past the next meal or cup of water. Like spoiled children they throw a fit at the first hint of anything that did not go their way. To counter that, Moses wanted them to "*remember how the Lord your God led you all the way in the desert these forty years.*" Moses was pointing at all the positives God had done for them. He wanted them to remember the miracles in Egypt, the great escape through the sea, water, manna, quail, victories over enemies, clothes that did not wear out and even feet that did not swell. God had His purpose in the forty years of wandering in the desert.

- **God wanted to HUMBLE them**. This meant following directions. This meant an attitude different than the one they started with. A humble person makes mistakes and learns from them, while a proud person will not admit their mistakes and will blame others like their leaders (Moses) and even say it is God's fault. Sounds like the Hebrews to me.

- **God wanted to TEST them**. God did not want them to fail. He wanted them to see what He would do for them. A test is designed to show a person how much they have learned. The Hebrews seemed to fail most of their tests. When they needed water a second time, they did not turn to Moses and God, but instead they turned against Moses and God. Every time God gave them a test to show how much they had learned, they showed how poorly they were paying attention.

- **God wanted to TEACH them**. They were so focused on the physical they never got to the spiritual. *"Man does not live on bread alone"* should have been a hint that there was more but they did not see they needed to focus *"on every word that comes from the mouth of the Lord."*

- **God wanted to DISCIPLINE them**. This is not about punishment but about love. *"As a man disciplines his son, so the Lord your God disciplines you."* God wants to be like a father to us. Jesus taught us to pray to Him this way. *"Our Father in heaven..."* This is about having a personal relationship with God.

They had now been under the direct leadership of Moses and care of God for forty years, and it was now time to see if they were ready to take the Promised Land. God had worked to humble them. He had tested them to get them ready for the real battles that were coming. He had worked to teach them to depend on Him and His promises. He had disciplined them so they would not be spoiled children but adults with faith in a living heavenly Father.

This you MUST DO! Deuteronomy 8.6-9

Moses wanted the people to succeed even though he was not going to be there for them. He knew what it would take and even though he had come up short he was a lot closer to God than they were. *"Observe the commands of the LORD your God."* Moses knew that obedience is the first step toward a lasting relationship with God, *"Walking in His ways."* It is more than a momentary obedience. It is a daily lifestyle that brings a person close to God. They were to *"revere Him."* The word revere can also be translated *fear* and has a deep hidden meaning within scripture. The fear of the LORD is the beginning of wisdom, knowledge and understanding. Yet when we *revere God* or *fear Him,* it does not mean we cower worried about His anger or might. *"To fear God is to hate evil."* (Proverbs 8.13) This means we love God so much we turn from evil. We cannot stand to have evil as part of our lives. If someone wants to be close to God they cannot have evil thoughts or actions as part of their lives. Moses was imploring the Hebrews to draw close to God with their whole hearts.

Then Moses turned to help the people see that following God was the way to their greatest desires and needs. They had complained about lack of water for forty years. Yet in a short while, they would enter a "*land with streams and pools of water, with springs flowing in the valleys and hills.*" The wilderness was not a punishment. It was a way to get them to where He wanted them to be. It was a way to a place where no one would ever be thirsty again. They had complained, grumbled and quarreled about the lack of food, meat, and bread. They had remembered the onions, garlic, watermelons, and fish they ate in Egypt. (Numbers 11.5) Just reading that list is a prescription for an upset stomach. God had prepared a "*land with wheat and barley, vines, and fig trees, pomegranates, olive oil and honey; where bread will not be scarce, and you will lack for nothing.*" What a contrast to Egypt and the daily acid indigestion. The Promised Land would make the wilderness worth the trip. Everything they wanted was in the plans of God. Yet they had to wait because of their grumbling, downcast spirits. They had missed seeing God in their presence day in and day out for most of forty years.

Getting Your Spiritual Focus (Psalm 42)

<u>They complained about the lack of water.</u> The Psalmist knew thirst, and he knew why God allowed it. "*As the deer pants for streams of water, so my soul pants for you, O God. My soul thirsts for God, for the living God.*" A spiritual thirst is part of God's plan for our lives. Three days is the limit of the human body without water and our spiritual souls are not designed to be any length of time without drinking with God.

They complained about the lack of meat. The psalmist knew what it was to eat at the table of God and what was needed to fill the soul. *"My tears have been my food day and night, while men say to me all day long, "Where is your God?""* The world does not know or see God so they ask where He is or if He even exists. The believer knows God and knows that as he or she bows in earnest prayer bringing needs and request to God, He hears and answers our tearful request. We are fed and strengthened by our relationship with God.

They complained about the leadership. The psalmist knew who he was following and why. "*Why are you downcast, O my soul? Why so disturbed within me? Put your hope in God, for I will yet praise Him, my Savior and my God.*" Here is the psalmist talking to himself again. He has caught himself looking down and allowing life to get to him. He is showing his human side. Then he remembers who he is following. It is not the human leadership he needs to focus on. They will always fail him. He needs to first focus on his Savior, this deliverer of his soul, the one who has removed the barrier between him and the throne of God. The Hebrews wanted Moses to talk to God for them. (Exodus 20.19) They did not want to have personal contact. Yet the psalmist knew it was this contact with God, the ultimate leader, which was vital in the toughest of times.

A spiritual thirst drives us panting to God. A spiritual hunger will bring us in tears on our knees before God. A spiritual person will follow the Savior who is his God. This is the God who humbles us, tests us, teaches us, and who disciplines us as part of His own family. We need to focus on Him and reject evil if we are going to receive all He has prepared for us.

Spiritual Food and Drink John 6.30-35

Those who gathered around Jesus were not much different than those who gathered around Moses. They reminded Jesus that Moses "*gave them bread from heaven to eat.*" They wanted Jesus to do a miracle and give them something to eat. Jesus refuted their belief system. *"I tell you the truth, it is not Moses who has given you the bread from heaven, but it is my Father who gives you the true bread from heaven. For the bread of God is he who comes down from heaven and gives life to the world."* Jesus knew that real life came not from having temporary physical needs taken care of but from a deep and lasting relationship with God. The people around Him were focused on physical hunger but Jesus was redirecting them toward spiritual hunger. Now the people wanted this new bread. *"Sir," they said, "from now on give us this bread."* They were ready, right where He wanted them to be. Now He would teach them one of the greatest lessons they could ever learn. *"I am the bread of life. He who comes to me will never go hungry, and he who believes in me will never be thirsty."* This is the lesson that they never learned in the wilderness. They focused on the physical and missed the spiritual. They were always thirsty and hungry. They gathered manna, bread, for forty years and never saw the correlation with God. They were always looking down, and missed the God of love that was watching over them day and night. They could have used a lesson from the Psalmist who talked to himself. Why so downcast. Hey, I will look up and see my savior. Now those around Jesus would have to make the decision. Jesus told them, "*I have come down from heaven not to do my will but to do the will of Him who sent me.*" (John 6.38)

Jesus, Jesus, Jesus!

<u>When you are thirsty,</u> remember the Samaritan woman and the living water that is Christ Jesus. Remember that He has promised that those "*who believe in me will never be thirsty.*" This points us to Jesus.

<u>When you are hungry</u> remember that Jesus is "*the bread of life.*" That anyone who "*comes to* [Him] *will never go hungry.*" This points us to Jesus.

<u>When you want to know whom to follow,</u> remember Jesus told his disciples, "*I am the way and the truth and the life.*"

Again and again, we read that He called those He met to "*follow me.*" Peter, James, John, Matthew and many more have done that and found the direction for their lives waiting for them. They are never lost or alone. There was the one who heard the call of Jesus to "follow me" who turned away and did not follow. He was too attached to the world and could not let go. "*He went away sad.*" (Matthew 19.22) The one to follow is Jesus.

The answer to the question is always going to be Jesus. You may want to know what Question I am talking about. It is the question the psalmist asks himself. "*Why are you downcast, O my soul?*" The answer was and always will be, Jesus. "*Put your hope in God, for I will yet praise him, my Savior and my God.*"

Review Chapter 6

Can you identify the following People or Places and tell how they are important to this week's lesson?

Moses

Aaron & Miriam

Joshua & Caleb

Balaam

Eleazar

Phinehas

Do you know the answer to these number questions?

How long did the Hebrews camp at Mt Sinai after Moses had received the ten commandments? ___________

How many years did Moses lead the Hebrew people? _________

How many years did Moses live? __________

How many spies went to check out the Promised Land? _____

How many days did the spies spend checking out the land? _____

How many years did they have to wander in the desert? _______

Age of those who could not enter the Promised Land? ________

Page numbers are from The Story

1. Who caused the problems, and what did they say they wanted? Page 72

2. What does this tell us about their lives and their relationship with God?

3. Page 74 How is being "face to face" with God explained here so that Moses does not die by seeing the face of God?

4. Page 75-78 How did most of the spies view the promised land? How did Caleb see the Promised Land? How did the people respond? How did Moses respond? How did God respond?

5. Pages 78-79 Here is a Leadership Lesson 101 - What did Moses and Aaron do wrong? Why was God so harsh with them? What should every leader remember in tough times?

6. Pages 82-83 What did the Hebrews do wrong here? How did Phinehas' actions please God? What can we learn from this?

7. Page 85 Here in Moses' final parting words can you find two statements that Jesus quoted in his ministry?

8. Why is each one important to Jesus and to us?

9. What do we learn about studying the Old Testament from this example of Jesus?

10. What one thing in this chapter did you learn that can help you on your personal faith journey?

Removing the Barriers
The Story Unfolds – Chapter 7

Barriers the Believer needs to deal with.

What can we do about barriers that divide us as believers? Sometimes we think barriers cannot be overcome. They separate us into groups. These barriers cause people to reject each other merely because they are different or do not fit into our group. Some people say that some of the biological barriers cannot be overcome.

Let me tell you about an example of such a barrier and the results. My son has an Australian shepherd he named Zoey. We take care of her sometimes. She spent seven months with us when he was stationed in Cuba with the U.S. Coast Guard. One day I took her out front with me. One second she was there and the next, well, she saw a cat. Zoey has a weak spot when it comes to cats. I call it a mental barrier. It is a wall she has not dealt with. The cat took off across the street with Zoey close behind. I shouted her name to try and get her to stop, but she was in full pursuit mode. She crossed the street and, luckily, there were no cars coming. Then she hit the neighbor's sidewalk. It was lined with solar night lights. Instead of going up the walk Zoey went through the solar lights. They were literally exploding as she ran through them. She took out the last light when she slammed into it as she disappeared into the hedges. Several minutes later she came trotting down the middle of the street. Now she does not have a tail so she has learned how to smile. She was smiling and looked really proud of herself, that is, until she saw me. It was then her demeanor changed. She knows she is not to chase cats or go into the road. She dropped low and made a straight line for the front porch. I let her in, went inside with her and hid, hoping the neighbors would not notice. NOT REALLY... I went across the street and rang the bell. I had never had to explain how a dog took out a row of solar light chasing a cat before. My neighbor just laughed and told me it was my lucky day. She opened the door wider and showed me eight new solar lights that were still in the boxes that she had bought the evening before. One day sooner and I would have bought new solar lights. One day later and I would have had to replace new solar lights.

Now, a lot of the barriers in life are the ones we just respond to. We learn them somewhere, and, just like Zoey, we often respond without thinking. They just set us off and, wham, we are off on a path of destruction. They can be very destructive in the church. I want to focus on two barriers in a person's life. The first is one that separates us from God, and the second is one that separates believers in the church. Both can be overcome. I want to focus on these barriers in the church that God has dealt with and we need to accept and grow into them as mature believers.

Jesus the REMOVER of WALLS Isaiah 11.1-11

Isaiah calls him the stump of Jesse. When you look at the family linage of Jesus in Matthew you see Jesse is there. Isaiah did not know that his name would be Jesus but he did know his line of heritage. Isaiah tells us that he will do two things in particular.

<u>The first is how he will judge</u>. He will judge with justice, righteousness, and will slay the wicked. When we think of justice we often are drawn to the modern concept of justice. The best lawyer can get even the guiltiest person off because of a technicality. This is not how God exercises justice. There are no technicalities that will get you off if

you are guilty. The righteous will be found innocent and the guilty or wicked will be found guilty. There are some who want us to believe that everyone gets into heaven and that the judgment and justice of God are just technicalities that will not leave anyone out. Isaiah says "*with the breath of his lips he will slay the wicked.*" This is justice. Those who have not dealt with the barrier between them and God will NOT get a free pass. When a judge in a courtroom speaks to the guilty person, his words carry justice and judgment. When Jesus speaks, his breath or words will "*slay the wicked.*"

The second thing that Jesus will do is to remove barriers. Isaiah says "*the wolf will live with the lamb, the leopard will lie down with the goat, the calf and the lion and the yearling together; and a little child will lead them.*" This is not about some future kingdom. It is how the church is supposed to be today. Before we become believers we are like a bunch of animals attacking and hurting each other. After we have experienced a new relationship with God, we are changed. Those people who would never have gotten along before are now part of the same family and are part of the living church. They are like leopards living in the same place with lambs, and no one getting harmed.

Jesus, the "stump of Jesse" will JUDGE and REMOVE barriers.

The 3 R's to Removing the Barrier between you and God

The first is **REDEMPTION**. The word means 'to pay the full price.' The price that is required for the sins of an individual is death. (Romans 6.23) Jesus died and gave his blood to pay the full price. We are often told that this is the free gift of God. We get the gift, but it cost Jesus his very life. This offer of being redeemed by the blood of

Jesus only covers those who accept it on a personal level. It is not a gift that covers individuals that have not called upon the name of the Lord. (Romans 10.13) This gift of redemption, through the blood of Jesus, has no value unless it is cashed in. It is like the refund check I got for a computer program last week. I paid $49.95 and received a check for $50.00 in the mail. This refund check has an expiration date on it. In three months, if it has not been cashed in, it will expire and have no value. The redemptive blood of Jesus is offered to each person, but it has a limit on it. You have to cash it in before you die. After you die you face the judgment. (Hebrews 9.27) When you are standing in front of the judge you cannot ask to have the blood of Jesus applied and be redeemed. Either you are or you are not redeemed when you stand in the judgment, but you do not get to make any changes after you die.

The second is **RECONCILIATION**. When two people reconcile, it means they mutually or both change. This is very different from compromise. When I am working with married couples who are having problems and come in for counseling, my goal is to help them reconcile and not to compromise. The United Nations gets nations to compromise. This means they stop fighting for now, but it is not about solving the problems. Postponing the war is only allowing both sides to get better prepared for a bigger fight. When people reconcile, it means they both have to make changes. This is true of people, and it is true when we are reconciled to God. Without the blood of Jesus in our lives, we are sinners, and God is our judge. When we are reconciled to God everyone changes. God stops being the judge and becomes our heavenly father. We stop being the sinner and become a child of God. We have both changed or have been reconciled. Married couples who reconcile are both willing to change. I would go so far as to say they both have to change if they are going to save a troubled marriage.

We can be reconciled to God because Jesus has paid the full price and has redeemed us. If we accept this free gift then we are reconciled to God. Reconciled means, God is the father, and we are his children.

<u>The third is</u> **RIGHTEOUSNESS**. After we apply the redemptive blood of Jesus to our lives and are reconciled to the father, we are to live our lives in righteousness. That means we make the right decisions and avoid doing the wrong things day after day. The person is to make godly choices a habit that they live by. It is about making the decisions that keep you right with God.

The barrier or wall that separates us from God is brought down. Sin, death, and punishment are dealt with. The Stump of Jesse has made it possible for us to face God as our heavenly Father after we die instead of a judge that will punish us. The righteous will live by faith. (Romans 1.17) This faith says we are ready to face God because of the blood of Jesus.

Jesus the REMOVER of Barriers (Galatians 3.26-29)

The first thing we need to know for sure is this was written to Christian believers. The principles here are for the church and will not work in the world without the blood of Jesus.

Conditional Promise

The Bible is full of conditional promises. These use the words, "*if*" and "*then.*" One thing depends upon another. It is clear that <u>*IF*</u> you are a child of God who has, by faith, been baptized and clothed in Christ, then you belong to Christ. This is a promise to everyone who is a believer.

Non-believers are not covered by this agreement. Those who are covered can know that <u>*THEN*</u> they are Abraham's seed and heirs according to the promise.

Several years ago my father, who at the time was in his seventies, came to visit. He was in his motorhome and brought along some things he wanted to give me. One was a white kitchen cupboard. It was not fancy or very large but it did belong to my grandmother. She got it from my grandfather when my father was a little boy. It was in every home my grandmother lived in after that. I remember if from her kitchen. My father carefully packed the glass so it would not break. The reason I got it was I am a heir. I am the oldest grandchild and my grandmother would want me to have it. My father wanted me to have it. I wanted it because it had become part of our family's heritage. It is special and because of my place in the family I got it.

IF you are a child of God <u>*THEN*</u> you get everything promised to Abraham. You get to go to a city whose builder is God. You get to live forever with God. As an heir you get what has been passed on to you from the father of faith. You are blessed and special.

The Three Barriers

There are not supposed to be any barriers between believers. This is true of all believers in Jesus. Yet, there are barriers that we need to be aware of, and not allow to be part of our fellowship. These barriers or walls are not to be part of the church. These barriers come in three basic types.

<u>First, we need to know that there *'is neither Jew or Greek*</u>." You may be thinking that you know for sure that there are no Jews or Greeks in your church, but that is not what it is telling us. The wall or barrier is about different

BACKGROUNDS. They should not matter in the church. People are born different; different colors, different nationalities, different gifts and abilities. These should not matter in the church like they do in the world. People react to each other because of the color of their skin, almost like Zoey reacted to that cat in the middle of the street. This should not be true in the church. Sadly, it is far too often true. How many churches are limited to those who have the same color skin? God expects us to look past the different backgrounds as brothers and sisters in Christ. This truth applies to all believers, and we should be setting the example for the world.

Second, we need to know that there "*is neither Slave or Free.*" In the church, there are no barriers between the rich and the poor. Whether you live in a mansion, a trailer, or are homeless, we are all one in Christ Jesus. There is no barrier of **STATUS** in the church. This was not true for the Church at Corinth. While the rich ate their meals, the poor could only look on in hunger. (1 Corinthians 11.20-21) They allowed status to come into the church and divide them. We need to remember that you do not become a believer because of your status or how much you have. You become a believer because you are a poor sinner who has applied the redemptive blood of Jesus to your life. You have been reconciled to God and are supposed to be living a righteous life. This includes not allowing divisions or barriers to be part of the fellowship of believers.

Third, we need to know that there "*is neither male nor female*" in the church. There are no **GENDER** barriers in the church. Well, there are not supposed to be any gender barriers in the church. The gender barrier came into this world because of sin, and it is to be removed in the fellowship of restored and forgiven believers. Eve was a helpmate to Adam and not his slave in any way. There are two genders. There are men and women. That is true no matter what the world is trying to say about it. Men and women are different physically, biologically, and emotionally, but within the church their gender is not supposed to matter.

It is vital for the church to regain these truths if it is ever going to be what God has intended it to be in this world. When background, status, or gender are allowed to be barriers in the fellowship of the church, we allow the worlds standards to stop the miracle of God's reconciling power to fully work. In the church we are changed and are different. We have been reconciled to God and are supposed to be reconciled to each other. That means we have all changed. We have not compromised, we have really been changed.

Jesus the REMOVER of ALL Walls and Barriers

Jesus is the stump of Jesse. His coming was predicted. That he would judge the world and remove the barriers was always part of the plan God had for his life. The redeeming power of His blood is a vital part of this plan to bring down barriers. He paid the full price to reconcile us to God, and then to be reconciled us to each other. We mutually change to become what God always intended us to be, living a life of righteousness day after day. This righteousness means we refuse the barriers of the sinful world. We need to reject background, status and gender as barriers, and see each other as God does. We are different from the world, and it needs to show in the church. We, in the church, are one in Christ Jesus without walls or barriers.

Review Chapter 7

Can you identify the following People or Places and tell how they are important to this week's lesson?

1. Joshua
2. Jericho
3. Ai
4. Rahab
5. Achan

Review — Number these in the order they appear and tell what they did . Bonus: How many wives can you name?

_____Adam

_____Abraham

_____Joshua

_____Isaac

_____Jacob

_____Moses

_____Joseph

_____Noah

Page numbers are from The Story

1. Who did God call to lead the Hebrew people after the death of Moses? Why was he chosen?

2. What did God promise to do for Joshua? (page 89)

3. What did God expect Joshua to do?

4. ______ sent _______ spies to check on the city of __________. When they arrived they were protected by

__________ who was a __________. They waited _______ days in the hills before returning to camp. What did she want in return for protecting them?

5. How long had the people of Jericho been waiting on the Hebrews to come and attack them? ______ Why were they afraid and unwilling to fight? (page 90-91)

6. What was the key to the Hebrews defeating the people at the city of Jericho? Pages 92-93

7. Why did the Hebrews first lose at the city of Ai? Why did they win the second time they attacked? (pages 94-95)

8. What miracle helped the people win when the Gibeonites needed help? (pages 96-97)

9. How old was Joshua when he died? Where was he buried?

10. What one thing in this chapter did you learn that can help you on your personal faith journey?

Christo-Scopophobia
The Story Unfolds – Chapter 8

Things We Fear As Christians

Did you know that *homilophobia* is the fear of sermons? It could better be describe, as the fear of what may be said in a sermon. I know people who do not go to church because they are afraid of what the pastor might say. They are afraid that they might be put on the spot. Some people are afraid of religion - *Theophobia*, some are afraid of Satan - *satanophobia*, some are afraid of spirits - *pneumatiphobia*. Some people have a fear of being seen or stared at - *Scopophobia*. You know the feeling you get when you look around and someone looks away quickly. There are people who live their lives in fear of being looked at. Then there is a fear that some believers have of being seen as Christians. I have named this *Christo-Scopophobia*. This means they are afraid of being seen as a Christian.

Are you afraid of being seen as a Christian believer? When someone asks you what you did yesterday and yesterday was Sunday, what do you say? "Well, nothing much." You should have said, "I went to church, and the pastor had a great message." The reason you didn't was you were afraid of how the other person might react to finding out you go to church and enjoy it.

There are no secret agent Christians or sleeper agent Christians in the kingdom of God. That is how some want to justify their not letting the world know they are Christian believers. Here is the news you need to know, Jesus said there are no secret agents. "*Whoever acknowledges me before men, I will also acknowledge him before my Father in heaven. but whoever disowns me before men, I will disown him before my Father in heaven.*" Matthew 10.32-33 So you may be afraid of being seen as a Christian believer, but you cannot say you are waiting until you are called up for duty.

Along with having a fear of being seen as a Christian believer many have a fear of producing fruit. They know what Jesus said about it but they still have a fear because they do not understand what it really means. Jesus said:

- ***Produce fruit*** *in keeping with repentance.* Matthew 3.8
- *I am the vine; you are the branches. If a man remains in men and I in him,* ***he will bear much fruit****; apart from me you can do nothing.* John 15.5
- *This is to my Father's glory, that* ***you bear much fruit****, showing yourselves to be my disciples.* John 15.8
- *I chose you and appointed you go and* ***bear fruit****.* John 15.16
- *By* ***their fruit*** *you will recognize them.* Matthew 7.16

Producing fruit is what a plant does when it has the right factors present. A plant needs light, food, water, and the right temperature. There is an old apple tree out back of the church in Olympia, WA where I pastor. It may be over seventy-five years old. It has produced fruit every year since I arrived here. That could be seen as a miracle, considering several years ago, it began to really show its age. It has been hollowed out by black wood eating ants. The branches had so many apples on it that they just broke off. For the last three years it has produced apples even though it has lost most of its branches. It does what an apple tree does; produce apples. It does not have to decide to produce apples. It is just what it does.

It is a natural part of the life to produce fruit. Producing fruit is what a Christian does when the right factors are present. Jesus was crystal clear when he said if we are connected to him properly, we will produce fruit. Now, I want to make it clear we should be producing fruit. If you are a Christian believer, you will produce fruit.

Hiding Out In A Wine-press Judges 6 11-16 (TS pages 107-112)

Israel was in a sin cycle. They would *sin*. Then God would remove His hand, and they would be *punished*. Then they would *repent* and God would *restore* them. Then Israel would sin and the cycle started over. The restoration would come with the leadership of a judge. Some of them were great leaders like Deborah who instilled faith and confidence. Others were badly flawed like Samson. Each one was the judge or leader during a period of needed recovery. Some of them did their jobs and some of them made matters worse.

During one particular period, Israel had been overrun by the Midianites. They were like locusts, devouring everything in their sight. Most of the people of Israel were hiding in the mountains and caves, living lives of fear. Gideon had grown a small crop of wheat that he kept from the Midianites and was trying to harvest and thrash it without being discovered. He took the wheat to an old wine-press where he was trying his best not to be discovered. It was here, beside the wine-press, the angel of the Lord came and sat down under a nearby oak tree and began a conversation with Gideon. Gideon will help us deal with our fears of being seen as a Christian believer, and our fears of producing fruit. When fear takes over it can be devastating to our lives and our usefulness to God.

Results of FEAR

People who are afraid often HIDE. Gideon was hiding out in the wine-press because he was afraid. Christians often hide out in their churches and their homes. This is where they go to feel safe. It is their modern day wine-press. They are places where we hope we will not be noticed. The world is not a very safe place for Christian believers. It is a place where they often feel out of place and alone. People who are not believers often stare and act as if the believer is the one who is out of touch with reality. These people can be strangers, co-workers, or, in many cases, they are unbelieving members of your own family. We often just want to be left alone and avoid any confrontation, no matter how small. That is why Christians often feel safe at church, and come out of their shells while they are there, only to retreat and hide their faith and belief in God the rest of their time in they are in public.

People who are afraid often feel DEFEATED. They are living secret lives. They do not want to be discovered. They hide their Christian activities much like Gideon must have hidden the crop he was growing. They feel like there is no hope. They are in survival mode instead of living victorious lives. This is a lot like a plant without the proper mix of light, water, soil and temperature. They stop producing fruit because they are not living as God intended them to live.

Christians, who are afraid, often live in DISTRESS. They worry about what the enemy might do to them next and what might be taken from them if they are found out to be believers. This fear of earthly powers and individuals cripples the lives of believers. It stops them from demonstrating any real outward faith in God. There is only the deep hope that things will go right and the deeper fear that they are only going to get worse.

Reasons for FEAR

When we listen to Gideon, he expresses the reason he is afraid. It is how he sees his world and how it has caused him to change how he is living his life. The first thing Gideon has allowed to happen is he has given in to the current CIRCUMSTANCES. He has allowed the physical world to become his guide and overshadow the spiritual world of faith and belief. Gideon looks around at the world he is living in with the Midianites everywhere and he asks the angel, "*Why has this happened?*" Gideon is looking through his physical eyes at the circumstances and seeing only his part of the world as the whole world. He is not aware or even considering that God has a greater plan. He is overcome with the present circumstances.

The second thing Gideon has allowed into his life is UNCERTAINTY. This lack of confidence or a disconnect between what we are experiencing and what we believe as a follower of Jesus causes us to begin to doubt. Gideon asked, "*Where are the wonders?*" He acknowledged what God did in the past but he also stated his uncertainty that it can happen again with the current circumstances. It may have worked for them in the past but what has God done lately?

Third, Gideon felt REJECTED and alone. He felt like God had forgotten him and Israel. He did not expect to hear from God and only expected to find some way to survive on his own. Gideon told the angel that "*The Lord has abandoned us!*" His circumstances led to uncertainty that left him feeling rejected. No longer living a life of faith in what God could do, he was now in survival mode. He was hiding out because of his fear. Even when confronted by an angel of the Lord he pulled back unwilling to listen or consider the possibility that God was still on his side.

Rejection of FEAR

Gideon needed to respond to the DIRECTIONS that were being given to him by God's messenger. Gideon had forgotten that it was not about him but about God. Believers who get caught up in fear often become self-centered. They forget it is God who directs their lives. They focus on those items causing their fear and forget about God. Gideon was told to "*Go in the strength you have.*" God does not provide until it is absolutely necessary. The red sea did not part until they were lined up ready to go in. The water from the rock only came when needed. God was not going to defeat Midian until Gideon and his followers were obediently in place. They would have to surround the enemy camp. They would have to carry the lamps and trumpets. They would have to blow the trumpets and wave the lamps. Only when all that was done would God defeat the enemy. The angel was telling Gideon to get out of the wine-press where he was hiding and go because God was "*sending you.*" You have to follow directions if you are going to be victorious for God. "*Go and make disciples*" Matthew 28.19 is not about waiting, it is about following directions. You do everything humanly possible and God will do all the rest.

Gideon needed to remove his DOUBT. How we see ourselves is often the greatest barrier to our success in serving God. "*How can I save Israel? My clan is the weakest in Manasseh, and I am the least in my family.*" Gideon saw himself as the world's greatest loser. He would have been picked last on the playground. That last kid who heard someone say, "You can have him." He ended up on a team because he was there. No one really wanted him. He saw himself as the least of the weakest. It is not about how you see yourself or how the world sees you. It is about how God sees you. He uses the least, the weakest, the forgotten, the youngest; the last one picked is often the first one on God's list. The last are always first on God's team.

Gideon needed to side with the DIVINE. Directions come from God. Doubts are erased when you switch to God's team. You need to focus on the divine and his commitment. Gideon makes excuses and God responds, "*I will be with you.*" You are not alone. I have plans that go beyond who you are. Gideon "*you will strike down all the Midianites together.*" This is how your will deal with the guys that you are hiding from and are the reason you are here. You will deal with them because you are on God's side. Jesus promised His followers that He was with them "*always even to the end of the earth.*" Matthew 28.20 All of the enemy was to fall because of Gideon's obedience.

Turning Fear into Faith Colossians 1.10-14

The first thing the angel said to Gideon was, "*The Lord is with you, mighty warrior.*" We need to listen to God and not to our fear if we are going to live a life of victorious faith. We are called to "*live a life, worthy of the Lord.*" We are to "*please Him in every way: bearing fruit in every good work.*" Being seen as a Christian believer and bearing fruit are tied together. When we do one the other one just naturally happens. We discover we are "*growing,*" "*being strengthened,*" with "*endurance and patience.*" Much like he rescued Gideon from his fears in the wine-press God "*has rescued us from the dominion of darkness.*" You are "*to share in the inheritance of the saints in the kingdom of light.*"

Gideon did not see himself as a mighty warrior, but God did. Gideon had to stop listening to his fears and start listening to God. If we refuse to listen to God we will live in fear. We will hide in our churches, defeated and alone, totally distressed, afraid to be seen as followers of Christ. We will suffer from **Christo-Scopophobia**. We will bear no fruit. We need to turn from the fear of being seen and listen to God's directions for our lives. We will begin to bear fruit naturally as believers. We will be surprised how easy it really is to be a follower of Jesus in this world today.

Review Chapter 8

Can you identify the following People or Places and tell how they are important to this week's lesson?

1. Gideon
2. Delilah
3. Barak
4. Ehud
5. Samson
6. Sisera
7. Purah
8. Deborah
9. Jael

What was the purpose of the Judges in Israel?

How many Judges can you name from The Story Chapter 8?

Page numbers are from The Story (TS)

1. According to the book of Judges (TS page 103) "another *generation grew up who knew neither the LORD nor what he had done for Israel.*" How could this happen and who would be responsible for this happening?

2. Deborah (TS 105-107) is said to have been a __________ who was ___________ Israel. (TS 105) How does this go against what we usually think of women in the Old Testament?

3. How can Deborah and Jael be seen as strong women of God?

4. What is one strength and one weakness of Gideon? (TS 108-112)

5. How would you describe Gideon's faith in God?

6. Why did God limit Gideon and his army? What lesson can we learn from this?

7. Samson (TS 112-119) was a tragic hero. What was his strength and what was his weakness? (Spiritually and physically)

8. How is honey from a lion's head a reminder of God's rewards for faithfulness to Him in tough times?

9. What lesson can be learned from the life of Samson and from his death?

10. What one thing in this chapter did you learn that can help you on your personal faith journey?

The Way or Not the Way
The Story Unfolds – Chapter 9

BLAMING GOD? Ruth 1.19-21 (TS 122)

It is as old as time. Something goes wrong in a person's life, and the first thing he/she does is blame God. Now, I have to admit that quite a lot had gone wrong in Naomi's life when she cried out, "*the Almighty has brought misfortune upon me.*" They had fled the country during a famine seeking a better life. Things seemed to be looking up when her boys both met local girls and got married. Then it started. Her husband died. Then both of the boys died, and her life was reduced to tragedy. She fled back to her own country and arrived with her daughter-in-law, Ruth, and a bitter heart. When recognized by the locals she asked not to be called Naomi but to be called Mara which means bitter. Oh, and she blamed "*the Almighty*" who, "has *made my life bitter.*"

Her path through life had come full circle and she was back where she started from and it did not seem to her it had been a very good trip. Everything and anything that could go wrong had gone wrong. A widow without a husband or sons to support her was literally without hope. Even the property she owned was attached to her daughter-in-law, Ruth, getting married. What man among the people of Israel would want to marry a Moabite woman and have her children split the inheritance with his own kids?

Four Paths Through Life

Path Number ONE: This is the path taken by people who follow God in GOOD times, and turn away from God in BAD times. These people want everything in their lives to be perfect, and the first sign of a problem they want to blame someone, so they just blame God. Physical sickness, financial problems, interpersonal failures, even a bad hair day can set one of these people off. So they turn away from God. It does not even have to happen to them. Something bad can happen to someone they know and, WHAM! They blame God and leave the church.

Path Number TWO: This is the path taken by people who follow God in BAD times, and turn away from God in GOOD times. Right after the attack on the twin towers in NYC on 9-11-2001, churches around the country saw an increase in attendance as people flocked in following the tragedy. Yet, it was not long, and those same people began to leave the churches, or, more correctly, to fade away. Everything was returning to normal, and they no longer needed God for comfort in a bad time. They just dropped Him and His church from their schedules. I have seen them come to the church in the worst of times. When family members were sick, they asked for prayer. When finances were bad, they were knocking on the door wanting help. When their marriages were falling apart, they came wanting help to put it back together. The list was long but they usually had one thing in common. They would not be there when everything got back to normal or the crisis was over.

Path Number THREE: This is the path taken by people who choose NOT to follow God ANY of the time no matter what is happening. They refuse to let God into their lives no matter what is happening. This group covers a wide spectrum of people. Some of them say there is no God. Some of them simply deny any personal contact. Yet, some of them acknowledge the existence of God, and even that they probably should do something about a personal relationship, but they refuse. They can find a million excuses or reasons not to have anything to do with God.

Path Number FOUR: This is the path taken by people who choose to ALWAYS follow God ALL the time no matter what is happening. These people are committed believers. They have stepped up and said that no matter what is happening in their lives, there is nothing that will draw them away. During good times, they are humble servants, and during bad times, they endure believing that there is a master plan and, even though they cannot see it, they believe God does, and will guide them for a greater purpose. People on this path are Isaiah 35 people. They see a path through life that may pass through the darkest parts of the world. They are encouraged to "*Be strong, not to fear.*" They believe "*God will come.*" For them everything will work out when left in God's hands. "*Then will the eyes of the blind be opened and the ears of the deaf unstopped. Then will the lame leap like a deer, and the mute tongue shout for joy. Water will gush forth in the wilderness and streams in the desert.*" They have discovered the way of God.

The Way of God

"*A highway will be there, a roadway, And it will be called the Highway of Holiness.*" Isaiah 35.8 NASB

There is the way, and there is not the way. These two ways are how the whole world is defined. Everything functions within these boundaries or limits. There is no exception to this no matter what you think or want to believe. If you believe in God, this is true. If you do not believe in God, it is still true. If I ask you what H_2O is, you would know that it is water. If it is not H_2O then it is not water. Either it is water, or it is not water. It does not matter if you believe in water or not. It still exists. Either it is water, or it is not water. There is the way, or there is not the way. This applies to both the physical world and the spiritual world. It does not matter if you believe in the way or not. It still exists.

There is the way to fly, and there is the way not to fly. Last year my wife and I were flying back east to see my family. We were sitting in our plane on the taxi way waiting to take off. There was a line of planes backed up everywhere. We were plane number 21 in the row we were in. There were other rows, and the planes were taking turns from different rows taking off. That is when I heard the announcement that made it the longest flight I had ever taken. Over the intercom came the captain with the following announcement. "This is your captain. We have turned off one of our engines to save fuel. We don't want to have to go back and get more fuel that would put us at the back of the line. By turning off an engine, we will have enough to make our final destination."

The laws of gravity say you need enough thrust to keep a plane in the air. You need to have fuel to get that thrust, and if you don't have fuel, you will not be flying. You will be crashing. When we finally touched down at our final destination, I was greatly relieved and breathed a great sigh of personal comfort of having arrived alive. I still wonder how much fuel was left in those tanks. How much further could we have gone?

Obey the rules or laws and you get <u>results,</u> and you are flying. Break the rules and there are <u>consequences,</u> and you are crashing. There are no law sabbaticals when you are flying. The law of gravity is not suspended so you can fly. The law of aerodynamics works with the law of gravity to make flying possible. The Wright brothers did not invent those laws. They discovered them and used them so they could fly. Obey the way and get results. Disobey the way and get consequences. This is the way it is. You don't make up the rules. You learn what they are, and, when you follow them you have success in life.

Spiritual Results and Consequences

Isaiah said there was the Highway of Holiness. It is the path chosen by those in the fourth group. It is the Path of Righteousness. The people on it make the right choices over and over, day after day, no matter what is happening, good or bad. This is the Way of God. It is the path that gets results and is approved by God. Yet it is the path that has the fewest people who take it.

There is what I have called Not the Way. It is the path chosen by the majority of people. They choose it when bad times come and they turn away from God. They choose it when good times return and they desert God. They choose it when they refuse to recognize or submit to God. They are choosing the Highway to Hell, the Path of Rejection, they have chosen to take the Not the Way and make it the path they follow for life.

He Has Made Me Glad!! Ruth 4.13-17 (TS 127)

Naomi came back with bitterness about all that had happened to her, but she was changed by remaining on the path. She had her meltdown with God and then went about a life of commitment that did not allow her to quit or turn away. She didn't see a way out of the situation but she also knew that this was the only path with a possible positive happy ending. God did not leave her because she stayed on the path. She chose the Highway of Holiness even though; it passed through some tough country. Boaz married Ruth, and they had a child who they named Obed. He will become the grandfather of King David, and was a direct relative of the Lord Jesus. She had a daughter-in-law who loved her "*better than seven sons*." She was praised by the women who gave God credit for all the positives that were happening in her life. They cried "*Praise be to the Lord*" as they saw the results of Naomi remaining faithful to God. She had the results of a life that had not left God out, even in the most difficult circumstances.

Choose a Path

Everyone has to choose a path for his/her life. The choice can be made by default. The person can just let it happen. This allows for circumstances to determine your relationship with God instead of being a personal choice. It allows for BAD times or GOOD times to come between you and God. It means that you can just find yourself on a path that excludes God no matter what. Those who choose the path to follow ALL of the time, no matter what is happening in their lives, have to make that choice early and often to make it stick.

There are two keys to having success. The first is to choose the correct path. That is more important than you think. Many people just go through life hoping everything will turn out. It is a personal choice that has to supersede all circumstances and happenstances. Second, you have to stay on the path. It is the path you stay on during all good times, and it is the path you are on during all bad times. It is the Highway of Holiness, the path of righteousness. It is the way of God. It is a life that stays committed. You need to choose the path, and you need to make the commitment to stay on the path, the way of God, for life.

Review Chapter 9

Can you identify the following People or Places and tell how they are important to this week's lesson?

Elimelek

Mahlon and Kilon

Naomi

Orphah

Ruth

Obed

Jesse

Moabite

Bethlehem

Judah

Guardian-redeemer

What is the key thing a person can learn from the story of Ruth?

Page numbers are from The Story (TS)

1. What caused the family of Naomi and Elimelek to leave Israel in the first place? There is an obvious answer and the reason this happened. Can you get them both?
2. What is the best thing that happens to the family in Moab? What is the worst thing that happens to them in Moab? (TS 121)

3. How does Ruth show her love for Naomi?

4. What qualities does Boaz see as important in the life of Ruth? (TS 125)

5. What qualities does Boaz display in his dealing with Ruth?

6. What is Ruth asking Boaz to do when she lays at his feet on the thrashing floor?

7. What is the responsibility of a guardian-redeemer? (Remember that the word redeem means to '*pay the full price.*')

8. Why did the first guardian-redeemer refuse to buy the land from Naomi? (TS 126) What does this tell you about him?

9. Ruth is the daughter-in-law of Rahab (the mother of Boaz). How do these two pagan women help us to understand the love of God?

10. What one thing in this chapter did you learn that can help you on your personal faith journey?

The Choosing of A King
The Story Unfolds - Chapter 10

What is the worst decision the people of Israel ever made? It is not a trick question. They made a lot of bad decisions but there is one that goes down as the absolute worst decision they ever made. In fact, they were never, ever able to recover from making it.

Israel's Leadership Crisis 1 Samuel 8.1-3

Samuel had grown old, and his sons were judging in his place. They had "*turned aside after dishonest gain and took bribes and perverted justice.*" The nation of Israel had a real leadership crisis. In property it is always about location, location, location. In everything else it is about leadership. That is true in running a nation, a business, a church or even a family. The right leadership makes the right decision and the wrong leadership makes wrong decisions. A great business with a bad leader will fail. A poor business with a good leader is likely to succeed. Yet Israel was at a low point in their leadership. The people in charge should have been in jail, not making decisions in the name of God.

Israel Demands A King 1 Samuel 8.4-5

The people wanted change and like so many people in such situations, they overreacted. They cited Samuel's age and the lack of integrity of his sons. Then they asked for a king. They wanted to be like the other nations around them. Their leadership had lost its influence with the people, and this caused a crisis of confidence. The people were willing to lower their standards to get the change they wanted. They were willing to leave God's leadership so they could have a king like other nations. The leadership of Israel needed to change, but they did not need a new king. They just needed to trust the one they had. God had served as the king for Israel and the judges had worked for him. Instead of wanting to keep God and change judges, they were now asking for God to step aside. They may not have known that was what they were asking, but they were.

Israel Rejects Their God & King 1 Samuel 8.6-7

Samuel knew the ramifications of Israel asking for a king like other nations. He knew that they were asking for the latest model of leadership. They were trading down in quality. They had come to the point of rejecting God so that they could fit in. They did not realize it, but they were making a major mistake. In fact, they were making a mistake so big the nation would never really recover from it.

Samuel was upset when he took their request to God. God wanted to calm Samuel down and deal with the hard hearts of the nation of Israel. God assured Samuel that they had "*not rejected you.*" God told Samuel that he was to "*listen to the voice of the people.*" God knew that they had rejected Him from "*being king over them.*" They were not just changing leadership. They were turning away from God. This major mistake would never be erased from the nation of Israel.

God Warns Israel One Last Time 1 Samuel 9.10-17

God wanted the people of Israel to know what they were really doing and what they were getting into if they took a king like the nations around them.

- It would cost them their FAMILIES. The king would take their sons and daughters. They would be forced to fight in his army, work in his fields, and produce whatever he needed for war. They would be his cooks, perfumers, and bakers. He would take over and run their lives.
- It would cost them their FIELDS. The king would get the best of their vineyards, olive groves and crops. The

taxes would go up, and there would be nothing in return except they would have a king to rule over them.

- <u>It would cost them their FREEDOM</u>. The king would take everything, including their servants. Then, when they had nothing else to give, they would find they had become servants of the king. They would no longer be free to make any decisions for themselves.

God was clearly warning the people of Israel what was coming if they rejected Him as their king and got a king like all the other nations had. The thought that they would get something for nothing was not real.

The king was going to take everything he wanted, and all they would get is a king who now owned everything. This is the same problem many nations face today where the people are expecting more and more from the government. That sounds good until you ask where the government is going to get everything it is giving to the people? The only place a government can get anything is from the people it rules over. If the people want food or shelter or medicine from their government, the only way the government can pay for this is to take from the people. They end up becoming the slaves for the little they are getting. The government always takes more than it gives.

When Egypt was going through seven good years, the people had to give to the government to prepare for the coming seven bad years. (Genesis 41.46-49) The Egyptian government did not pay for this. They took it from the people. Then when the seven bad years came, the government did not give it back to the people they took it from. The people were forced to pay for it. First with their money, then with their land, and, finally, they all became the slaves of pharaoh to buy the food that used to belong to them.

This is what God was warning Israel would happen to them if they continued the course they were on and got a king like the other nations around them.

Israel Refuses God's Warning 1 Samuel 9.19-20

Even with all that Samuel warned them about demanding a king, they "*refused to listen.*" They said, "*No, but there shall be a king over us.*" They wanted a king so they would be like the other nations around them. He would judge them, go before them, and fight their battles. They were excited about this change and they were not willing to acknowledge that it might not be such a good idea. They were saying to God, "You don't have to do these things for us anymore because we will have a king to do it for us now." They were telling God to back off, to get out, that his leadership was no longer needed. The new king would take care of this from now on. They were willing to do this no matter what it cost them.

God Rejects Israel 1 Samuel 8.18

God was very clear on what was going to happen if they chose a king over Him. "*Then you will cry out in that day because of your king whom you have chosen for yourselves, but the LORD will not answer you in that day.*" God did not pull his punches there. He told them exactly what was going to happen. It would not be the result of anything He did. It would be because of the king they wanted. After their new king had taken their families, fields and freedom they would turn to God for help and God was clear He would not be there. He knew that they would cry out to Him for help. It would be because the very king they chose, they needed God's help, and God had already decided they would "*not be heard.*"

Life Without God

It cannot be stated strongly enough, they had just made the worst mistake that they could make. It was a tragedy with long range consequences that the Israeli nation would never recover from. They had rejected God as king and replaced Him with a man. Their kings were failures from the beginning. Saul was not the strong leader they needed, and, in the end, he went mad throwing spears at people in his palace. David is often seen in a positive light, but, when you look at his leadership, he used his power to commit adultery, to kill a loyal commander, and was so violent that God would not let him build the temple. His son Solomon became king, and threw off all limits, breaking the rules of God. Then the kingdom was split in half under the leadership of Jeroboam and Rehoboam. The nation suffered under the leadership of bad kings for the rest of its history. Then, in 722 B.C., the Assyrians captured the Northern Kingdom and, in 586 B.C., the Babylonian Empire captured the Southern Kingdom and destroyed the great temple of Solomon.

The rejection of God as their king was the end of His protection, and He kept his word by not responding to their prayers. Israel would spend the next 1,000 years without God as their king. During the last 400 years God would be silent. Between the end of the book of Malachi and the Angels bringing the news of the coming birth of Jesus, God was silent. God kept His word, and Israel suffered under the kings they had chosen over God.

Keys to What Happened

They had REJECTED God as their king. Then they REPLACED God with a man. Even when God warned them, they REFUSED God's warnings. This brought God's RESPONSIBILITY to the nation of Israel to an end. When they chose a man over God, it was like replacing a pit bull with an attack hamster. Everything went wrong that could go wrong. God went silent and let them live their lives without His help.

The King Returns John 18.33-37

Jesus is standing before Pilate. The conversation is often overlooked, but it is vital when we remember that Israel has now been without God as their king for over one thousand years. "*Are you the king of the Jews*?" Pilate asked Jesus. Jesus wants to know why Pilate is asking the question. Did he want to know or did someone else put him up to asking this question? Pilate deflects the question and reminds Jesus it is the Jews who have had him arrested. Then Jesus sets up one of the most important things He will ever say. He outlines that He is NOT going to rule any earthly kingdom, that His kingdom is a heavenly kingdom. He has spoken of this heavenly kingdom and is cited 31 times in the book of Matthew making reference to this heavenly kingdom. Jesus says Pilate is "*right in saying I am a king.*" Jesus says this is the reason He was born. He was born to be a king. This is the reason that God has come into the world as a man. He plans to reestablish Himself as king of His people; not of a nation or a region but of a spiritual kingdom that is tied to heaven.

After one thousand years the King has returned. The king who had said one thousand years earlier He would not listen or answer their prayers, has returned. Now He is saying, "“*Whatever you ask in My name, that will I do, so that the Father may be glorified in the Son.*" (John 14.13-14)

Choosing a King to Follow

- Israel REJECTED God as their King but now the opportunity exists that you can ACCEPT Jesus as your king.
- Israel REPLACED God with a man, but you can ACKNOWLEDGE Jesus as your God.
- Israel REFUSED to listen to God's warnings, but you can ADHERE to God's word as the guide for your life.
- When Israel rejected, replaced, and refused to listen to God, His RESPONSIBILITY ended, and He

> stopped listening to their cries for help. Now, when people accept, acknowledge Jesus as their king, and adhere to his word, God's AUTHORITY returns. Once again He is with his people. He will judge them, guide them, and fight their battles. He will listen to their prayers and answer them. He will be their king.

The Kingdom of Heaven has a king. That king hears and answers our prayers. That king is Jesus. Israel rejected God as their king, and it never recovered from that mistake. You can avoid making the same mistake by serving the King of Kings and Lord of Lords, Jesus.

Review Chapter 10

Can you identify the following People or Places and tell how they are important to this week's lesson?

1. Eli
2. Hannah
3. Peninnah
4. Elkanah
5. Hophni and Phinehas
6. Samuel
7. Kish
8. Saul
9. Nahash
10. Jabesh Gilead
11. Jonathan
12. Joel and Abijah
13. Agag
14. Ramathaim

Page numbers are from The Story (TS)

1. What was the relationship between Hannah and her husband Ekanah? Between Hannah and Peninnah? Between Hannah and her son Samuel? (TS 129-131)

2. How is Hannah's devotion to God rewarded over and over? (TS 129-131)

3. What were Eli's strengths? What were his weaknesses?

4. What were Samuel's strengths? What were his weaknesses?

5. How did the sons of these two last great Judges of Israel reflect the culture of their father's values?

6. What reason did the people give for wanting a king? (TS 135-136)

7. What were they willing to give up to have a king? (Both physical & spiritual) (TS 135-136)

8. How were the physical qualities of Saul deceptive when compared to his leadership skills? What was the final straw for Samuel? Why was this the wrong thing for Saul to do?

9. Why would God have preferred to have judges leading the Hebrews instead of them serving a king?

10. What one thing in this chapter did you learn that can help you on your personal faith journey?

Dealing with the GIANTS in Your Life
The Story Unfolds - Chapter 11

How do we handle the BIG problems in our life?

Read 1 Samuel 17
The problem with life is there are problems in every life. Now, that may seem obvious but most people live their lives trying to avoid their problems. That can be a huge mistake when you consider the results of ignoring or refusing to face your problems. They usually get worse, or they take over your lives to the point of making you incapable of functioning or having any level of success or happiness.

I have always liked to root for the underdog. That may be why I make such a good fan of Seattle sports. We had the Sonics, but now they are playing ball in the mid-west. We have the Mariners who were 1/2 game out of first place at the all-star break, but now are 20 games back and fading. We have the Seahawks who did make it to the Superbowl and LOST! I root for them for the same reason I can root for a number 16 seeded team to win the NCAA basketball tournament. I like rooting for the underdog. The Bible details one instance when what appeared to be the biggest or smallest underdog won. That was David over Goliath. We all know the outcome, but do we know why David won, and why it helps us live our lives today? How can studying little David help us overcome or deal with real problems today? It would be good if you read 1 Samuel 17 but, even if you don't, I can help you.

What are the Giants we could face in our life?

- Giants are problems, issues, hang-ups, hurts, habits, obstacles
- Giants taunt us... intimidate us...frighten us
- Giants stand in our way
- Giants keep us from living the life God has for us.

- Giants can be relationship issues (family, marriage, friends)
- Giants can be addictive bad habits; a crutch we use to escape (alcohol, drugs, food, sex, TV, internet, sports)
- Giants can be a fear that you are unwilling to face
- Giants will paralyze us into doing nothing day after day
- Giants are battles we are afraid to fight.
- A Giant:
    - can be a spouse who is mistreating you
    - can be a boss/supervisor who is harassing you
    - can be a church member who demands their own way, and no one will deal with them
    - can be an adult taking advantage of a child
    - can stop you from dealing with sin
    - can be an excuse to keep you from serving God
    - can be a money issue (too little or too much)
    - can be a health issue (yours or a loved one)
    - can be loneliness, fear, doubt, lack of confidence, insecurity,...etc.

The simple fact is, we all have giants we have to deal with, and often don't. Giants can stop individuals, families, churches, and nations. One giant stopped the nation of Israel and made them run in fear every time he came out to taunt them. That is something giants are good at. They like to taunt, they want to be noticed, and they want to make sure you are afraid of them.

NEGATIVE PEOPLE

There is a person you will have to deal with before you ever face your next giant. That is the well-meaning friend, family member, co-worker, or fellow believer who just has to tell you why you cannot deal with your giant, and why it is not a good idea to even try.

First David has to deal with his negative brother Eliab. “What are you doing here? Have you left the sheep to die? You are so wicked and conceited. I bet you came down here just to see the battle.” Eliab knew every reason that David should not be here dealing with his giant. Eliab could not deal with the giant and I am sure he did not want to be made to look bad by his little brother. Negative people just seem to know how to push your buttons and to get you where it will hurt.

Then David has to deal with King Saul. ‘Hey, David, you are too young. You are too small. You don't have the experience to handle a giant.’ David has to decide if he is going to be stopped by negative people and their words, or if he is going to trust God for his strength and courage. It is only after you have dealt with negative people that you can deal with the real problem, the giant.

FACING YOUR GIANTS

When you are preparing to face your giants you need to

- FACE them as quickly as possible, or they will paralyze you with fear. The longer you wait, the harder it will be. Fear eats away at your confidence, and the longer it takes you to act, the more of your confidence it can erode.
- FACE them, or they will taunt you. The taunts will be waiting for you when you wake up, and will be there when you are trying to go to sleep at night. The army of Israel heard it first thing in the morning and the last thing at night. They were being overpowered by the taunts (negative thinking) of the giant.
- FACE them in your own way. You cannot wear the king’s armor. Your abilities and experiences are different from others. You need to be able to defeat the enemy, not learn a new way of life.
- FACE them in the name of the LORD God Almighty. You are a child of God, and He wants you to be a

winner. The real battle is His. He is the one who guides and teaches you how to deal with giants. You must remember you are never acting alone. Leave the negative people with their negative thinking behind and move forward with God.

WHAT YOU GET FOR FACING YOUR GIANTS

David wanted to know what he was going to get if he defeated the giant. He was told to expect to receive wealth, the princess and no taxes for life. You may not expect to get rich facing your giants. Your wife will not let you keep the princess, and I know the government is not going to let you go on without paying taxes, but there is a greater reward. Any time you defeat a giant in your life you are able to move forward and enjoy life free from the taunts and hindrances that come with such big problems. You will be free from fear. You will not have those negative thoughts every morning and every evening. You will discover that there are great rewards waiting for you beyond where you are now. You will be able to move on and live your life.

WHY GIANTS USUALLY WIN

Giants usually win, not because they are so big, but because of how we respond to them.

- We forget to trust God. We see the giant and forget our God is bigger. Not David, he served a victorious God.
- We remember our past defeats and failures and project them into the future. Not David, he only remembered his previous victories.
- We trust in armor that is not made for us. Not David, he used his God given gifts and life experiences against the giant.

- We believe the negative words of others. Not David, he ignored his brothers, and rejected the negative words of King Saul.

- We listen to the taunts of the giant. Not David, he knew no one was invincible.

- We don't consider the rewards. Not David, there was money, a princess, and no new taxes.

Not one of these should stop us, but usually they do. We don't lose to our giants because we are smaller; we lose because we let the giant win. It is not part of God's plan for giants to win over believers.

WHAT TO DO WHEN YOU WIN

Most people don't know what they are supposed to do when they win. David knew what to do and how valuable a win was to his future. Most people are overcome by the negatives in their life. They stew over them so much and so long that they are ingrained into their very being. We need to learn how to let go of our losses and how to use our wins. As a boy David kills a lion. No small feat for anyone. What does David do? He mounts the lion's skin on his wall. Every day he can be reminded of his victory. As a boy David kills a bear. What does David do then? He mounts the bear skin on the wall so that every day he can look at it and be reminded that he is a winner. When David is confronted with a giant, what does he remember? He remembers that he has a bear skin and a lion skin on the wall at home. Why not put a giant's spear up there too? David did the three things we have to do with any victory. First he *CELEBRATED* his victories. I can just see him dancing around the dead lion and bear. He skinned them and ate the meat. Then he took the hides and put them up on his wall at home. That way he could *CHERISH* these victories over and over. He could replay them in his mind, and every time someone came over, he could retell the story of his victories. Finally, he *COPIED* his victories. Hey he killed a lion, why not a bear. Hey, he killed a lion, and a bear, why not a giant? Winners learn how to win and how to keep on winning. They copy their success and avoid repeating their losses. Each victory should be CELEBRATED, CHERISHED, and COPIED.

DEALING WITH YOUR GIANT

1. FACE your giant head on. Warning: this will place you in a situation you have been trying to avoid. The closer you get to your giant, the bigger the giant gets. You have to face your giant up close and personal if you are going to be a winner.

2. RESPOND quickly, or you will be paralyzed with fear and negative thoughts. You have to fight to win, and you cannot fight if you are so afraid that you cannot do anything.

3. VISUALIZE your life without the giant. Great dreams require personal action. What can you do when you have dealt with your giant? How much better will life be? How well will you sleep at night knowing that there will be no taunting giant waiting for you tomorrow? It can and should happen.

4. FOCUS on a great big God who loves you. He wants to help you deal with your giant.

The choice is yours. Are you going to defeat the giant, or are you going to continue to listen to the negative taunts of defeat? Gather up your stones and go get the giant that is stopping you. Discover the freedom of a life without giants, and don't forget to CELEBRATE, CHERISH and COPY this victory.

Review Chapter 11

Can you identify the following People or Places and tell how they are important to this week's lesson?

1. Saul
2. Jonathan
3. David
4. Goliath
5. Michal
6. Nathan
7. Uzzah
8. Obed-Edom
9. Ish-Bosheth
10. Jesse

Page numbers are from The Story (TS)

1. Name the four sons of Saul, and tell what happened to each one.

2. What criteria does Samuel want to use to select the next King? How is this different from the way God would make the choice? (TS 145-146)

3. What three things did Saul promise to the person who could defeat Goliath? (TS 148)

4. Contrast the attitudes of Goliath and David as they faced each other for battle. (TS 149))

5. Why did Saul have so much trouble with David? (TS 151) What does this tell us about his relationship with God?

6. How does David treat Saul even when Saul is trying to kill him? How does this show David's character and his relationship with God?

7. Why is the Ark of the Covenant so important to the nation of Israel and to David, the king?

8. Why is David so excited to be able to bring the Ark of the Covenant to Jerusalem? Why did this event upset Michal?

9. What promise does God make to David that stretches all the way into the New Testament? (TS 159)

10. What one thing in this chapter did you learn that can help you on your personal faith journey?

A Congregation of Crocodiles
The Story Unfolds - Chapter 12

What should a church do if they are going to stay in God's will?
There are different nouns to describe the various groups of animals, birds and insects. Here are some I found...

Antelopes – A HERD of antelopes
ANTS – A COLONY or an ARMY or a SWARM
Apes – A SHREWDNESS of apes
Baboons – A TROOP or FLANGE or CONGRESS
Badgers – A CETE of Badgers
Bats – A COLONY or A CLOUD
Buzzards – A WAKE of buzzards
Caterpillars – An ARMY
Clams – A BED
Cockroaches – An INTRUSION
Crows – A MURDER
Dolphins – SCHOOL or POD
Gerbils – A HORDE
Kangaroos – a MOB
Mosquitoes – A SCOURGE (as far as I am concerned one Mosquito is a Scourge)
Parrots – A PANDEMONIUM
Pelicans – A SQUADRON
Porcupines – A PRICKLE
Rattlesnakes – a RHUMBA
Wombats – A WISDOM
Vultures – A COMMITTEE

But, the one that I found the most fascinating was what they call a large group of crocodiles. You know, when you see them on those programs gathered in the river waiting to eat the wildebeest. A group of crocodiles is called a CONGREGATION of crocodiles.

What is the collective noun for a group of Christian believers? They are called a church. Jesus said "*where two or three come together in my name, there am I with them.*" Matthew 18.20 We need to remember that the church is not a building, though the church often meets in a building. The church is made up of Christian believers.

Now, if the church is made up of Christian believers, then what is a Christian believer? It is a person who has accepted the atoning sacrifice of Jesus for their sins. It is a person who has made a personal commitment of faith to listen to God and God's Holy Spirit. It is a person who is being obedient to the teachings of Jesus, starting with baptism, and then, living life as a servant and being the hands of God in this world until they are called home and life here ends. Then the Christian believer, standing before God, wants to hear just two words; WELL DONE.

The question remains. What are believers supposed to be doing as they meet together as the church? Most would answer that they are supposed to worship God, but I think that does not answer the question. It is a way of avoiding the real answer. First, let's take a look back at someone who was not doing what he was supposed to, and see how that turned out.

Where You Are, Is Important!

"*In the spring, at the time when kings go off to war, David sent Joab out with the king's men and the whole Israelite army. They destroyed the Ammonites and besieged Rabbah. But David remained in Jerusalem.*" 2 Samuel 11.1 You may not be a big fan of war, but if you are the king of Israel you have your responsibilities. King David was at the wrong location at the wrong time. Let me explain.

My wife is into watching house hunters. I would rather watch Star Trek again, but she says after the 300th time it is getting a little old. Who would have thought that was possible? She really likes the International House Hunters. We record the new ones on the DVR. It is always about location. They choose a country they want to move to, and then they choose a city they want to live in. They want to be in the city near the market, or in the country, or near the ocean, or near the mountains, or they want to be near mass transportation. But it is always location, and then the inside of the house or apartment. What is their view going to be? One couple wanted to see the ocean from their place. After seeing the apartment they asked about the ocean view. They were taken to a side window and told to lean out and look down the street. There, between two rows of buildings, was a sliver of ocean about two miles away. Yet, in that country, that was considered an apartment with an ocean view. So, where you are is very important.

Where you are makes a great difference, and where David was made a really big difference in his relationship with God.

David's Dangerous Decisions 2 Samuel 11.2-5

David decided to LINGER in Jerusalem instead of going off to war. He sent others to do his job, and thought that would cover the bases for him. Then it happened. One evening he was walking around on the roof and LOOKED and saw a woman bathing on her roof. (I heard an old preacher say that a look is not a sin but to look again is giving in to temptation. He also said that if the first look is too long it is the same temptation.) David must have looked away, but then he LOOKED again and saw she was very beautiful. Then he LOOKED a 3rd time. He wanted to find out about her, so he started asking questions. Then David took a CLOSER LOOK and sent for her to come to him. He was the king, and she had to do what he said. David had his LIAISON, or one night stand and then tried to cover it up with the LIE by sending her home and acting like everything was back to normal. He was going on the 'no harm, no foul' principle of adulterous relationships. Then someone slipped him a note from Bathsheba, and David's personal LESSON of cause and effect kicked into full swing. It all started when David stayed home and did not do the right thing to start with.

Too bad David did not have the book of James to read. He would have known that "*each one is tempted when, by his own evil desire, he is dragged away and enticed. Then, after desire has conceived, it gives birth to sin; and sin, when it is full-grown, gives birth to death.*" James 1.14-15 Yet David did what most people do when they have done something wrong and are about to get caught. David tried to cover it up. He tried deceit by bringing Bathsheba's husband, Uriah, home, but that failed, so he had Uriah killed and then quickly married Bathsheba. Problem solved! Well not really.

Nathan, the prophet, shows up with a problem that he needed some help with. A guy with a lot of sheep had stolen a lamb from a family who had only one. Before Nathan could finish telling the story David had reached a boiling point and passed judgment. David was outraged! The guy who did this will pay back four for one. There, Nathan, problem solved. That was not so hard now was it? David was king and he had handled it. That is until those four famous words pierced David's soul. Nathan pointed to David and said "*You are the man!*"

You could have heard a pin drop in the throne room that day. David was caught. No more covering it up. No more lies. David had passed judgment on himself. Four of his sons would die starting with the baby he had with Bathsheba. Three of his sons would die very violent deaths. Remember, 'Where You Are, Is Important.' "*In the spring, at the time when kings go off to war...*" What was a king supposed to do? A king was supposed to GO. Instead David stayed and strayed and everything else went wrong from there. So, back to my question, 'What are Christian believers supposed to do?'

Christ Cherished Church

Jesus said "*I will build my church and the gates of Hades will not overcome it.*" Matthew 16.18 We need to see the four keys to the church here if we are going to know what we, as believers, are supposed to do. Remember that the church is made up of Christian believers. The church is not a building.

- Jesus will BUILD the church: It is not something we can do, but we can be part of what He is doing if we are part of the church He is building.

- Jesus OWNS the church: He is very clear when He says, "*my church.*" The word church is a Greek word for assembly or a group of people gathered together for a specific purpose. You are only part of His church if you are one of His followers.

- Jesus EMPOWERS the church: It will be able to stand up against the worst evil there is because of who He is. He is the force behind the church. He is the force in front of the church. You can turn on the light switch in your house but, without electricity, there will be no light. Without Jesus, evil wins. Without Jesus, there is no church.

- Jesus GUARANTEES the church: *'Will not'* is a powerful statement. Jesus is telling us how much effort he is willing to put into the church. He will not let it fail. He will not let it be defeated. Even when we read Revelation, chapter 20.7-10 and the believers are completely surrounded and about to be destroyed, God deals with all evil. *"But fire came down from heaven and devoured them. And the devil, who deceived them, was thrown into the lake of burning sulfur, where the beast and the false prophet had been thrown. They will be tormented day and night for ever and ever."* The church is victorious. Jesus guarantees it.

This brings us back to the question again. What is a group of Christian believers, the church, supposed to be doing?

Let me add this question; How is the church supposed to stand up against the gates of hell?

Jesus' Disciples' Directions Matthew 28.18-20

Here is Jesus after his resurrection, standing with his disciples, giving them last instructions, before returning to heaven, and then sending them the Holy Spirit to be with them. What is the most important thing He can tell them? He gives them instructions for the church to follow. It is a blueprint that can be used by any church, in any time, and any place.

- Jesus is in CHARGE: The very first thing He wants every group of believers to know is that He has all authority. It is not our church. It is His church, and what He says, goes. The directions He is about to give are not suggestions, but they are, well directions to follow.

- The church is to **GO**: The church is to "***GO*** *and make disciples of every nation.*" **This is about COMMUNITY**! This is about taking the message of Jesus' forgiveness and sacrifice, along with his kingship, to the world outside of the local community of believers. We must do more than meet together. We must take the good news to those who live around us. This is the mission of the church. It covers the people next door, and the people on the other side of the world. No church is too large or too small to be involved. The church I pastor in Olympia, Washington has a strong mission's support program that has developed over the fifteen years I have served as their pastor. This has grown over the years and even though it is a small church, it has done great things for its size. This week we received that annual giving report from our home office in Anderson, Indiana. Sonrise

Church of God, here in Olympia, WA, is number twenty in all churches in North America in per capita giving for 2011. We support missionaries in Europe, and we support children in Colombia. We support the united effort to reach around the world with the message of Jesus. We reached out with disaster relief for the church following the tsunami in Japan. This national giving does not include our local missions support for youth, battered women's shelter, crisis pregnancy center, and our strong regional support as part of 50 churches in the Northwest U.S. Yet, as I reminded the church this past Sunday, this alone is not enough. We are still required to go into our local community to our families, friends, neighbors, and co-workers with the message of Jesus. We cannot pay someone to do it for us. If we think that is enough, then we are making the same mistake King David made when he sent Joab off to war, and he stayed home.

- <u>The church is to **BAPTIZE**</u>: When people become disciples we are to baptize "*them in the name of the Father and the Son and of the Holy Spirit.*" **This is about CHRIST!** To make disciples means they make a commitment to follow Jesus as their Savior and their Lord. How many people want forgiveness but never accept the Lordship of Jesus. They want the benefits without the responsibility. They want new life without a new direction. It does not work that way. It is like cleaning out the soul of a person and removing the evil that has been in charge and then leaving it unoccupied. Without Jesus moving in the old evil comes back, checks out the place, and "*Then it goes and takes with it seven other spirits more wicked than itself, and they go in and live there. And the final condition of that man is* *worse than the first.*" (see Matthew 12.43-45) Baptism is about obedience and submission to Jesus. It is the first public act of a lifetime to the Lordship of Jesus in a person's life.

- The church is to **TEACH**: We are to teach the new disciples "*to obey everything* [Jesus] *has commanded.*" **This is about the CHURCH!** This is about Christian believers coming together and growing in their relationship. This is about them learning the teachings of Jesus so that their lives can be distinctly different from those who do not know or follow Jesus. This is about Jesus being in the midst of them. It is about their worship, obedience, sacrifice, and willingness to follow directions of their Lord and Savior, JESUS. This is where they prepare to *go* into the whole world to reach their family, friends, and everyone who will listen. This is part of the cycle of life in the church that Jesus lay down as a blueprint for success. How each church does it will differ, but the end results are always to be new disciples.

- Finally, we need to remember it is about Jesus: He is always with us even to the very end of the very end. He promised "*whoever lives and believes in me will never die.*" John 11.26 To believe in Jesus is more than to acknowledge his existence. It is to live in such a way that others recognize the presence of Jesus in your life.
  The first time this happened was when "*The disciples were called Christians... at Antioch.*" Acts 11.26 They were so changed that people looked at them and saw the influence of Jesus Christ, and they were called 'Christ like' or 'Christians.' That is the goal of our lives. We are to become more like Jesus every day, and follow the directions he has

given us as the church to *Go* and *Baptize* and to *Teach all nations.*

The Gates of Hades Luke 10.1-18

When the church is really the church, the results are remarkable. In fact they are so powerful that the gates of Hades cannot stand against them. You want proof? Jesus is traveling down the road with his disciples and a large crowd. He "*appointed seventy-two others and sent them out two by two ahead of him to every town and place where he was about to go.*" They were sent to minister, to go and do what he had directed. They were the hands and feet of Jesus ministering in thirty-six different locations. Later "*the seventy-two returned with joy and said, "Lord, even the demons submit to us in your name.*"" They had faced the enemy, and won. Yet, they did not know how big the win really was. They could only see the results of the time spent traveling and being obedient to the directions of Jesus. It is what Jesus saw that was the really important part of the story.

They come back all excited and then Jesus says, "*I saw Satan like lightning from heaven fall.*" People often misread what it says here. It is in two parts. What happened, and then it is explained how it happened. First, what happened; Satan fell. The power he had was broken. When the disciples were casting out demons it was Satan who was losing his power and hold over the world. Now, the followers of Jesus were casting out his followers and setting people free. Satan was no longer in charge of this world. Second, it is how it happened. It was as fast as lightning coming down from heaven, or the sky. This is not about the throne of God. It is about how fast the overthrow of Satan's power came about. One minute he is in charge. Jesus sends out his disciples. The disciples of Jesus have power over the demons and, WHAM! Satan has lost his position of authority.

I had a friend who was preaching about this at a youth camp over fifty years ago. He was reading with some excitement about this. "*I saw Satan like lightning from heaven fall.*" When BOOM...lightning hit a tree outside of the tabernacle where he was preaching. He said every kid got saved that night. It was sudden, unexpected and it was the end of the power of the enemy. Now, Satan is fighting to stay alive, but he has fallen and Jesus in now in charge no matter how it looks to those who do not know Him. I guarantee, He is the one in charge.

The gates of Hades are broken down. They flew apart centuries ago when some disciples found out they had power over demons. Nothing has changed since then. Satan is still not in charge. The gates of Hades are a pile of rubble, and the church is on a mission.

"*I will build my church and the gates of Hades will not overcome it.*" The church should see herself as a CONGREGATION of CROCODILES where sinfulness is afraid to swim. King David stayed home and fell into a sinful lifestyle. It was a downward spiral that ended in disaster. It would be almost 1,000 years before another king would come that could remove that stain and replace a tarnished earthly kingdom with the church of believers and a spiritual kingdom. Not a building, but the collective of believers that would be called to walk right up to the gates of Hades and demand they be opened, and those held captive be set free. We, the congregation of believers, are the church. We have been called to GO and to BAPTIZE and to TEACH. Let us be obedient. Let us do as directed by our savior and our Lord Jesus. Let us be the CHURCH!

Review Chapter 12

Can you identify the following People or Places and tell how they are important to this weeks lesson?

1. David
2. Bathsheba
3. Uriah
4. Joab
5. Abishai
6. Ittai
7. Jedidiah
8. Absalom
9. Nathan
10. Solomon

Page numbers are from The Story (TS)

1. What was David supposed to be doing when he started his adulterous relationship with Bathsheba? (TS 161)

2. How did David try and cover up what he had done? (TS 161-162)

3. How did Nathan trick David into passing judgment upon himself? (TS 162-163)

4. Even though he had sinned against God, how does David's response show a deep love for God? (TS 163-165)

5. What are the direct results of David's sin?

6. How would you characterize the relationship between David and Absalom?

7. How are the actions of Joab a positive? A negative? For Israel and King David?

8. How does the death of his son, Absalom, show David's heart and his soul? (TS 168-169)

9. Why was David prevented from building a house for God?

10. What did he do instead?

11. What one thing in this chapter did you learn that can help you on your personal faith journey?

The Seasons of LIFE
The Story Unfolds - Chapter 13

How can you balance your life between the Positives and the Negatives? You may have more of a choice in the matter than you think. My wife collects antique wind up clocks. Well, they call them antiques now, but I remember when they were new. They are loud when they are all wound up and ticking. Thankfully my wife realizes that many clocks ticking at the same time are a great way to drive anyone crazy. So they have all wound down and are only right twice a day for a minute at a time. Yet, they represent how we measure time. Solomon wrote about measuring time in seasons. He said, "*There is a time for everything, and a season for every activity under heaven.*"

How Wise was Solomon?

That is a question with two different answers. He showed his lack of wisdom when he stacked the deck against himself with the odds being one thousand to one. 700 wives and 300 concubines, all with different gods, and is it any wonder that he had trouble making right decisions? He was seen as the wisest man in the world, but anyone who would think he could handle 1,000 women is, well, not that bright. Yet, we learn that Solomon learned from his mistakes and wrote about it so we would not have to make the same mistakes. He said it was "*better to live on the corner of the roof than share a house with a quarrelsome wife.*" Proverbs 21.9 So we know that at least one of those 1,000 wives was not the best person to spend a life with. There must have been one that was even worse than that because he wrote it was "*better to live in a desert than with a quarrelsome and ill-tempered wife.*" Proverbs 21.19 She must have been something else to stand out like that in a crowd of 1,000 other women.

Yet, we also see he learned and grew. He wrote Ecclesiastes about his life experiences, and what he had learned. He observed that life was a balance, or contrast, between negatives and positives. They seem to come much like the seasons, with one following the other and never, ever, really being able to say exactly when one started and the other ended for sure. Ecclesiastes, chapter three, is all about the seasons, and how to balance life.

What about TIME?

"*There is a time for everything and a season for every activity under heaven.*" Chuck Swindoll, in his book "*Living on the Ragged Edge*"[5] helps us understand time. He asks what would you do if you were given $864 a day, every day, for the rest of your life? There are restrictions, and the $864 has to be spent by midnight, or whatever is left over is lost. You cannot carry one penny over to the next day. Could you do it? That is $6,048 a week or almost $315,000 per year. How much would you fail to spend, and lose, and how much could you find to do with your $864 every day? Remember, I said this is about time and not money. You get 86,400 seconds every day. When the day comes to an end you cannot carry any time over to the next day. So everyone wakes up and has the same allotment of time to spend during the day. The richest and the poorest have exactly 86,400 seconds to spend before the day is over.

That figures out to be about one trillion seconds every 31 ¾ years. So a person will have spent two trillion seconds by the time they reach sixty-four and if they make it to 97 they will have lived over three trillion seconds.

Some of that time will slowly creep by. Three years ago, my daughter had her first child. My wife and I waited in, you guessed it, the waiting room, while she gave birth. It took forever, just sitting and waiting. Hours, minutes, seconds ticking off the clock spent waiting. Did I tell you it took forever? Recently my grandson, now almost three, was over to our house, and we played for six hours. Building tinker toy houses, playing with cars and trucks, coloring, and making a mess in the kitchen playing with two sinks filled with water that we splashed everywhere.

Time flew by, we were having so much fun. His mom came to pick him up, and I was not ready for him to go home. The same guy who took forever to get here when he was born helped me spend some of the fastest and most joyful hours of my life.

I have a favorite movie that my wife hates. It is "Groundhog Day" with Bill Murray and Andy McDowell. Bill, who plays Phil, keeps living the same day over and over. It is February 2nd and he is in Punxsutawney, Pennsylvania. He has to live the day over and over until he gets it right. Then, finally, he learns all his lessons and stops being a self-centered jerk, and starts caring for other people. That is when he gets to February 3rd, and life goes on. The movie tries to show that, if you could just do it over and over enough times, you could get your life right. The problem, or the truth of the matter is, you don't get to live those 86,400 seconds over again. That means you need to learn from your mistakes a lot faster than Phil did. That is also part of the problem. Many people repeat their mistakes day after day, week after week, month after month, and they wonder why things are not working out. These people wish they could get a do over, or a mulligan. They wish for a time machine, like the one Marty McFly used in 'Back to the Future.' They wish they could go back and fix the mistakes, and correct the world that Biff messed up for them. Time goes in one direction. When it is used up, it is gone. There are no do overs in life, but there is the chance to learn from our mistakes, experiences and grow. That is what Solomon did, and it is what we should do.

Solomon's Outline for LIVING

When we read Ecclesiastes three, we are hearing from the life experiences of Solomon. He broke life down into fourteen sets of events. He then put them into seven sets of mirrored or shadowed pairs. He was able to take the complicated lives of everyone who ever lived or who would ever live and compress them into just a few lines. Solomon knew that everyone had the same amount of time, and when it came to the final say everyone was making the same type of decisions. He knew that everyone would face certain events or circumstances, and how each person handled them would directly impact how they used their allotment of time. If we are going to be successful we have much to learn from Solomon.

Beginnings and Endings of LIFE

There is "*a time to be born and a time to die,*
A time to plant and a time to uproot."

It may sound trivial, but every living thing has a beginning and an end. Plant or animal; there is a moment or point when they get their start or shot at life. This is the beginning of the cycle of life. This same cycle then ends with a person dying or a plant being uprooted. These bookends of life mark the outer perimeters of living here on earth. It is said there are only two guarantees in life: death and taxes. You can cheat on your taxes, but in the end, you cannot cheat death. There is coming, for everyone who is born, an appointment with death. Solomon knew that living happened between these two points.

Starting Over AGAIN?

There is "a time to kill and a time to heal,
a time to tear down and a time to build."

Life is often about starting over or rebuilding. My grandson, who will be three in a few months, has a favorite television show. In fact, if it is on, he will not want to leave until the current episode is over. It is not a cartoon, but it is the Canadian Mike Holmes and his show "Holmes on Homes." Mike Holmes evaluates the needs of homes, and what it will take to repair them. He does home inspections and shows how much was missed by someone who claimed to be a home inspector. The show has three parts: First, there is the evaluation of the needs of the home. Several home owners have been reduced to tears when they learned how much trouble their home is in. Second, Mike and his crew come in and rip out everything that has to go to get to the problem. One small leak recently led to a whole house being gutted. The attic had asbestos for insulation. The wiring was so bad it could have caused a fire at any time. The plumbing was leaking, and there was not any ventilation for the sewer lines. The outside foundation, by the basement, was crumbling, and had to be dug up around the entire house. All the carpet in the house was backed by asbestos padding, and the roof had three layers of shingles that were leaking. Mike and his crew ripped everything out and did it right. The problems could not have been fixed until the old was torn out. Then it was time to rebuild. That is the third phase. You often have to remove the old in life if you are going to start over. You have to deal with what is there before you can do anything else.

Solomon knew this. He knew that doctors often make you feel worse so you can get better. He knew that in order to remodel you have to tear down so you can rebuild. In life, there are the times when you have to drastically deal with the situation if you are going to get the desired results. You have to kill the cancer cells if you are going to heal. You have to rip into the house if you are going to rebuild and make it new again.

Those Pesky FEELINGS

There is "*a time to weep and a time to laugh,*
a time to mourn and a time to dance."

We all have them, men and women; those feelings. Women show them in public more often than men, but we all have them. According to Solomon, they come in two forms. The first are the spontaneous emotions that just happen. When you are given bad news that someone has died, you just start weeping. It happened to Jesus when he heard about the death of Lazarus, his friend. Those who were there said that "*Jesus wept.*" John 11.35 It was not planned. It was a response to the moment. It was a release of his emotions. It is the same thing when something funny happens, and you laugh. You just start laughing because of what has happened or what was said.

Second, are the planned emotions. I know we don't usually think of them in this way but that is what we are doing. When a family is planning a funeral or memorial service, they are planning for a time of mourning. They are planning on a final good-by for a loved one. They are planning for an emotional release with family and friends. It is the same when a family plans a wedding. They are planning their emotions. This time it is to rejoice and celebrate, and using the words of Solomon, they are planning to dance.

Our emotions are there for a purpose. They are what God has given us to cope and to deal with the pressure of life. We weep to release sudden and unexpected emotional pressure. We laugh to share our joy and to stimulate our health and the health of those we love. We mourn to deal with shared pressure and emotions and to allow us to deal with sadness and hurt. If we keep these bottled up inside they will destroy us. We will overload, and melt down from grief if they are not allowed to come out. We dance and enjoy life together. We need these times and they should not be avoided. People who never take vacations, and are consumed by their jobs, are making a great mistake. There are times to weep and mourn, and there are times we need to laugh and dance.

Dealing with PROBLEMS

There is "*a time to throw stones and a time to gather them, A time to embrace and a time to refrain.*"

When you look around this world, there seems to be a lot of different types of people. Solomon broke all the people in the world down into three groups. There are the <u>wise people</u>. They listen, learn, grow, and contribute to life, and are the ones you want as friends. They can be trusted, and their advice will help guide your life and make you a better person. There are foolish people. They talk a lot about things they know little or nothing about, and will give you advice, even if you don't want it. Foolish people are a drain on your resources and your emotions. They are not necessarily evil but, according to Solomon, they can go that way very easily. That brings us to the third group of people. These are the evil people. They feed on power and position. They want to dominate, and they are the ones Paul wrote about in Romans, chapter one who do evil and disobey God, and spend their lives working to get others to do the same.

In the ancient world small cities defended themselves by putting up walls, and having a supply of stones on the top of the walls. When the city was attacked, the gates were closed, and the people would throw stones down on the enemy. The key to this working was having stones on top of the wall when there was no enemy nearby. You could not wait until the enemy showed up and gather stones. We find that history often repeats itself. A country wins a great war or battle and defeats the enemy. Then, during the time of peace there are those who want to enjoy the peace, and who believe that there will not be another enemy. They see no need to gather stones, or prepare for the next battle. There will always be another enemy, and the wise person will make preparations for that time. The foolish one will think there is nothing to worry about, and the evil person will hope that this is his/her opening to take charge.

We may not use walls and stones, but the principle still applies. You have to keep your guard up against evil people, and hold fools at arm's length. Solomon knew that there are people to keep close and people to keep at an arm's length, and there are people whom you should keep outside the walls, or you will surely suffer.

Jesus did tell us not to worry about tomorrow, but he never told us not to prepare for it.

Weighing the CHOICES

There is "*a time to search and a time to give up, a time to keep and a time to throw away.*"

The AMBER alert system is in place to help law enforcement officers rescue kidnapped or abducted children before they can be harmed. Not all children who are missing, and get an AMBER alert, are in danger of bodily harm or death. Of all the AMBER alerts in one recent year, only 30% were actual abductions by strangers. Most of the rest were custodial disagreements between estranged parents. Some were misunderstandings of where a child was supposed to be. Yet, of those who are in physical danger, 75% of those killed happened in the first three hours. That is why it is so vital to find a child as quickly as possible. The longer a child is missing, the greater the danger to their health. Literally every minute counts. Yet, there comes a time when an AMBER alert is no long valid. It is past its time of effectiveness. They are cancelled. This is also true of mountain rescues. I live where we can see Mount Rainier. It is majestic at over fourteen thousand feet. The mountain dwarfs the surrounding hills. This past winter a couple of back country skiers got lost on the mountain in a storm. The rescue squads searched for several weeks through some terrible weather. Then came word that the search was called off. One reporter said they would probably find the bodies after the spring when some of the snow melted.

In this life there are times to try with all our might. The times we should do everything we can to find someone, to solve a problem, or to make peace. But there comes those times when hope is lost. We have to make the tough decisions to get on with life.

This principle also applies to stuff. You know all that stuff you have stored in your garage, attic, or under your bed. Last Monday I asked my wife if she wanted to go to an antique store. That was a big mistake, not in asking her, but in what I found. Everything I had thrown out for the last forty years was in the antique store at astronomical prices. Everything I had kept and treasured was considered junk. I guess it is finally time to throw it away.

Solomon knew that we have to make choices. Sometimes we have to move on, and sometimes we need to deal with the stuff in our lives. It is when we refuse to move on and cling to something that is beyond our control we find our life bogging down. It is when we hold on to everything until we are buried and controlled by taking care of our stuff. It is then that we get in trouble.

Working with PEOPLE

There is "*a time to tear and a time to mend,*
a time to be silent and a time to speak."

When things were at their worst, the people in the Old Testament would just tear their clothes, sit down, put on sackcloth and ashes, and mourn. They did not deal with the problem. They just became emotional. Remember, emotions are part of God's plan. Then, after a period of mourning, they would get up and deal with life again. They would work to correct the problem. This is why David is found lying on the floor begging God for the life of his and Bathsheba's child. Yet when he heard the child was dead, he rose, washed up, and started to mend. He had heard from God, and he accepted God's answer.

There is a great difference between a fool and a wise person when you read Proverbs.[6] The wise person knows when to keep silent and the fool cannot shut up to save his life. There are times we need to listen, learn and evaluate the situation. When the right time comes, then we can speak. We should also speak for those who cannot speak for themselves. This includes those in prisons around the world who are being held for their belief in Christ as their Savior. This includes the 1.3 million babies that will be aborted, this year who cannot speak for themselves. We need to be the voice for the 55 million and counting that have been killed before they could even draw their first breath.

Solomon knew about grief and mending relationships. He knew about keeping quiet and about speaking with a strong voice for matters that were important.

Conflict MANAGEMENT

There is "*a time to love and a time to hate,*
a time for war and a time for peace."

There are some Christians who say they do not believe in war. They believe it is not Christian to fight in a war, or stand against evil people. They say we are to turn the other cheek and do nothing. I have to respectfully disagree with them. Jesus does not want us to give in to our enemies. He wants us to be smarter than they are. Let me see if I can show this to you. He told us that when someone "*slaps you on your right cheek, turn the other to him also.*" Matthew 5.39 In the culture that Jesus lived, there were no toilets, toilet paper, or any of the things we take for granted. The right hand was for life and the left hand was for private matters and was not to be used in any interaction with other people. The turning of the other cheek was a way to shame a person. When they turned the other cheek, it required that they use the other had to hit you. If they hit you they had broken the rules. If they did not hit you, they were shown as being weak. In either case they lost. Jesus had shown them how to deal with the Arab culture and win. Then he says "*If anyone wants to sue you and take your shirt, let him have your coat also.*" Matthew 5.40 Here is the picture of a person who has won a legal judgment against you, and who has just taken your shirt, or the garment that is worn closest to the body. So Jesus says, "*give him your coat also.*" Now, if you have never thought about this; the person without their shirt and coat is naked. Yet, who is going to be seen as responsible for their being naked? It will be the person who sued and forced them to give up their shirt. Here, Jesus is dealing with Jewish law, and the probation against viewing a naked body. The Jew who took another Jew's clothes would have been sinning in the eyes of God. Then Jesus says, "*Whoever forces you to go one mile, go with him two.*" Matthew 5.41 The Roman army occupied the nation of Israel at the time of Jesus. It was Roman law that a Roman soldier could force any conquered person to carry his pack for him the distance of one mile. It was also Roman law that the soldier would be in violation of the law and could be punished if he had the citizen carry the pack any further than one mile. Here is Jesus saying you have to carry the pack, but when you get to the end of the mile, don't give the soldier his pack back. Keep going. Now you have placed this oppressor on the defensive. If he allows you to continue, he may face severe punishment. Make him take the pack from you. Make him think twice about forcing anyone to carry his pack.

Jesus said we should be smarter than your enemies. Even when they think they have won, turn the other cheek and force him to dishonor himself or to give in. Even when you lose in court to a Jew, use his religious beliefs to defeat him. Even when you are completely oppressed, be smarter than your enemies.

When possible, love, even your enemies, but you need to hate sin and all it does. You need to fight against evil, even when you have no walls to stand on, and no rocks to throw down. At least, be smarter than your enemies. We are to "*be shrewd as serpents and innocent as doves.*" Matthew 10.16 Now that is conflict management the Jesus way.

Why Even TRY?

"*What does the worker gain for his toil?*"

There are those times in life when you want to know if it is even worth trying anymore. All the negatives in the world are piling up, and you don't seem to catch a break. You know Solomon spoke about fourteen negatives and fourteen positives, but you feel like you are only getting the negative. You find your spirit bound up and weighed down. Family, money, and work, it just does not stop. If it can go wrong it does, and it happens again and again. You want to ask, "Where is God?" but you are afraid to ask because if God gets mad at you that could make matters worse, if that is possible.

After a recent tornado in the Midwest, a woman was being interviewed by a reporter. It was a striking picture. There she stood holding her baby, her husband at her side, and behind them the foundation where their house had stood hours earlier. A house, that if someone had tried to break into the night before and rob, would have upset her greatly, now it was gone. Surrounded by splintered trees and debris, the reporter asked her what they would do now. Her reply was classic, "We'll start over. What else can we do?" She did not have 'quit' in her vocabulary. Sure, it was terrible, but she and her baby and her husband were still alive. They were within the bookends of life. Surrounded by negatives, she was going to start building new positives. She crossed the negatives of the worse day of her life off the list and decided right there, in the midst of tragedy, she would not be defeated. If you would have asked her, "Why should you try, look at this mess?" She would have replied, "Because I am alive and I don't want to live a negative life."

When you are on God's TIME

"*He has made everything beautiful in its time.*"

There are only 86,400 seconds in a day, and some of those days are filled with negatives, but if you are a believer, you are on God's time. You make choices, based not on circumstances, or how many negatives there are in life, but on your relationship with the Creator. Sometimes, life stinks. That is a fact that we all have experienced. Yet, there is the truth that life is not all negatives. There are just as many positives. In fact, when you look at it closely, even the negatives are to our advantage. When you weep or mourn, it is for your emotional health. When you fight an enemy and throw rocks down on his head, it is for your physical well-being you are doing it. When you tear your clothes and just sit down silently it is so you can spiritually get in touch with God and discover what is next. He has a plan to turn your life around.

"*He has set eternity in the hearts of men.*"

We, as believers, in effect, function on a different time line than the rest of humanity. They might get up to three trillion seconds of life if they are really lucky, but we get eternity. We are on course to step outside of time, and enjoy only positives forever with God.

It is your TURN, and your TIME

"*I know that there is nothing better for men than to be happy and do good while they live.*"

Happiness is all relative. What would make one person happy could make another one sad, yet those who know God can be happy in all circumstances, knowing that God has a plan even when things are tough. You are currently between the bookends of life. You have passed birth and are not yet dead. Sorry to be so blunt and use the word 'yet.' The life you face will have its share of negatives, and if you work through them, they are followed by positives. It is the people who let the negatives win who do not get to the positives. You are alive, and it is your turn and you still have time. In fact, you will have another 86,400 seconds tomorrow. How will you use them? Well, remember, you will not get them back, and there are no DeLorean time machines or 'do over' groundhog days. So, take it from Solomon, who made his share of mistakes. *There is a season for everything, and a time for everything under the sun.*

Review Chapter 13

Can you identify the following People or Places and tell how they are important to this week's lesson?

1. David
2. Abishag
3. Bathsheba
4. Solomon
5. Hiram
6. Queen of Sheba
7. The Temple
8. Ark of Covenant

How old was Solomon when he became king? ______
How many years did he reign as King? _______

Page numbers are from The Story (TS)

1. How was the reign of Solomon different from that of his father David?

2. What was the greatest accomplishment of the reign of Solomon? Why was this so important?

3. How is the wisdom of Solomon demonstrated to the people of the nation of Israel?

4. Why was it necessary to put the Ark of the Covenant in the temple?

5. How does God deal with a nation that has turned against Him? How can this be applied in modern times? (TS 188-189)

6. What does it take for God to restore a nation when it has turned away from Him? (TS 188)

7. Solomon was a man of great wisdom. Yet he made one great misstep that caused him and the nation to turn from God. What was that misstep and why was it so devastating? (TS 191-192)

8. Which of the proverbs of Solomon listed in The Story is your favorite? Why? (TS 179-183)

9. How does Solomon's declaration at the dedication of the temple show his understanding of the nature of God? (TS 186-187)

10. What one thing in this chapter did you learn that can help you on your personal faith journey?

Choosing Leadership
The Story Unfolds – Chapter 14

What is one of the most important decisions a church can make? That decision is in their choice of leadership. To understand how important this is, we need to take a look back at the Hebrew people and learn a valuable lesson about leadership from them. The Hebrews demanded Samuel appoint a king to rule Israel. Samuel warned them that this was a mistake, and would eventually cost them their freedom and their precious relationship with God. They refused to listen and decided to do it their way. The result was they ended up with one bad king after another. The modern church needs to know that God has set standards for leadership that every group needs to apply.

Comparing Leaders & Leadership Styles

1 Kings 14.25-28 &; 1 Kings 15.16-19

The difference between leaders comes down to character and purpose. Comparing two Old Testament kings should help set the stage for understanding the need to follow God's direction for choosing church leadership. Rehoboam and Asa both served as kings for the nation of Judah. They both ruled from Jerusalem and both had prolonged wars while they were king.

Rehoboam fought against Shishak of Egypt. Everything was taken from the Temple, even the gold shields that Solomon had made when Shishak conquered Jerusalem. After Shishak left, Rehoboam had bronze shields made so that when he went from the palace to the temple he would look the part of a king. His troops would take the bronze shields that had replaced the gold ones and parade through the streets as if nothing had happened. Rehobaom was so concerned about his pride and position that he worked to put on a show, even in front of his defeated and suffering people. He had forgotten the PURPOSE of LEADERSHIP. He saw himself as so important that he had to put on a show to cover up what everyone knew about him. He was a phony when it came to caring about the people. He was a lousy leader.

Asa fought against Bassha of Israel. Baasha had boxed Asa in, and was applying pressure hoping to defeat him. Asa called in his officials, and had them scour the temple for any hidden gold or valuables. Then he had them go through his palace and find any of his personal gold and valuables they could. He emptied the temple and the palace of all gold and valuables, and sent them to Ben-Hadad in Damascus, who had a treaty with Baasha. Asa knew if he could get Ben-Hadad to break the treaty, then Baasha would have to withdraw, and there could be peace in Judah. The plan worked, and Ben-Hadad broke his treaty with Baasha and signed one with Asa. There was peace. The war ended, and the people were freed from the fear and burden of a long war. He remembered his PURPOSE of LEADERSHIP and did not worry about personal pride or position. He gave up everything for the people he was leading. He became a servant leader willing to sacrifice for the good of his people.

The difference between Rehoboam and Asa is striking. Rehoboam was worried about appearance, and it made him weak. Asa was not worried about appearance, and it made him strong. Rehoboam lost everything, and got nothing in return. Asa gave everything away, and won the war and the love of his people. Rehoboam wanted to look strong with fake shields. Asa did not care how he looked and ended up strong. Rehoboam was worried about his personal pride and position, and allowed this to trump his responsibilities as a leader. Asa saw his purpose of leadership clearly, and would not allow his personal pride or his position as king, to stop him from doing what was right. Rehoboam was a king with servants while Asa was a king who was a servant. Servant leadership led to peace and lifted the people's burdens.

Understanding Types of Church Government (Polity)

There are three basic forms of church government in use today. The first is the Episcopal, or the form used by the Catholic Church. Here, all authority eventually rests with one person. This form of church government is directed from the top down. The second is the Presbyterian, or the Calvinistic form, of church government. In this, the church is run by an elected body or synod. The leadership has a broader base, but is limited to those selected either as ministers or elected lay-leaders. The third form is the Congregational, or the Independent form of church government. Authority for making decisions rests with the members of the local church. They often approve an annual budget, and then the leadership is directed to work within that budget for the year. Now, here is the part most people do not want to admit. Not one of these forms of church government is in the Bible. Every group will argue that they have Biblical church organization or government and will point to scripture to prove it. Here is my argument; *there is no Biblical basis for any form of church government, but there are Biblical standards for church leadership, no matter how the church is organized*.

Church LEADERSHIP Standards [1 Timothy 3.1-7]

Paul is writing to the younger pastor, Timothy. He sets up the basis for leadership qualifications or standards within the local church. He gives the list that those, who are going to serve as church leaders, need to meet in order to serve the church. When we look at the New Testament there are lists of titles used to describe church leaders. They are called elders, deacons, deaconesses, overseers, shepherds, and bishops to name the most prevalent ones used. The problem that comes to us today is the varied ways these titles are used. In one church an elder is a pastor only, while in another an elder is anyone serving on a leadership board. In one church a deacon is a worker in the church, while in another church the deacons are in charge of running the church. I pastor a church without deacons, elders, or any of the others. We have a

Leadership TEAM that guides the life of the church. I serve on it with five elected members of the church. I have a friend who will not allow women into any position of leadership, while I believe that when Paul wrote that "*there is neither... male nor female*" Galatians 3.28 this applies to all parts of the church including leadership. Yet, however your church is organized, and whatever titles you use for your leadership, there are Biblical qualifications they need to meet in order to serve in those positions. These qualifications or standards can be broken down into five simple statements about church leadership that should apply to every church leader.

A Church Leader MUST be...Committed to GOD

Paul said they must *not be a new convert* and should be tested by time. 1 Timothy 3.6 They first have to be a believer and be in right relationship with God. They should not be a novice to the faith. This is vital, and means they have demonstrated their relationship to God over a period of time. They need to be *free from the love of money.* 1 Timothy 3.3, Titus 3.7 It does not say they do not have money, but that it has not become their God. They use it as a tool in life, and it is not their life's purpose. They must *hold fast the faithful word.* Titus 1.9 This places them in regular contact with the foundational directions given them, and the church from God. They must be *holy.* Titus 1.8 Their lives are clearly tuned to their call and relationship with God.

A Church Leader MUST be...Committed to SELF

This may seem to contradict the call itself, but it is vital the church leader demonstrate *self-control* 1 Timothy 3.3, Titus 1.8 and be *temperate* 1 Timothy 3.2, Titus 1.8 or show personal discipline under pressure. They are *not to be addicted to wine* 1 Timothy 3.3, Titus 1.7 or have *a quick temper* Titus 1.7 Both show the personal control a person is exercising in daily living. They are to *love what is good* Titus 1.8 or they are to make the right choice between good and evil, even when no one is watching.

A Church Leader MUST be...Committed to FAMILY

They are to *manage their own household well,* [1 Timothy 3.4] or they will not be qualified to lead the church. They must *have one spouse* [1 Timothy 3.2, Titus 1.6] and their *children need to be under control and believe.* [1 Timothy 3.4] A church leader can be a single adult or a married individual with or without children. The key here is that their home life must reflect their commitment and belief in Jesus as their personal savior.

A Church Leader MUST be...Committed to OTHERS

They must *have a good reputation with those outside of the church.* [1 Timothy 3.7] A person who does not live his relationship with Christ in his daily life, as he or she interacts with the world, cannot serve as a leader of the local church. As a church leader deals with non-believers he or she must be *just* [Titus 1.8], *non-violent* [1 Timothy 3.3, Titus 1.7], *hospitable* [1 Timothy 3.2], *respectable* [1 Timothy 3.2], and *not self-willed* [1 Timothy 3.2], or not putting themselves first, but considering the needs and wants of others.

A Church Leader MUST be...Committed to CHURCH

When a person has been selected as a church leader, he/she is to *willingly serve the church.* [1 Peter 5.2] The church leader needs to serve the church following the example of Asa's servant leadership, and not like Rehoboam. They are in the position of leadership as servants, not as masters or bosses. To serve in church leadership means to be a servant leader. They are to *watch and shepherd the church.* [Acts 20.28] The shepherd is a protector of the flock, and a guide who loves the sheep, and would place himself between the flock and danger. The church leader is to serve as an *example to the church.* [1 Peter 5.3] The reasons the qualifications are so high are to make sure the person will succeed, and that the person will serve as a pattern of the Christian life for the other members of the congregation. They will take the study of the word seriously so that they can *teach sound doctrine* 1 Timothy 3.2, Titus 1.9 and to *refute* Titus 1.9 those who oppose the truth.

A Church Leader MUST be ABOVE REPROACH

1 Timothy 3.2, Titus 1.6-7, 1 Timothy 2.13

There can be no secret lives or places in the life of a church leader. Every part is open and reflects their relationship with the risen savior, Jesus. This means that their commitment to GOD is dedicated, and the leader represents God openly. Their commitment to SELF is about being motivated and growing as a believer. Their commitment to FAMILY means they protect and cherish these vital relationships. Their *commitment to OTHERS* reflects the knowledge that Christ died for them too. Their *commitment to the CHURCH* means they believe in the potential of the local fellowship.

In his book '21 Irrefutable Laws of Leadership' John Maxwell talks about the five people who add tremendous value to your life and your leadership. People serving in leadership need to be able to look around the table at their leadership meetings, and see people who bring tremendous value to their lives. The church I serve has a six person Leadership TEAM. That means there are five people who sit at that table with me and whom I need to respect, listen to and whom I can count on as dedicated Christians and dedicated leaders of the local church. They are there because they meet the high standards inspired by the Holy Spirit. Each year, as we prepare the names to be presented to the church for consideration as members to serve on the Leadership TEAM, we check off five distinct categories. We use these questions to see if a person is qualified to serve. Here is our check list and how we explain each one.

1. The church leader *must be a born again believer.* (God) This must be evident in how they live their lives. There are no secret agent Christians in the kingdom of God. Jesus said if we deny him before

the world he would deny us before the father. Matthew 10.33

2. The church leader must have a visible moral character. (SELF) The person must demonstrate self-control and a willingness to make right decisions as a regular part of their daily living. Each of us is called to be holy. This is especially true of the church leader. Ephesians 4.1
3. The Church leader *must have a stable home life*. (FAMILY) The need to live the Christian life with those who are closest to the leader is vital. Jesus knew the importance of the each believer and their witness to their own family. Mark 5.19 A stable Christian home is a vital part of the life of any Christian leader.
4. The church leader *must be a person who works well with a group*. (OTHERS) The person who is going to serve in church leadership needs to work well in a committee type structure. "Do they play well with others?" is the way we ask it in our meetings. There are people who get along and work well on a committee or in a team experience, and there are those who do not. A key part of leadership is working with others. It means they bring a spirit of support and cooperation to the time spent working on church matters. The goal is "*to bring all things in heaven and on earth together under one head, even Christ.*" Ephesians 1.10
5. The church leader *must support the local fellowship.* (CHURCH) We look at three areas here. First, are they regular in their participation in the local church activities, including being regular in their attendance of church services? Second, are they involved beyond showing up? This means they have a ministry or a way that demonstrated their commitment to the local church. Third, are they

> supporting the church financially? Where a person's treasure is where their heart is. Matthew 6.21 A person who is not supporting the local church should have no say in how the local finances are handled. How much money a person has is never the question. We want to know if they are faithful with the money they have, no matter how much or little, including their support of the local church.

The people of the Old Testament turned their backs on God's personal leadership, and put in place the leadership of kings like the other nations had. They paid dearly for this mistake. The church must hold its leadership up to the Biblical standards. It does not matter the form of church government as much as the way qualified Christian leaders are selected. When it was time to choose people to wait on tables, after the dispute between the widows, they were very careful not to choose just anyone. They chose those who were known to *be full of the Spirit of wisdom.* Acts 6.3 We should do no less when we select our local church leadership.

Review Chapter 14

Can you identify the following People or Places and tell how they are important to this week's lesson?

1. Jeroboam
2. Rehoboam
3. Abijah
4. Asa
5. Baasha
6. Naamah
7. Maakah
8. Samaria
9. Bethel & Dan
10. Jerusalem

Page numbers are from The Story (TS)

1. When Solomon died what two men replaced him as king and why was the country divided between them?

2. How was Rehoboam like is father, Solomon? How was he different? (TS 193-195)

3. What did Jeroboam do to strengthen his hold as king? (TS 196-197)

4. What did he do that angered God? (TS 196-197)

5. How did God plan to deal with Jeroboam for all the evil he had done? (TS 197-198)

6. How were the standards and the leadership of Judah impacted by their sins? (TS 198-199)

7. How did the leadership of king Asa in Judah differ from the leadership of most of the kings of his time? (TS 199-201)

8. What did it cost King Asa to gain peace and end the war with Israel? (TS 200)

9. What does this tell us about King Asa and his leadership?

10. Why is Samaria so important to Israel? (TS 201-201)

11. What one thing in this chapter did you learn that can help you on your personal faith journey?

Your Faith Journey
The Story Unfolds - Chapter 15

Have you completed the first three steps in your personal FAITH JOURNEY?

It may be hard to believe, but most people stop before they really get started on their personal faith journeys. Your faith journey is like the amazing race. You arrive at a location, and you have to complete the task before you can go on to the next location.

Elijah and Elisha the FAITH JOURNEY 2 Kings 2.1-14

Elisha had been selected to replace Elijah as the prophet of Israel. They were on their final trip together. Three times Elijah asked Elisha if he wanted to wait at a location along their path. These three locations each represent a place we as believers must visit if we are going to make a true and successful spiritual FAITH JOURNEY. First there is Bethel. This is where we will meet Jacob and learn who is actually in charge of each life. The trip continues to Jericho where we learn to deal with the barriers to victory in our lives. Finally, we need to travel to the Jordan where we have to decide if we will serve God, or watch from a distance.

The trip to BETHEL

Jacob is a real character when we look at his life. He cheated his brother out of his birthright. That is equivalent to getting the key to the family safe deposit box so that when dad passes away you have the inside track to all the cash on hand. Then, he tricks his dad into giving him the blessing of the eldest son. That is like getting the will changed, and getting yourself named to get the biggest share of the whole thing. After pulling these both off, Jacob takes off for the back country because he is afraid that his brother, Esau, is going to kill him. As Jacob travels he is alone and running for his life. He stops, and during the night, has a dream or a vision of a stairway reaching up to heaven with angels going up and down. At the top of the stairs, he sees the Lord God of Abraham and Isaac. Genesis 28.13 He sees God as the God of his grandfather and his father but he is not his God at this time. Jacob is so impressed he calls the place Bethel or 'the house of God'.

Jacob, who has pulled the wool over his father's eyes, and tricked his brother, now decides he has a deal for God. The first part says "*If God will be with me and watch over me on this journey I am taking and will give me food to eat and clothes to wear so that I return safely to my father's house...*" Genesis 28.20-21 Jacob is setting the conditions and telling God what he expects of him. It is all about Jacob. Jacob laces this small conditional phrase with I and me, making it plain who is important here. Jacob even says if God takes care of him, when he gets back there are two things he will do for God. The first is, "*Then the Lord will be my God.*" Genesis 28.21 Wow, he will give God permission to be his God, that is if God takes good enough care of him. If that is not enough, he reduces God to a table waiter. He says for taking such good care of him, he will give God ten percent. So God is supposed to make Jacob rich, and get him home safely and Jacob will give God a tip. Most people give the person waiting on their table at the restaurant a better tip than that.

Jacob takes off for the back country. He gets rich, marries Leah and Rachel, and starts back home with his wives, wealth, flocks, and kids. He is running from his father-in-law, whom he has tricked out of most his best flocks. On the way home, word arrives that Esau, his brother, is on the way with four hundred men to meet him. Jacob devises a plan that should at least keep some of his family and possessions safe if Esau is coming to settle the score from years before. Jacob divides up his flocks, and servants, and sends them on ahead in two groups. That way if one group is attacked the other one can get away. "*That night Jacob got up and took his two wives, his two maidservants and his eleven sons and crossed the ford of the Jabbok."* He sends them on their way in two groups with the same plan in place. If they are attacked, then, at least part of them can get away, and he will be able to escape. This is when scripture reminds us that *"Jacob was left alone."* After all the years and all he had acquired, Jacob is back where he started. Alone, just Jacob and a messenger sent from God. Reduced to nothing, now, he has learned a very valuable lesson. Jacob now knows he will have to serve God on God's terms. Everything he has can be taken away, but he still needs God. It is here his name is changed from Jacob, or the one who deceives, to Israel, or the one who wrestles with God.

The next day Jacob meets Esau, and finds that he has been forgiven. He has accepted God on God's terms, and he has returned to Bethel where the whole thing started. Genesis 35.6-7 Jacob has learned the hard way that you serve God on God's terms, and when you set conditions on God he just leans back, smiles, and waits till you have backed yourself into the corner. Many people give God their terms and, when things don't work out, they want to blame God. It is not God's fault when you live your life in your own strength on your terms. The bottom line for Jacob was, no matter what he had, he was nothing without God.

It is here at Bethel that Elijah asks Elisha if he wants to wait. Elijah wants to know if Elisha has made the commitment to surrender his life to God. If Elisha has held anything back, he needs to stop at Bethel and get it right. It is no use leaving Bethel till you have it all worked out on God's terms. If you leave, you will have to return and settle up with God before you can go any further on your spiritual faith journey. Elisha is ready to continue on his journey with Elijah.

The trip to JERICHO

Jericho was a fortified city that was in the path of the Hebrews when they first entered the Promised Land under the leadership of Joshua. Jericho had to be dealt with before their conquest could continue. The Hebrews were instructed to walk around the city once a day for six days and then, on the seventh day, they were to walk around the city seven times. "*When the trumpets sounded the people shouted, and at the sound of the trumpets when the people gave a loud shout, the wall collapsed.*" Joshua 6.20 The battle of Jericho was a victory of surrender and faith.

Jericho represents the inner obstacles of our lives that have to be dealt with. They are often well fortified and not easy to deal with. We see them as impenetrable and massive. Jericho represents the hidden inner sins or addictions that people hide within their lives. These areas are well fortified, and no matter how hard we try in our own strength, they cannot really be dealt with. The Hebrews walked around the walls, but when they called out, in the strength of God, He brought the walls down.

People often believe that they will deal with the problems in their lives themselves and then they will serve God. The problem is, their hidden city is what is keeping them from serving God and from personal spiritual victories. You have to deal with the Jericho in your life before your spiritual journey can continue.

Elijah asked Elisha if he needed to stay and deal with anything in his life that was keeping him from serving God. It was a time of reflection that Elisha needed to take. If he did not deal with Jericho, he could not really serve God. There was no need to go on until he was really ready. Each of us has to make sure there is nothing hidden in our inner life that stops us from serving God. We have to surrender and allow God to bring down the walls if we are going to really be of any use to Him.

The trip to the river JORDAN

The river Jordan separated the wilderness from the Promised Land. It also represents the fear of the unknown. The Hebrews first came to the Jordan 40 years earlier when they had first been set free from the oppressions of

Egypt, under the leadership of Moses. They had sent in a committee of twelve spies to determine how to proceed. The report from the committee of spies was ten against going in, and two for following God's directions and entering the Promised Land. Instead, they listened to the report of the ten. This made God mad. He sentenced them to one year for every day of spying and 40 years later they were at the river Jordan again. When anyone does not get it right with God or for God, they get to do it over again until they get it right. Jacob got to go back to Bethel. The Hebrews found themselves back at the bank of the river Jordan. Their fear and lack of faith translated into a long trip to learn a lesson. People often exercise zero faith and then wonder why they are so lost, and always haplessly wandering around.

When the Hebrews returned forty years later, they did not send in a committee, but they sent in a team of two spies to get the lay of the land for them. It was not a matter of if they were going into the Promised Land. It was merely a matter of where to go in at. Rahab told the spies that they had been waiting for their attack for the last 40 years, ever since the Hebrews left Egypt. Finally the morning to cross the Jordan came. "*Now the Jordan is at flood stage all during the harvest. Yet, as soon as the priest who carried the ark reached the Jordan and their feet touched the water's edge, the water from upstream stopped flowing. It piled up in a heap a great distance away.*" Joshua 3.15-16 Here is faith in action. The parting of the waters at Jericho was the beginning of the new life in the Promised Land. This had to happen before anything else could be accomplished.

Elijah tells Elisha to wait and be sure before going to the Jordan. Its waters only part for those who have surrendered at Bethel. The waters only part when the person has dealt with the inner forts that have to be removed like Jericho. Elijah parts the waters of the Jordan, and they both cross over on dry land. Now comes the test for Elisha as he returns without Elijah. Like the Hebrews, he has to part the waters or be trapped in the wilderness. He picks up Elijah's cloak, walks forward, and in his first act of personal faith parts, the waters of the Jordan.

Faith is learned in a group setting, but must be practiced on an individual basis. Until he was willing to exercise it himself, he was like the school of prophets who stood at a distance and watched, but never seemed to get any further.

The Three Places We Must Visit

Elijah wanted to make sure that Elisha knew the personal commitment and the journey he was on. It was not just a walk down the road. It was a walk of growth and faith.

- Elijah knew that each person had to enter into a personal relationship with God. He knew that any such relationship must be on God's terms. Every person must go to Bethel and meet with God one on one. You have to let GO and let God take CHARGE when you come to Bethel. "*Submit yourselves, then, to God. Resist the devil, and he will flee from you. Come near to God and he will come near to you*" James 4.7-8

- Elijah knew that each person has to deal with those areas of their life that hinder spiritual growth. They are never easy or small, yet, with God, it will happen. It may take time. It took the Hebrews thirteen trips around Jericho and seven days, but it was well worth it in the end. Every person has to deal with Jericho if they are going to be victorious in their personal spiritual life. You will have to deal with your personal sins and temptations if you are going to bring down the walls of Jericho. "*Those who belong to Christ Jesus have crucified the sinful nature with its passions and desires.*" Galatians 5.24

- Elijah knew that each person must cross over and face or deal with their fears. We may watch as others practice their faith and part the waters in their lives, but until we cross over ourselves, we are only observers. God has called each of us to pass through the waters on dry ground. We will either pass through the waters by exercising our faith or we will wander in the wilderness with our fears. The basic fact is you must have faith to cross the river Jordan. "*And without faith it is impossible to please God, because anyone who comes to him must believe that he exists and that he rewards those who earnestly seek him.*" Hebrews 11.6

Every time Elijah challenged Elisha to wait, it was not as a setback, but as a confirmation of completing the next set in the faith Journey. Elijah knew that to pass one by was merely an exercise in futility. Jacob had been forced to return 20 years later and surrender to God. The Hebrews had to return 40 years later and, again, face the same river they had faced. The person who refuses to surrender, or to deal with their personal sins and temptations, or who will not surrender their fears to faith, will be called back again and again until they gets it right or quit.

Where Are You On Your Faith Journey?

Each person is on a faith journey. It does not end at the Jordan, but you have to get there before you can go any further. Will you choose to come to Bethel and surrender to God, or will you, like Jacob, try to out deal God? Will you deal with the Jericho in your life, or will you allow the city of sin to stand, stopping any possibility of real spiritual victory? Will you have the faith to cross the river Jordan, or will you allow your fears to push you back into the wilderness to wander? Each person needs to make sure they are ready to go on, or they will just make a large circle, and come back to the same place again. You need to, first, surrender to God. Then, you need to deal with all the sin in your life. Then you need to step out in faith and discover the deeper life of victory.

Review Chapter 15

Can you identify the following People or Places or Items and tell how they are important to this week's lesson?

1. Elijah
2. Elisha
3. Adab
4. Jezebel
5. Gehazi
6. Amos
7. Hosea
8. Prophets of Baal
9. Mt. Carmel
10. Kerith Ravine

Page numbers are from The Story (TS)

1. Name two things that Elijah did that made King Ahab & Queen Jezebel angry enough to want to kill him. (TS 203, 205)

2. At the battle with the prophets of Baal, how did Elijah remind the people who the real God was? (TS 205)

3. How many of the miracles of Elijah can you name?

4. How and why did Elijah's attitude change after defeating the 450 prophets of Baal and the 400 prophets of Asherah? (TS 206)

5. Elijah thought he was alone, or the last follower of God left in the nation. Yet God said that ________ had not bowed their knee to Baal. God saw it was time for a new prophet. How did God replace Elijah and why do you think he did it in such a dramatic manner? (TS 207-209)

6. How many of the miracles of Elisha can you name?

7. How did Elisha defeat an entire army and bring peace to the country? (TS 211-212)

8. How do the prophecies of Amos and Hosea set the stage for a coming defeat of Israel and Judah? Why was God going to allow this to happen?

9. What one thing in this chapter did you learn that can help you on your personal faith journey?

Beyond Showing Up
The Story Unfolds - Chapter 16

What does it take to discover the deeper life of the Christian believer? Most people are happy in their Christian experience to just show up at church and listen to the message. They are so overcome by the daily activities of the living that they are numb when it comes to spiritual feelings or adding anything to their lives. They function like a soaked sponge. The only way something is added is if something drains out. There is a deeper life for the Christian believer that is more meaningful and fulfilling than most are experiencing now. This deeper life passes through this dark world, and is clearly marked out for us by God, yet few follow the path, or choose to discover the victories and joy that it can bring to their lives.

Two Real Question

How close to God can a believer get? That may sound dumb, but many believers act like getting too close to God will cause them to burst into flames. Isaiah, the prophet, was an average believer for his time. He served in the court of the king like many other prophets. He was an adviser in spiritual and military matters. Yet, he was average. The real question you have to answer, and the one Isaiah would face, is, how close to God do you want to get? If you want to go deeper, you have to be willing to accept what comes with getting closer to God. It means a new path. It means a new attitude. It means making changes, and it means being changed by God. If you want to go deeper, you can go through the same process Isaiah did. These seven steps can bring you closer to God and put you on the deeper path of commitment and faith. Isaiah 6.1-13 challenges us to follow the prophet into a deeper walk with God.

Evaluate Where You Are

This is about putting things into proper perspective. "*In the year king Uzziah died.*" This is where Isaiah found himself. People have life points that they never forget. Generations remember Pearl Harbor, when Kennedy was shot, the moon landing, the Twin Towers, and the Japanese Tsunami because they are personal and overwhelming. My mother tells of listening to the radio as the reports came in on that Sunday when Pearl Harbor was attacked. Now, in her late seventies it is like it was yesterday. I remember when my son rushed into the house and told us that planes were flying into buildings in New York City. We watched the television most of the day. It still seems unreal. How things change. My mom listened to the radio about an attack that was over even before she heard it was happening. I watched the twin towers collapse live on television. The world communicates today with email, twitter, skype, facebook pages, and it seems like every kid I see has a cell phone. Last week I watched as the homeless guy who holds up a sign on a local street corner answered his cell phone. Isaiah watched Israel, the northern kingdom, go into captivity. The nation of Judah was in shambles, under constant attack from enemies. Then the king died. He is confronted with the reality of life and begins to evaluate his spiritual life.

Establish Contact With God

Isaiah says, "*I saw the Lord seated on a throne, high and exalted, and the train of his robe filled the temple.*" Here the seraphs with their six wings cried out "*Holy, holy , holy is the LORD Almighty; the whole earth is full of his glory.*" The word holy has a three part meaning. It means to be physically pure, to be spiritually pure, and to be mentally pure. The angels are declaring God is completely pure. God is the Lord. This is the God who is sovereign. He is the creator of the world and is always here. He is the "I AM" of time. He was, is, and always will be. He is called the Almighty. He is the final authority for everything. This fact alone keeps many people as far away from Him as possible. They want to be in charge of their lives. It is a scary thing to establish contact with God. Most people spend their lives avoiding God, and here Isaiah has seen God. The problem with seeing the holy Lord almighty is what you look like in His presence. That is what Isaiah found out.

Examine Who You Are

When you find yourself in the presence of the holy God it can be a terrifying experience. When Isaiah found himself in front of God he cried out "*Woe to me! I am ruined! For I am a man of unclean lips, and I live among a people of unclean lips, and my eyes have seen the King, the LORD Almighty.*" Isaiah was ruined, completely cut off; in comparing himself to God he was destroyed. He and everyone around him were not capable of standing in front of a holy God. He had unclean lips. Jesus spoke to the matter of unclean lips. "*What comes out of a man is what makes him 'unclean.' For from within, out of men's hearts, come evil thoughts, sexual immorality, theft, murder, adultery, greed, malice, deceit, lewdness, envy, slander, arrogance and folly. All these evils come from inside and make a man 'unclean.'*" Mark 7.20-23 The inside of Isaiah was unclean. Isaiah could have blamed the society he lived in. The problem was not the world he lived in. It was Isaiah himself. He was not living up to the standards of God. Most people, confronted with this truth, just move away from God as quickly as possible. Isaiah realized he was a fake in a world of fakes. Having examined himself he had to choose whether to turn away from God, or to make changes.

Eliminate the Negatives

If you discover you are not acceptable to God you have choices to make. You can walk away and continue to live your life out of step with God. You can try to fix it yourself. This approach says when I have improved enough then I will serve God. The third choice is to allow God to make the changes that are needed in your life. You may be able to cover up the sin on the outside but only God deals with the root cause. One of the angels took a coal from the altar of God and flew to Isaiah. He touches Isaiah's lips or deals with the personal sin making him pure. The angel declares "*your guilt is taken away.*" This is dealing with the mental state of Isaiah or his conscience. This makes him pure in mind. Then, we learn that Isaiah's sin is atoned for making him pure in Spirit. This means the God who is Holy, Holy, Holy, has made Isaiah Holy (in body), Holy (in mind), Holy (in spirit). God has provided a way for the impure Isaiah to come before Him without guilt or fear. Jesus has made this purity and holiness available to any who call on His name.

This is about being changed by God. In 1958 people were still drafted into military service. You received a letter from the local draft board that called you up for two years active military service and then four years in the reserves. That year soldier number 53-31-07-61 entered the service. He was walked to the induction service by his mother and girlfriend Anita. Then he was put on the bus and taken to the first stop, where, he got the famous military haircut, and went to basic training at Fort Hood Texas. He was then assigned to a tank battalion and sent to Germany as his first service station. That is where he met his future wife, Priscilla. As famous as this soldier was, he did not get to skip the haircut, basic training, or wearing the uniform. He had to conform to military standards as a U. S. soldier. Elvis Presley may have been famous in the world, but if you look at his military pictures he is every bit what was expected of him. He rose to the rank of sergeant while serving in the Army.

If you are going to serve God, you have to fit with the expectations of the commander, the Lord Almighty. This means we have to know and meet the conditions set by God. Elvis was given his haircut free of charge. He was bussed to Fort Hood free of charge. He was given a ticket to Germany on a ship which he did not pay for. He was even paid $78 a month as a private in the army even though had made over a million dollars the year before.

Here is the key point. What he needed to be a soldier was provided for him. What we need to make the transformation is provided for us by God. We do not earn it. We do not pay for it. We cannot do it ourselves. The Army transformed Elvis into a soldier. God almighty transforms us into a holy person. We cannot do it ourselves. God eliminates the negatives from our lives.

Enlist For Service

God does not change us so we can sit in a church and do nothing. God did not change Isaiah to make him feel better about himself. He changed Isaiah to put him into service. Yet, it was still Isaiah's choice to serve God or turn back to the world he had just been cleansed of. God looks around and asks, "*Whom shall I send*?" God is searching for those who will respond to his call. He gives a call that will allow Isaiah to respond. "*Who will go for us?*" It is still a personal choice. No one is forced to do anything for God.

Isaiah responds, "*Here I am, Send me.*" With one sentence he established contact and signs up for his assignment. Yet none of this would be possible if he had not been changed by God. He is making a public declaration. We are called to do the same thing. Jesus said, "*Whoever acknowledges me before men, I will also acknowledge him before my Father in heaven. But whoever disowns me before men, I will disown him before my Father in heaven.*" Matthew 10.32.33 Even after we step up, God wants to be sure we really want in. We need to volunteer to serve. He will not force us to do any of this.

Explain the Truth

Isaiah is told to "*Go and tell this people.*" It will not matter how they respond. God already knows they are *"dull of hearing.*" You can train yourself to hear God. You can also train yourself to ignore God. Much like a husband, who can tune out his wife's voice, people tune God out. They do not want to hear God's voice or change. Their *"hearts are calloused"* and it will not be easy to reach them with the truth. In fact it may be impossible. If we are going to respond to God's call we need to know up front that most people will not be receptive to our message. They see you as a door-to-door salesman working for God. They have signs on their souls that read, NO RELIGIOUS SOLICITATIONS EVER!!! Their *"eyes are closed"* and they refuse to see the positive and focus on the negative. Even when the truth is right in front of them, they will not see it. Even the obvious truth of God is ridiculed and rejected. These are the people God was calling Isaiah to speak to. These are the people God is calling us to *Go and tell this people* about Jesus.

Endurance That Last

Isaiah has just learned that the people he will be sharing with will reject everything he is trying to tell them. So, he asks the logical question, "*For how long, O Lord*?" Isaiah was faced with preaching the coming judgment of God to the nation. Even, as things got worse he was required to preach the truth, this even as more and more pull away from the living God in their search for universal happiness and self-satisfaction.

How long? Elvis only had to give two years of active service. Right here is where a lot of people stop. It is when they begin to hear the commitment that it takes. They hear how hard the battle may be, and they just bail. Jesus faced this as he was going down the road, and began to lay out the commitment that it would take to follow Him. It was not going to be easy. He ups the score and lets them know it will get more difficult if they continue to follow Him. That is when it happened. "*From this time many of his disciples turned back and no longer followed him.*" John 6.66 They just walked away. They wanted the easy road, a short enlistment, and a cushy assignment. Instead, Jesus told them the same thing God told Isaiah.

How long? God tells Isaiah 'UNTIL'... Until the cities are ruined. Until the houses are empty. Until everyone is far away. Isaiah has just had the greatest religious experience in his life. Then he is told he will preach to these people 'UNTIL'. Not two years, or six years, but 'UNTIL'. That is a long time. Tradition says that Isaiah was sawed in half with a wooden saw by the evil king Manasseh. So Isaiah's until was until he was sawed in half. How long are you called to serve God? You are called to serve *'UNTIL,'* even if that means until you are sawed in half with a wooden saw.

That is why those disciples following Jesus stopped and walked away. They heard Jesus say they had to follow him until.... They looked at Jesus and said, "See you later, we are outta here!" They were there for the suppers by the lake. They liked the scenic boat trips. They were there for the healings, and the excitement of following Jesus, but they were not going to follow and serve UNTIL...

The great Christians I have known in my life, and there are not a lot of them, all were people who were serving until. They had endurance that last. Their stories are not of fame but of endurance and obedience. The famous preachers of large churches do not measure up to these saints who live for God day in and day out. They know and understand that "*All men will hate you because of me, but he who stands firm to the end will be saved.*" Mark 13.13 Standing firm to the end means until...

Emphasize the Essentials

We can learn a lot from the encounter that Isaiah had with God. We need to put it all together:

- Evaluate where you are - NOW
- Establish contact with God - ALMIGHTY
- Examine who you are - UNCLEAN
- Eliminate the negatives - HOLY (X's 3)
- Enlist for service - VOLUNTEER
- Explain the truth - POSITIVE
- Endurance that last - UNTIL....

This is what it takes to discover and live the deeper life of a believer. It means you are signed up until............

Review Chapter 16

Can you identify the following People, Places or dates and tell how they are important to this week's lesson?

1. Hezekiah
2. Isaiah
3. Uzziah
4. Shalmaneser
5. Sennacherib
6. Hoshea
7. 722 B.C.
8. Assyrians
9. Israel
10. Judah

Page numbers are from The Story (TS)

1. __________ became the last king of the Northern Kingdom of __________when he was defeated and 27,000 were deported to Assyria to live as slaves. Why did this happen and could God have prevented it? (TS 219-220)

2. __________ was the king of the Southern Kingdom of__________ when it was attacked by the Assyrian king. He boasted of his power and the weakness of the Hebrews. (TS 221-222) How did God deal with the Assyrian army? (TS 224)

3. Why did God help Judah and allow Israel to be taken captive by the same nation?

4. Why is godly leadership so important to a nation?

5. How can ungodly leadership hurt a nation even in these modern times?

6. Isaiah was a prophet to the Southern Kingdom for 60 years. His greatest prophecies were about the coming Messiah. What do we learn about this messiah from the writings of Isaiah? (TS 228-230)

7. Israel made the logical choice of Egypt as their ally uniting with a strong military against another strong military nation, while Judah chose to rely on God, which, on the surface, seemed foolish. Why was one the wrong choice and the other the right one?

8. What one thing in this chapter did you learn that can help you on your personal faith journey?

Remember to Look Up
The Story Unfolds - Chapter 17

The Life and Times of Jeremiah the Prophet

How can an Old Testament prophet help someone deal with difficult people in his/her life? Well, if that Old Testament prophet is Jeremiah you could learn a lot from him about dealing with difficult people. Jeremiah had one of the toughest assignments ever handed out by God to any prophet. He told the truth, and suffered physical, mental, and spiritual abuse at the hands of God's people.

Overview of the life of Jeremiah

He was called as a young man Jeremiah 1.5 and was given the assignment of bringing a very negative message to the Israelites. Often called the weeping prophet, he was the voice of God in a very difficult time. His ministry opened with visions given him by God. One was of an almond tree that showed that God was watching the nation as they turned away from him. The other was of a boiling pot Jeremiah 5.19 being spilled out toward the north. This represented the coming attack and brutal captivity that would follow. Jeremiah was so upset with the vision about the coming captivity. Jeremiah begged God to change his mind. God told him if he could find one righteous person in Jerusalem, God would spare the nation. Jeremiah 5.1 This was done to allow Jeremiah to look closely at how far the nation had moved away from God. Jeremiah visited a potter's shop and watched him make clay pots. Jeremiah 18.1-6 Later, God showed him that, as the potter fashions the pots and removes the impurities, so God would fashion the people and remove the impurities. God told Jeremiah that he needed to tell the people about the coming judgment. Jeremiah did this by buying a large pot and carrying it around with him until he got a crowd to follow him out of town and down the road to a nearby valley. When he got there, he raised the pot over his head and smashed it against the rock. Then he proclaimed that the pot was the nation, and God was about to smash it for their sins. Their response was to beat him, and put him on public display in stocks, so people could pass by and spit on him. Jeremiah 20.1-2

Jeremiah found that he was the most unpopular man in the nation. The people became angry when he preached to them. He became so upset that he complained to God. "*O Lord, you deceived me, and I was deceived; you overpowered me and prevailed. I am ridiculed all day long; everyone mocks me.*" Jeremiah 20.7 Jeremiah had answered the call of God to preach truth and had thought he would be well received. He thought being a prophet of God might be a cushy job. Instead, it turned out working for God was the toughest job in the world. God helped Jeremiah understand that the prophet's comfort was not the top of the list when the nation was going down the tubes. Then God gave Jeremiah a message of judgment and hope all in one. The captivity that was coming would last seventy years. Jeremiah 25.11 That was God's judgment, and many would not live to see it come to an end. It was a message of hope, in that, it would not last forever. God was promising not to forget his people.

Jeremiah wrote a book to tell the nation about what was going to happen. The king heard about it and ordered it confiscated and read to him in his palace on a cold winter evening. Jeremiah 26.20-32 The king would listen for a while and then have the part that had been read burned in the fire. When Jeremiah heard about it he wrote the book again because there were no backup copies. The second time he wrote the book he had several copies made and then sent them out to be read to the people.

Jeremiah took a yoke from an ox and began wearing it around his shoulders as he continued to preach about the coming judgment. Jeremiah 27.2 He told them, like an ox has to go where he is directed, so the Israelites would have to go where they were directed, when they were conquered. Another prophet, Hananiah, yanked the yoke off of Jeremiah, broke it to pieces, and declared that Jeremiah was a false prophet. Jeremiah told Hananiah that, for going against God's prophet, Hananiah could talk it over with God face to face. A short time later Hananiah died. Jeremiah 28.13

Usually all's well that ends well, that is except for Jeremiah. The people became so tired of his negative message they dropped him into a mud filled well and left him there. Jeremiah 38.1-13 When he was finally rescued from the well, he told the king to surrender or his family would die, and he would suffer under the coming invaders. Jeremiah 38.13f The king listened instead to other court prophets who told him God was on his side. That was the wrong move on his part. The city was captured. The king's family was killed in front of him, and he was taken away into captivity, after having his eyes gouged out. Jeremiah is spared captivity by the invading king. He must have thought, "finally I am safe," but, wouldn't you know it, some of the people left behind rebelled against the invaders. They became frightened and decided to leave for Egypt to escape being punished. The last thing they did, before leaving Jerusalem, was to grab Jeremiah and force him to go with them. Jeremiah 43.4-7

Don't cry for me, Argentina, I mean Jeremiah. Here is Jeremiah taken to Egypt by the people who beat him up, put him in stocks, spit on him, dropped him down a well and burned his book. So, what does this weeping prophet do? He writes the book of Lamentations or, his book of tears, to tell the story of what went wrong. Here he is, the prophet of God, who did nothing wrong. He just lived in an evil time, surrounded by evil people, who did evil things to God's servant, when he preached the truth. That was the life and times and calling of Jeremiah the prophet. He was called to preach the truth and weep for God before the people.

The Salvation of the Lord Lamentations 3.14-26

The way Jeremiah was treated was quite different from the way Jeremiah saw God. In fact, after his meltdown, he turned around. When he wrote Lamentations in Egypt, he remembered the tough times. "*I became the laughingstock of all my people they mock me in song all day long.*" He speaks of broken teeth and being trampled in the dust. "*I have been deprived of peace; I have forgotten what prosperity is.*" Yet, through it all, he knew God's presence. "*Because of the Lord's great love we are not consumed for his compassions never fail.*" He saw the benefit of serving God in the toughest times. Those who remain faithful know that "*the Lord is good to those whose hope is in him, to the one who seeks him; it is good to wait quietly for the salvation of the Lord.*" Jeremiah learned much in his lifetime of service and suffering.

The Little Red Hen

I have read this story over and over to my grandson. My wife has read it to him. I am sure you remember the story. The Little Red Hen finds some seeds and wants help planting but no will help. She wants help harvesting the crop, but no one will help. She wants help grinding the meal and making the bread, but no one will help. She wants help baking the bread, but no one will help. Then, when all the work is done, everyone wants some of the fresh baked bread, but the Little Red Hen says, NO WAY, and eats the bread she has worked so hard for herself.

The Little Red Hen & Jeremiah the Prophet

You may not think of these two in the same sentence, but they have a lot in common, just the opposite is true. They both had a job to do. They both worked alone. They both received zero respect for all the work they did. They both had an end goal in mind. They both asked for help many times. They both turned out to be popular in the end, and they both, alone, got the reward. The Little Red Hen enjoyed the bread, and Jeremiah ended up with God in eternity. I can see Jeremiah, tired and alone, living in Egypt after a lifetime of weeping and preaching truth, with little to show for it. He closes his eyes and dies. When he opens his eyes again, he is at the gates of heaven. They swing open and, as he walks in, everyone is lined up on both sides of the entrance clapping and cheering. Tears again fill his eyes. This time they are tears of joy. The weeping prophet is home.

The Little Red Hen, Jeremiah the Prophet & YOU

We live in a broken country surrounded by those who are rejecting the message of God, and, who see us as foolish and backward. The message of truth we share runs in the exact opposite direction of this world. We often wonder if it is worth it. You are not alone in this struggle, and God is still on his throne. The key to your life is that, in the end, you get to eat the bread. You get to spend eternity in heaven.

Jeremiah, the Little Red Hen, Jesus and You

Jeremiah knew that "*the Lord is good to those whose hope is in him, to the one who seeks him; it is good to wait quietly for the salvation of the Lord.*" Lamentations 3.25-26 We must always remember to keep our eyes on God and not allow this world to decide our values or direction. If we do our part we get to eat the bread in the end. "*Then Jesus declared, "I am the bread of life. He who comes to me will never go hungry, and he who believes in me will never be thirsty.*" John 6.35

When you are at the bottom of the well in this life you need to remember one thing. Look up. The sky you see may seem so very far away, but it represents the living God who has not forgotten you. You may be up to your armpits in mud, but there is coming a day when you will enjoy fresh baked bread in heaven. The very people who reject you, also will call on you for help when they have a spiritual problem. Even if they drag you to Egypt, remember, you will end up in heaven.

Review Chapter 17

Can you identify the following People, Places, or dates and tell how they are important to this week's lesson?

1. Ezekiel
2. Jeremiah
3. Nebuchadnezzar
4. Zedekiah
5. Josiah
6. Babylon
7. Egypt
8. Judah
9. 586 B.C.
10. Manasseh

Page numbers are from The Story (TS)

1. Manasseh represents the way most kings of Judah acted. List some of the things he did that angered God and led to God giving up and punishing His people. (TS 231-232)

2. What caused Manasseh to turn back to God? Why will people who turned to God, as he did, never really serve God? (TS 232)

3. Ezekiel's message was one of defeat and doom that preceded the eventual restoration of the nation. (TS 235-237) Eventually, God showed him hope even though he had been taken as a hostage to Babylon. How does God describe the rebirth of the Hebrew nation? (TS 245-247)

4. Jeremiah, the weeping prophet, stayed in Jerusalem with the remnant of the poor, and eventually was taken to Egypt with them. Things had already gone from bad to worse in Judah. Why could Jeremiah not give the people any hope with his messages? (TS 237-240)

5. God declares that, "I, myself, will fight against you with an outstretched hand and a mighty arm in furious anger and in great wrath." (TS 242) How and why would a loving God respond to his own people in this way?

6. Why doesn't God just wipe the nation out and start over with a new people? (TS 244—245)

7. Which would have been harder to be: Ezekiel, taken to Babylon, or Jeremiah, and taken to Egypt? Why?

8. What one thing in this chapter did you learn that can help you on your personal faith journey?

How Much Faith Do You Need? The Story Unfolds - Chapter 18

How much faith do you need to survive? Faith is vital to the believer's life, yet, if you ask most to define it, they cannot. If you ask them to explain how faith impacts their lives, they don't do much better. There are some basics you need to know about faith. Throughout the Old Testament faith is evident in the lives of those who serve and follow God. It is evident in the lives of the Hebrews who were taken to Babylon as captives, after the fall of Jerusalem in 586 B.C. Here, Daniel, Hananiah, Mishael, and Azariah find themselves in a battle to maintain their relationships with God while serving evil and pagan kings. They are challenged to maintain purity when told to eat the king's food. They are challenged with unknown dreams that need to be interpreted if they are going to live. They are challenged when confronted with a golden image they are told to kneel and worship. They are challenged when told to worship the king or be thrown into the fiery furnace. They are challenged when their regular prayer times become illegal. They are challenged when thrown into the lion's den. Yet, in each case, they each lived a life of faith and remained faithful. We will look at one of these challenges to help us lay the foundation to understanding what faith is.

Faith Trumps Fear Daniel 3.1-15

Nebuchadnezzar sets up a ninety foot gold statue, and orders everyone to bow down or die. He has been convinced, by those around him, he is a god, and everyone should worship him through this statue. It was really a trap to catch the Hebrews. The other officials wanted them out of the way, and this was how they were going to get rid of at least three of them. The day arrived and everyone bowed down. That is, everyone, but Shadrach, Meshach, and Abednego—they stood tall. The astrologers who had set up the trap made a bee line to tell Nebuchadnezzar of the three Hebrews refusal to bow to the golden statue. The three are brought before the king and given one final time to bow down or be thrown into the fiery furnace. He even asks them "*what god will be able to rescue you from my hand?*"

If we are going to understand faith, we will start by seeing how they responded to the king. Standing there with the image on one side and the fiery furnace on the other, "*Shadrach, Meshach and Abednego replied to the king, "O Nebuchadnezzar, we do not need to defend ourselves before you in this matter. If we are thrown into the blazing furnace, the God we serve is able to save us from it, and he will rescue us from your hand, O king. But even if he does not, we want you to know, O king, that we will not serve your gods or worship the image of gold you have set up.*"" They stood their ground and refused to bow. To understand how deep their faith was and why they could be so confident in facing death, we will need to better understand what faith really is.

Five Faith Facts Hebrews 11.1-40

Faith Fact Number ONE: **Faith is always about the future**. "*Now, faith is being sure of what we hope for and certain of what we do not see.*" Hebrews 11.1 Yesterday my son, Aaron, ran in the Capital City Marathon. He ran the ½ marathon while his girlfriend ran the 5K. At the end of the race, my son got a t-shirt, a cup coaster, and a dog-tag necklace that were all engraved with the information about the race he had finished. Everyone who raced started at the same place, but at different times. The marathon runners started first, then those running the half-marathon started, then those who ran the five K race went next and finally the kids' race started. They all had the same goal: to finish the race. They all had to run the course that was laid out for them, and would all have to cross the finish line to get their reward. When the race started, the reward was in the future, and the only way they could get it was to run the race and finish. This is also true about faith. Faith is about the race we call life, and our relationship with God. We are running toward the finish line where we will stand before God and hear, "Well done, come on in." We are not there yet.

Faith Fact Number TWO: **Faith is a requirement in your relationship with God**. "*Without faith it is impossible to please God, because anyone who comes to him must believe that he exists and that he rewards those who earnestly seek him.*" Hebrews 11.6 If you want to please God the only way you can do that is through faith. You have to believe in God. That may sound trite, but there are many who do not know God or who are searching for God in all the wrong places. Many of the Hebrews turned from God to Asherah poles, serving Baal and worshipping strange Gods on high places. You have to believe in 'the' God and his Son Jesus, who is the promised Christ. If you believe in Him, then you can also know that He rewards those who believe. In the race, the rewards often come at the end.

Faith Fact Number THREE: **Faith is not about anything that you can hold. It is a promise**. "*All these people were still living by faith when they died. They did not receive the things promised; they only saw them and welcomed them from a distance.*" Hebrews 11.13 According to the dictionary a promise is a declaration, or assurance, that one will do a particular thing, or that it will happen. God has given us His promise in the written word. Through the scriptures we learn of all his plans and even the coming rewards that will be given to those who believe in Him. The promise was delivered in the form of His son, Jesus, and paid for with his death on the cross. The resurrection is the way we know that God is able to keep His promise. When a young man meets a young lady they first talk, then they date, then they fall in love, and eventually, if she is the right one, he asks her to marry him. Then, they are engaged. An engagement is a promise to marry. It means they are not going to date anyone else, and they are telling everyone that there is no one else they want to be with. When we make a commitment to God, we are getting engaged to God. We are making a commitment to Him alone. God is also making a commitment to us. This commitment, or promise, will be fulfilled in the future when we arrive in heaven. This future date is when we will attend the great wedding feast that is being planned by God to celebrate the marriage of Christ to His church, the church which you are part of.

Faith Fact Number FOUR: **Faith 'can be' living a victorious life**. "*Through faith* [they] *conquered kingdoms, administered justice, and gained what was promised; who shut the mouths of lions, quenched the fury of the flames, and escaped the edge of the sword; whose weakness was turned to strength; and who became powerful in battle and routed foreign armies. Women received back their dead, raised to life again. Others were tortured and refused to be released, so that they might gain a better resurrection*" Hebrews 11.33-35 When you read this section you want to shout, "Put me in the game coach." You feel ready to face danger, fire, lions, or enter a battle without any doubt of anything, except victory. Right here is where a lot of preachers stop their messages. This is where they start the messages of health, wealth and happiness. They preach that every believer is supposed to be rich and healthy and so happy that the world will envy us for what we have received from God. Yet, that message is just not true. When someone believes they are supposed to be rich and it does not happen, they can become discouraged. Then they begin to believe their faith is not strong enough. Finally, they give up and walk away from the church and a personal relationship with Christ. They have checked out of the race because of a misleading message. I would not want to be that preacher when he stands before God in the judgment. The warning is clear, "*Not many of you should presume to be teachers, my brothers, because you know that we who teach will be judged more strictly.*" James 3.1 Those who teach false doctrines, even to itching ears, will have to give account for their words and the resulting effect it has on people's lives. Faith can raise the dead, win battles, defeat lions, and stop all sorts of things from happening to the believer, but that is not promised. The average preacher and person reading Hebrews, the 11th chapter, often stop at verse 35 where women are getting their dead raised back to life, but what follows in verse 36 is vital to understanding what faith is.

Faith Fact Number FIVE: **Faith 'can be' a life of suffering and dying**. "*Others were tortured and refused to be released, so that they might gain a better resurrection. Some faced jeers and flogging, while still others were chained and put in prison. They were stoned ; they were sawed in two; they were put to death by the sword. They went about in sheepskins and goatskins, destitute, persecuted and mistreated— the world was not worthy of them. They wandered in deserts and mountains, and in caves and holes in the ground. These were all commended for their faith...*" Hebrews 11.35b-39a This also is faith. It can be a life where you are called on to endure and to live with hardships. It is a choice that God makes for us. In the race of life, God chooses who gets to run a 5K race. He chooses who gets the half and full marathons. He even allows some to run in the kiddie race. The full marathon race is much tougher and longer than the 5K race some people get. When you think you have it tough, you need to remember people like Jeremiah. He did not get a 5K, or a half marathon or even just a 26.2 mile marathon. Jeremiah is the guy who got beat up, spit on, dropped in a well. He was dragged down to Egypt by the people who did that to him. Jeremiah had to run an Iron Man Triathlon for his race. The triathlon starts with a 2.6 mile swim. That is followed by a 112 mile bike ride and, if that is not enough it is followed by a full 26.2 mile marathon. Jeremiah thinks that people who complain about getting a marathon race chosen for them are wimps.

Faith Never Changes Hebrews 11.39-40

"*These were all commended for their faith, yet none of them received what had been promised. God had planned something better for us so that only together with us would they be made perfect.*" The best definition of faith says, "Whether I live or die, God is my God and Jesus is my Savior." That is what the three Hebrews facing the fiery furnace believed. They may have not known His name but they believed just the same. You may be thinking that they could not believe in Jesus because He wasn't born yet. That is partly true. He had not taken on human form, but He already existed. We know that "*Through him all things were made; without him nothing was made that has been made*" John 1.3 Jesus was there at creation, and He was there with the Hebrews as they faced Nebuchadnezzar. Remember what they told him. "*The God we serve is able to save us.*" They also knew that He might not do it. "*If he does not*" was not their lack of faith, but showed they had real faith. If they lived or died, they still believed. Their faith was not based on this world, but was based on the promise of the end of the race, and the wedding banquet. It did not matter if they lived or died. They would not bow to the statue. They knew of the coming reward that was promised in their future.

The king was so mad he had the furnace heated seven times hotter than usual. When the soldiers threw the three Hebrews in, the soldiers were consumed by the heat of the furnace. The king bowed down and looked in to see what happened, and was astonished at what he saw. "*Look! I see four men walking around in the fire, unbound and unharmed, and the fourth looks like a son of the gods.*" Daniel 3.25 When the heat gets turned up is when people see Jesus in our lives. It is in the most difficult situations that bring us closest to the Lord.

Five Faith Facts

1. Faith is about the **FUTURE**!
2. Faith is **REQUIRED** to be a believer
3. Faith is a **PROMISE** from God
4. Faith <u>can be</u> living a **VICTORIOUS** life
5. Faith <u>can be</u> a life of **HARDSHIPS**

Faith says:

"Whether I live or die, God is my God and Jesus is my savior."

Review Chapter 18

Can you identify the following People, Places or dates and tell how they are important to this weeks lesson?

1. Daniel
2. Ashpenaz
3. Darius
4. Nebuchadnezzar
5. Belshazzar
6. Azariah, Hananiah, Mishael,
7. Cyrus
8. Jeremiah
9. Babylon
10. Medes

Page numbers are from The Story (TS)

1. Daniel's, Hananiah's, Mishael's and Azariah's first test was one of purity and commitment. They wanted to remain faithful and not give in to the Babylon ways. How did they show wisdom in their dealings with Ashpenaz the chief of the king court? (TS 249-250)

2. How was Daniel able to interpret King Nebuchadnezzar's dream? How did Daniel show his dedication to God throughout the process? (TS 250-254)

3. Why was the Golden image erected and how did the three Hebrews show their faith in God when confronted with a death sentence? (TS 250-250)

4. Who came to save the Hebrews when they were thrown into the fiery furnace? (TS 256)

5. Why was Belshazzar punished? How do we know that this punishment came from God? (TS 257)

6. Why did the other leaders working with Daniel get the King to sign an order against praying for thirty days? How did Daniel respond when he was told about the order? (TS 257-258)

7. The seventy years the Hebrews spent as captives under various rulers was determined in advance by God. What do you think was God's purpose in holding them there for so long?

8. What one thing in this chapter did you learn that can help you on your personal faith journey?

One together – Worship Explained The Story Unfolds – Chapter 19

What does it mean to Worship God? When a church gathers together on a Sunday morning, it is usually called the Sunday Morning Worship Service. Yet, what makes it worship? The elements necessary for worship can be seen simply as praise, prayer, and preaching.

When the Israelites had begun to return to Jerusalem from captivity, their first goal was to rebuild the temple. They got off to a quick start, but then were sidetracked and did not get back to the project for sixteen years. When they finally finished the project, it was seventy years since it had been destroyed. That fulfilled the prophecy of Jeremiah. They also worshipped God on the foundation of the temple.

Point Of Perspective

We often see the world from our point of view and fail to understand that everyone does not see things the same way we do. The prophet, Joel, understood this, and, in his famous prophecy that is quoted by Peter on the day of Pentecost,(Acts 2) he points this out to anyone who will listen. Joel wrote *"In the last days, God says, I will pour out my Spirit on all people. Your sons and daughters will prophesy, your young men will see visions, and your old men will dream dreams."* (Joel 2.17 & Acts 2.28) God understands this point of perspective and wants us to see it in our lives and in our churches.

The need to prophesy, or to proclaim the truth for God, is often the responsibility of the young. It takes a lot of energy and commitment. It is not that older people do not have that zeal, but they are less likely to take up the cause. Peter knew that as he preached that day and quoted Joel.

The difference between visions and dreams is about point of perspective and the age of a person. First, we need to look at the lives of people. If a person is young he/she has little to base his/her decisions on and still has most of his/her life in front of him/her. Everything he/she sees and hopes for is in the future. He/she has more life in the future to live than he/she has life experiences. So a twenty year old who may live to be eighty has three times as much life in the future than the time he/she has been alive so far. His/her life is about vision for the future.

A person who has lived a longer life has less future and more memories. He/she has less time for visions about what will happen in his/her life in the future and his/her memories are what his/her dreams are made up of. We need to remember that most of what we dream about is based on life experiences and what has already happened to us. I still have one recurring nightmare. I am in high school and cannot find my locker. After I find it, I cannot remember the combination to the lock. Then I decide to go to class, but do not know which class I am supposed to be in. So I wander the halls of my high school until I wake up exhausted. So a person who is sixty has a much shorter vision window, twenty years, and a greater life experience to draw from or to dream dreams about.

Here is the prophet, Joel, telling us that, together they cover or span a great distance. They have visions that reach far, into the future and they have dreams that reach far into the past. Young men have limited experiences, but their whole lives are in front of them while old men have dreams and a lifetime of memories, but a limited future.

Three Elements of Worship

There are three elements that make up a worship service. There is praise where we connect together with God. There is prayer where we call on God, and there is preaching where we learn about the contract from God for our lives.

PRAISE

"*Speak to one another with psalms, hymns and spiritual songs. Sing and make music in your heart to the Lord, always giving thanks to God the Father for everything, in the name of our Lord Jesus Christ.*" Ephesians 5.19-20 A key to worship comes in our time of praise. This is most often expressed in our fellowship in music. The three words used, all refer to this. The word *psalm* comes from the word 'to strike' and is in reference to the use of musical instruments as part of the worship experience. The second word *hymns* is about the words that are put to the music. We often think of hymns from the old hymnals, but that is not the meaning here in scripture. The third word (s) here is *spiritual songs,* or the including of music, words and scripture to worship.

A problem arises when different people use different types or styles of music and declare that theirs is Christian music. There is no Christian music, but there is music that is Christian. There is nothing sinful about music, but there are sinful ways to use music. If the music is being used to the glory of God, it can be considered religious music. I love the old hymns, and I love the contemporary music that is being written today. I am not a fan of rap or heavy metal music, but both can be used to glorify God. At least that is what people who love Jesus and listen to Christian Rap or Christian Heavy Metal tell me.

A problem develops when a group begins to believe that everyone should enjoy their music, or that their type of music is THE Christian music. Someday, the church historians will look back at the great music wars as a low point in the life of the Christian church. The European church dominated the development of the church music, and missionaries took their music with them. Their style of worship and music was seen as 'Christian music,' until the second half of the twentieth century. One of the differences between the old and the young is dreams and visions. Another difference is the style of music they like.

Every generation has their own style, and that style can be used to praise God in worship.

PRAYER

"*I urge, then, first of all, that requests, prayers, intercession and thanksgiving be made for everyone—*" 1 Timothy 2.1 Timothy is told there are at least four different ways to express ourselves before God. We can make *requests* for our basic needs. There are *prayers* that are directed toward God. We may think that all prayers are to God, but "*The Pharisee stood up and prayed to himself: 'God, I thank you that I am not like other men—*" Luke 18.11 It is remarkable what we learn here. The prayer was not directed to God, but to the Pharisee who saw himself as God. He was so self-righteous he no longer needed to pray to the real God. Real prayer is directed to God. Then Timothy was told *intercession* was part of the prayer life of every church. Intercession is the bringing of special petitions or concerns to God. These may include physical needs, spiritual concerns, or even personal struggles someone is dealing with. Then the church, and each believer, needs to bring *thanksgiving* for all God has done for them. Thanksgiving is often the toughest part of our prayer life. We have often forgotten what God has done for us, and we have moved on to new requests or intercession needs.

PREACHING

Paul told Timothy to "*devote yourself to the public reading of Scripture, to preaching and to teaching.*"1 Timothy 4.13 Every worship service needs to have, or to include, the *Word of God* or *scripture*. This is the foundation of all truth for the church. It is included on the list first because scripture is of the first importance to the church. Timothy, as a leader in the church, is responsible to *preach* the truth. He is to exhort, encourage, and urge people to respond to the truth of the good news. It is not the preacher's responsibility to get the person to say yes. It is his responsibility to bring each person to a place where he/she can make an informed decision. Each person has to say yes or no but the preacher is there to share the truth of the word. Then, there is the *teaching*. This is to share and to instruct those who have made a commitment in the doctrines of the church. My father taught me how to use a hammer. That may sound like anyone could figure it out, but, when you are a little kid, and your dad catches you using one of his crescent wrenches for a hammer, he needs to teach you how to use a hammer. Every Christian needs to be taught the basics and the foundations[7] of the church and how to use them correctly in his/her life.

The Foundations of the Church

When it comes to the church and worship there are certain things that must be preached and taught. They are what the scriptures call the elementary elements or the foundation of all every believer needs to know. Hebrews 6.1-2 tells us that there are six foundational teachings. They are:

1. Repentance from dead works - The Christian life begins when a person responds to the truth and his/her life changes directions.

2. Faith toward God - We need to learn what faith is if we are going to live a successful life as a follower of Christ. Faith simply says, 'whether I live or die, God is my God and Jesus is my savior.'

3. Christian washings - The word can be translated either washings or baptisms, and includes; water baptism; the baptism of the Holy Spirit; foot washing, and the baptism or washing through suffering.

4. The laying on of hands - There are six reasons for the laying on of hands in the New Testament. They are all related Christian service and ministry.

5. The resurrection of the dead - There is that moment in time when a person dies. That is when he/she is transformed and receives a new eternal body.

6. Eternal Judgment - Everyone will face the judgment after they have received their eternal bodies. Some will go away into eternal life, and others into eternal punishment. If you don't believe me, you might believe Jesus. (see Matthew 25.46)

This is an outline of the Christian life. It goes from the day of repentance to the day of arrival and entrance into eternity with God. It covers the obedience of the washings we are to go through. It covers the ministry symbolized by the laying on of hands. These six are the basis for the whole life of a believer.

Worship Is Always the Same Ezra 3.11-13

The Israelites had returned from captivity to rebuild the temple. At the laying of the foundation we find all the elements we have discussed here.

Prayer - Praise - Preaching

"*With praise and thanksgiving they sang to the LORD: "He is good; his love to Israel endures forever.*" Here they were praising in song. They were praying a prayer of thanksgiving. They were proclaiming the truth of God as they quoted the word of God.

The Foundation of Truth

"*And all the people gave a great shout of praise to the LORD, because the foundation of the house of the LORD was laid.*" The foundation of the temple was the foundation of the truth of their relationship with God. The foundation of the six basic truths is the basis for each of our Christian lives.

Dreams & Visions

"*But many of the older priests and Levites and family heads, who had seen the former temple, wept aloud when they saw the foundation of this temple being laid, while many others shouted for joy.*" Their various points of perspectives caused them all to respond differently at the laying of the foundation of the temple. The older believers remembered all that had brought them this far. Their dreams of how they had endured and served God were being rewarded. They wept for joy. The younger ones saw the coming future. Their visions of ministry and blessing from God had them shouting for joy.

Worship

"*No one could distinguish the sound of the shouts of joy from the sound of weeping, because the people made so much noise. And the sound was heard far away.*" Together they were worshiping God, the young and the old. Their visions and dreams merged into joyful worship. The past and the future united to form a great sound that everyone could hear and recognize as worship. They sang their praises; they prayed to God almighty, and they shared the Word of God.

It has not changed. Worship is praise, prayer and preaching. We may not always see it when others do it, but I guarantee God always sees it, and it is sweet to Him every time it happens. Whether it is the Israelites on the foundation of the incomplete temple or our modern worship service, it is pleasing to God.

Review Chapter 19

Can you identify the following People, Places or dates and tell how they are important to this week's lesson?

1. Zechariah
2. Nebuchadnezzar
3. Cyrus
4. Darius
5. Haggai
6. Sheshbazzar
7. Tattenai
8. Trans-Euphrates
9. Persian Empire
10. Temple

Page numbers are from The Story (TS)

1. Why did Cyrus king of Persia, allow the Israelites to go home and to rebuild the temple? (TS 264)

2. When the temple foundation was laid, how did the different groups of people respond? Why was their response so different? (TS 265)

3. The prophet, Haggai, was not happy with the Israelites who had returned. What had they failed to do that they should have done? What had they done instead? (TS 266-267)

4. Through the Prophet Zechariah, God tells the people twice they are not to be afraid. What will God do for them, and what are they to do for each other as part of turning from fear? (TS 269)

5. Tattenai, the governor of Trans-Euphrates, tried to stop the Israelites from rebuilding the temple. How were his plans turned against him when he wrote to King Darius? (TS 270-273

6. The temple was finished being rebuilt on March 12, 516 BC. Why is this date so important when you look at how long it had been since it was torn down? (TS 273 Also TS 261)

7. What distracted the people from their work on the temple, and how can you relate this to your life?

8. How did the pressure of non-believers help get the people back on track to finish building the temple?

9. What one thing in this chapter did you learn that can help you on your personal faith journey?

What to do with BAD DAYS
The Story Unfolds - Chapter 20

How should a believer respond when the pressure is on? The Hebrews, living in Babylon, had to navigate the tough waters of the society they were surrounded by. The Christian believer today lives in a country that is very similar to the ones of ancient Babylon. The believer today is ruled, or governed, by religiously neutral people. Those in power want to stay in power. They are focused on making sure they have a strong voter base and a cash flow so they can run for the next election. They cater to special interest groups that often have an agenda that is anti-religion or at least anti-Christian. With such leadership, it only gets worse when you examine the culture which is made up of non-believers. This is not saying they are not spiritual, but "just 8% of the adult population, in 2006, fit the criteria"[8] of born again evangelical believers. That places 92% of the population in varying degrees of conflict or disagreement with the beliefs of dedicated believers. This leads the culture to have a noticeable anti-Christian bias. The news is filled with stories of crosses, which have stood on public property for decades, being removed due to lawsuits. A California teen has sued her high school to stop the graduation from being held in a local church. The graduation has been there for the last twenty years. When believers hear the phrase 'separation of church and state' they cringe to think what will be coming next. It usually means they are about to come under attack by a group of non-believers, who want to impose their belief system on the entire society. The 8% feel, and are often, a persecuted minority, in a larger population that calls itself Christian but fails to meet even the basic requirements set forth by Jesus in his teachings. Much like Esther and Mordecai, they are often hiding in plain sight while trying to blend in with the surrounding society. Believers try to live their lives as quietly as possible while keeping a low profile. They are uncomfortable in the world and afraid to speak up.

The Challenge Esther 4.1-16

Esther and her uncle Mordecai were Hebrew believers who were hiding in plain sight. He, her uncle, worked for the king and she had been elevated to Queen of Babylon. Many of those close to them had no idea they were from Israel, or of their religious beliefs. Then it happened. Haman tricked king Xerxes, Esther's husband, into signing an order that would, in effect, allow the destruction of every Israelite in the Babylonian empire. Mordecai learned of the order and put on sackcloth and began to mourn. His interaction with Esther included his challenge for her to approach her husband, the king, for help in undoing the order. She responded in fear of the possible consequences if she was unsuccessful. Mordecai put her on the spot. Either she helps, or God will find someone else to take her place. Finally she called for fasting and prayer, and responded in faith by declaring, "If I Perish, I Perish."

So You Are Having (another) Bad Day

There is a song by Daniel Powter called "Bad Day." The words go:
You stand in line to hit a new low.
You're faking a smile with the coffee you go.

You had a bad day
The camera don't lie
You're coming back down and you really don't mind.
You had a bad day. [9]

That song describes how a lot of days go for believers. They feel like they are having one bad day after another.

As a pastor I get text messages that often start, "Pastor please pray for...." Someone is having a bad day. When someone asks me, "Pastor, why do you think this happened to me?" They want to know why they were chosen for a bad day. That phrase, "Pastor, I need to talk to you" usually means someone needs help with another bad day. Sometimes, it seems I spend more time trying to help with the bad days than the positive side, but people don't need much help when they are having good days. They need help getting ready for, and handling, the bad days.

Mordecai was having a bad day. He may have wondered why it was happening to him. What he needed to know was God "*causes the sun to rise on the evil and the good, and sends rain on the righteous and the unrighteous.*" Matthew 5.45 Tough times happen to everyone, but the believer can expect they are coming. Believers are outnumbered, and many times are easy targets.

Choices in Making Decisions

Mordecai has to confront Esther when she hesitated when challenged to step up, and help her people. She was hiding in plain sight, and wanted to keep it that way. Mordecai tells her there are three possible choices.

Choice #1 was just to REMAIN SILENT. The choice is to be like the German prison camp guard in the old TV series, Hogan's Heroes. Whenever something came up he would say, "I see nothing." Esther's first choice was to see nothing and do nothing.

Choice #2 is to LET SOMEONE ELSE DO IT. If you don't do it, then God can get someone else and you will not have to risk anything. The only problem is, if you don't step up, it may cost you everything. This is the warning that Mordecai gave to Esther. If she does not get involved, God will use someone else, and will hold her responsible for refusing to get involved.

Choice #3 You can ACCEPT YOUR RESPONSIBILITY. When you have a clear opportunity, and the need is real and vital, it is your responsibility to step up and get involved. Every Christian believer is called to be involved. Some may only need to fast and pray and hold up others. Still, if you are called to step up and fill a gap you have to make a choice. Everyone has a responsibility to be involved in God's kingdom.

This Means WAR

You need to know that you are not alone. Esther called for all the other Hebrew believers to start a period of fasting and praying. In a spiritual battle you need to remember that you are not alone, and no battle is put on only one person. "*Let us not give up meeting together,... but let us encourage one another.*" Hebrews 10.25 One of the reasons we gather together is to strengthen our lives for the battles we will face during the coming week. This time together is also a way to remember that we are not alone, and that bad days are not the norm for believers. It is here we remember that Jesus has promised to be with us "*always, to the very end of the age.*" Matthew 28.20

This is a spiritual battle, and we should be using spiritual weapons. Esther wanted the Hebrews to fast and pray. This is because the ultimate battle will not be won or lost on the physical level but on the spiritual level. Paul wrote about this spiritual war to the Ephesians. The battle is not against flesh and blood. It is not the people we face in this battle. It is who they are serving we must be aware of. We are fighting against forces of evil that are often located in high places. The spiritual weapons that Paul lists are truth, righteousness, the gospel, faith, salvation, the word of God and all kinds of prayers. Each one of these must be part of the believer's life if he/she wants to win the battles he/she will be part of.

We will have to step out in faith if we are going to win the battle. Esther said, "If I perish, I perish." She understood that faith says 'whether I live or die, God is my God, and Jesus is my savior.' Reading Hebrews, chapter 11 makes it clear that living a life of faith may mean dying for God. Esther is putting the results into God's hands. She will do all she can, and then she will wait.

God moves when we are obedient. King Xerxes could not sleep so he remembered all that Mordecai had done for him. The Gallows that Haman had prepared for Mordecai were used against Haman instead. Esther was the hero because she steps forward and did what was right, leaving the final results in the hands of God.

When you are fighting a spiritual war, you have to be smarter than your enemies. Jesus told his disciples that he was "*sending* [them] *out like sheep among wolves. Therefore be as shrewd as snakes and as innocent as doves.*" Matthew 10.16 Jesus told his disciples to turn the other cheek to shame their enemy. He taught them to go the second mile to force them to be afraid that they would have to pay a price for taking advantage of a believer. He showed them how to embarrass the enemy when they took their coat by giving the robe also. The person would be stark naked and their enemy would be embarrassed into giving it all back. This is not about submission to your enemies. It is about being shrewd and outsmarting them. The believer has to also remain innocent. "*Everyone has heard about your obedience, so I am full of joy over you; but I want you to be wise about what is good, and innocent about what is evil.*" Romans 16.19 We must never compromise doing what is right to win the battle against evil. We are not to sin.

Esther was shrewd in her dealing with Haman, but she did not violate her relationship with God. She was smarter than her enemy, and that is why she won the battle.

God At Work

Esther could not have known how it was going to turn out but she had to believe it was being handled by God. "*And we know that in all things God works for the good of those who love him, who have been called according to his purpose.*" Romans 8.28 How often do we, as believers, limit God? We don't trust him all the time. We think that there are places where God cannot help us. We forget that we are God's children and He loves us and He wants only the best for us. David faced a bear and a lion that God had put there preparing him for a giant. He could have thought of it as a bad day in the field but looking back, it was all part of God's plan. Moses spent forty years taking care of sheep on the back side of the desert. Talk about a string of bad days! Moses found himself demoted from prince of Egypt to watching over smelly sheep. That was 14,600 bad days in a row. Yet, God was at work getting Moses ready to lead his people out of Egypt. John was sent to the Island of Patmos where the enemy felt he had silenced him. Yet, God had plans to let John see visions that the church needed. The solitude of the island was exactly where God needed John to be and He allowed the enemy to pay for the trip and give him a place to stay.

Hillsong Australia has a song called 'Salvation' that says:

> God above all the world in motion
> God above all my hopes and fears
> And I don't care what the world throws at me now
> I'm gonna be all right.

You have been called to be a believer in times such as these. Your bad day in God's hands is a battle about to be won. It's part of a great plan he has for your life and for his kingdom. It's gonna be all right.

Review Chapter 20

Can you identify the following People, Places or dates and tell how they are important to this week's lesson?

1. Queen Vashti

2. Haman

3. Mordecai

4. Xerxes

5. Esther

6. Zeresh

7. Susa

8. Persia

9. Jews

10. Feast of Purim

Page numbers are from The Story (TS)

1. How is the absolute power of King Xerxes of Persia demonstrated in how he dealt with his wife, Queen Vashti? (TS 275-277)

2. How can the selection of Esther be seen as the providential guiding hand of God?

3. What are the weaknesses of Haman? (TS 279-285)

4. What are the strengths of Mordecai? (TS 279-285)

5. What was the root cause of the conflict between Haman and Mordecai (and the Jews)?

6. How is Esther's statement, "If I Perish, I perish" a statement of complete faith? (TS 282)

7. How does Proverbs 16.18 "*Pride goes before destruction, a haughty spirit before a fall.*" apply to Haman and his family? (TS 283-284)

8. How does Esther and Mordecai fulfill Isaiah 66.2, "This *is the one I esteem: he who is humble and contrite in spirit, and trembles at my word?*"

9. How does King Xerxes fail in leadership by listening to Haman?

10. What one thing in this chapter did you learn that can help you on your personal faith journey?

Rediscovering the Foundation of Joy The Story Unfolds – Chapter 21

Why does it always seem you never arrive in your spiritual journey? That must have been how the Israelites felt in the time of Ezra and Nehemiah. After decades of captivity they get to go home. Then they have to lay the foundation of the temple. Then they find out they need to build the temple. There is no time to sit back and relax. No way! Now, they have to repent and grow spiritually. What's next? They have to build the walls around the city. Then a prophet, called Malachi, shows up and says they are not where they should be spiritually. It is always something else. Just when one thing is taken care of, along comes the next challenge. There is always something else to do for God.

The Reading of the Word Nehemiah 7.73-8.3; 8.9-10

The Israelites had strong leadership; Leadership that had been selected for them by God. There was Ezra, the priest, and Nehemiah, the cup bearer to the king. We would call Nehemiah a layman working for God. The prophets Joel and Malachi were also prominent figures in their lives. On one occasion, Ezra called the people together and began to read the Law of Moses to them. Many of them had never heard it read. Ezra read it to the people all day. As they listened and realized what they had lost they began to weep. Nehemiah had to step up and interrupt Ezra. He called to the people to stop weeping and mourning, but have joy because they were returning to God. That day, they crossed over a barrier and were changed. They were changed from a group of people listening to a priest, to God's people worshiping together. This was not about the three elements of worship (praise, prayer and preaching) as much as it was about what happened to the people on that day.

The ASSEMBLY of Believers

"*The people assembled as one man*" as they gathered together on that day. They were changed from a crowd, or group of people, into a unified group of believers. This was no small step for them to take. It was a gift given to believers by God. Paul knew this, "*May the God who gives endurance and encouragement give you a spirit of unity among yourselves as you follow Christ Jesus, so that with one heart and mouth you may glorify the God and Father of our Lord Jesus Christ.* Romans 15.5-6 This unity was a foundation Jesus wanted to build his church on.

Jesus called the unified believers the 'church.' He said, *"I will build my church, and the gates of Hades will not overcome it.*" Matthew 16.18 We take the word church for granted and think of it as the religious term describing where believers meet together, but are as far from wrong as it is possible to get. In Jesus' day the term church was a common word. The word was 'ekklesia.' It is a Greek term meaning 'an assembly of people united for a common cause.' The cities would call an assemble or ekklesia to handle their business. Jesus said that His assembly or ekklesia would be so strong that it could even go up against the gates of Hades. Literally nothing can stop a unified church, assembly, the ekklesia.

The same word was used in Acts when they came together to bring charges against Paul in Ephesus. The city leaders called the assembly or ekklesia to meet. When the people of the city finally got there "*the assembly* (ekklesia) *was in confusion; Some were shouting one thing, some another. Most of the people did not even know why they were there.*" Acts 19.32 This was the assembly, ekklesia or church run by man. It was full of confusion, noise, and ignorance.

Remember those listening to Ezra were "*assembled as one man.*" They were united. The church Jesus is building will be given the *"spirit of unity.*" They will be united to fight against evil, and to follow the directions of their Lord, Jesus.

Going by the BOOK

Ezra was reading from "*the Book of the Law of Moses.*" It was the foundation of all they believed. When they heard it their hearts were stirred. Yet, we, as Christian believers, have a higher level to live by, "*For the law was given through Moses; grace and truth came through Jesus Christ.*" John 1.17 What a contrast is presented here. Moses gave them rules, but Jesus gave grace and truth. Grace is the free, unearned, and undeserved gift of God to the believer. Truth is the final knowledge that rises above debate and settles the matter. We are told that "*sin shall not be your master, because you are not under law, but under grace.*" Romans 6.14 We are not guided by rules and lawyers (Pharisees). We are under the grace of God and are guided by the truth of Jesus, who is the promised Christ. They go by the Law of Moses. We go by the directions given us by Jesus. We have His early disciples and followers who have shown us what it should be like. We are people of the book, only a different part of the book applies to us.

Why Does Everyone UNDERSTAND Differently

Ezra was reading the Book "*in the presence of men, women and others who could understand.*" Their unity, as believers, had placed them in a position of being in tune with God and God's word. As believers, "*we have not received the spirit of the world but the spirit who is from God, <u>that we may understand</u> what God has freely given us.*" 1 Corinthians 2.12 There are two different ways of looking at something. First, there is the world's way. Those of the world "*are <u>darkened in their understanding</u> and separated from the life of God because of ignorance that is in them due to the hardening of their hearts. Having <u>lost all sensitivity</u>, they have given themselves over to sensuality so as to indulge in every kind of impurity, with a continual lust for more.*" Ephesians 4.18-19 Then, there is the way of those surrendered to God, whom the spirit gives understanding. They are sensitive to the consequences of a life lived with "*a continual lust for more*" impurity.

This was clear on an interview show I watched yesterday. The host asked two guests the same question: Is this nation getting better or worse as we go along? The first guest said that everything was getting better. With the removal of many of the moral taboos, the nation was healthier than it had ever been. The second guest disagreed. He said that the removal of the moral taboos was, in itself, an indication of the disintegration of the nation. Well, if your thinking has been dulled then you have "*lost all sensitivity*" and there is no gauge that says anything is wrong. If you drive down the highway at night with your lights off, and you don't know the bridge is out, you aren't afraid. What you are, is ignorant. If you are living your life like there are no boundaries, and God does not exist, or does not care, you will perish "*because of the ignorance that is in* (you) *due to the hardening of* (your) *heart.*" Just because you don't know the bridge is out does not mean you will not crash. Just because you deny God does not mean you will survive His judgment.

The card that came in the mail from the local crisis pregnancy center on Friday had two facts on the top line. One in three babies born in our local county is born to an unwed mother. The second fact is that the STD (sexually transmitted disease) rates are climbing steadily for 15-19 year olds. The world understands this as progress because of their hardened hearts. The believer understands this as sin and as unacceptable because of grace and truth.

It Just Makes You to Want To Cry

Remember, the people heard the reading of the law and began to mourn and weep. They saw the outcome for all who did not turn back to God. Their hearts were broken by the way the world was living. They had begun to focus on the negative. Nehemiah stopped the reading and called out to the people, "*Do not grieve, for the joy of the LORD is your strength.*"

There are two types of Joy

When we think of joy, we often see it as temporary or momentary. For some, this is true, but for the committed believer, that is not enough. In the parable of the sower Jesus talked about temporary joy. "*The one who received the seed that fell on rocky places is the man who hears the word and at once receives it with joy. But since he has no root, he lasts only a short time. When trouble or persecution comes because of the word, he quickly falls away.*" Matthew 13.20-21 Here is joy that is based on feelings or emotions. It is momentary and passing. It is shallow and easily uprooted. The person with this type of joy "*lasts only a short time.*"

The second type of joy is not momentary or based on feelings. It is a gift from God. It is given to every believer. "*But the fruit of the Spirit is love, joy, peace, patience, kindness, goodness, faithfulness, gentleness, and self-control. Against such things there is no law.*" Galatians 5.22-23 Did you see what God gives us right after he gives us love? He gives us joy. This grace of God is so great it even comes with a full dose of joy built right in that will last a lifetime.

No wonder Nehemiah called on the people to stop weeping and turn their hearts to joy. The world should not drag you down with its revised attitudes about what is acceptable. You have been given a gift of joy that is designed to overcome the negative world we live in.

Restoring What Has Been Lost

Over the next days and weeks they stayed close and listened to Ezra as he read to them. "*They found written in the Law, which the LORD had commanded through Moses, that the Israelites were to live in booths during the feast of the seventh month.*" Nehemiah 8.14 Something that was lost or missing had been shown to them. It needed to be restored. It was their responsibility to do this. The lost must be found.

Jesus taught about searching for the lost in the fifteenth chapter of the book written by Luke. The whole chapter was about the lost. The lost sheep wandered away by paying no attention but it still needed to be found. The lost coin slipped away as it was mishandled, but it still needed to be found. The lost son ran away to pursue a life of sin but he still needed found. The church of believers needs to discover anew that "*the Son of Man came to seek and to save what was lost.*" Luke 19.10 He also wants us to seek the lost. That was why His final instruction to the believers is to "*go and make disciples of all nations.*" Matthew 28.19 It is directions to find the lost and what to do with them when they were found. The father of the lost son said, "*We had to celebrate and be glad because this brother of yours was dead and is alive again, he was lost and is found.*" Luke 15.32

Imagine what it would be like if we took restoring the lost as seriously as they did of restoring the lost practices and festivals. If we saw our place as helping others find this gift of joy and freedom, what a different world it would be.

Coming Before God

The Assembly of Believers is united in their stand with God as one people. The church, like the people with Ezra and Nehemiah, are united. They are the assembly; the *ekklesia* of God. God's people are people of the Word. This foundation truth is vital to their living in a world that is confused and living lives of distorted reality. They have a different understanding than the world. They are not confused by what is right and wrong. Their lives are not billboards, approving sin with every deed and thought. They live by the grace of God. The joy of the Lord is their strength. This gift from God is not earned. It is given to every believer. It is not temporary or based on feelings. It is a permanent part of their lives. The modern believer is on a search and rescue mission in this world looking for the lost. They are everywhere but are so hard to find because they like being lost. They have wandered away, slipped away, and even run away and bringing them back is a tough task, but it is our task.

We have far to go on this spiritual journey. When we come before God, it must be as one people of the word, who understand and celebrate with joy, the restoring of the lost sheep, coin, son, or soul.

Review Chapter 21

Can you identify the following People, Places or dates and tell how they are important to this week's lesson?

1. Ezra
2. Nehemiah
3. Malachi
4. Artaxerxes
5. Geshem, Sanballat & Tobiah
6. Persia
7. Jerusalem
8. The Law of Moses
9. Samaria
10. Transjordan

Page numbers are from The Story (TS)

1. King Artaxerxes was the stepson of Esther, the Queen of Persia. She had saved the Jews from destruction from Haman when she acted in faith. How does Artaxerxes help the Jews? (TS 293-294, & 295)

2. What was the mission of Ezra when he went to Jerusalem? (TS 291-294)

3. How was the mission of Ezra different from the mission of Nehemiah?

4. What was the mission of Nehemiah when he went to Jerusalem? (TS 294-299)

5. What was the greatest challenge Nehemiah faced while he was in Jerusalem?

6. How did Ezra help the people celebrate the completion of the walls around Jerusalem? (TS 300-301)

7. God sent a prophet named Malachi to the people living in Judah. What questions did the people ask God in Malachi's prophecies? (TS 302-303)

8. What was the final prophecy, or promise, that came from the prophet Malachi? (TS 304)

9. How is this prophecy later fulfilled? See Matthew 11.13-14

10. What one thing in this chapter did you learn that can help you on your personal faith journey?

Who's In Charge
The Story Unfolds - Chapter 22

The birth of Jesus is usually draped in the Christmas season with children's choirs and presents. Songs like 'The First Noel" and "Silent Night" are playing in every store you walk into. Yet these are not the real themes of Christmas. In fact the birth of Jesus is all about one question, 'Who's in charge?' To understand this we will need to take a trip back in time.

THE WAY BACK MACHINE

There used to be a cartoon with a really smart dog named Peabody and his friend, Sherman, a little boy with thumbs to operate the machinery. The two of them would get in the Way Back machine and travel through time. They would travel through history to discover some great truth that Sherman needed to learn. Mr. Peabody usually had to fix history to make it come out right.

FRAMING EVERYTHING

Each of the four gospels takes a look back at the origins of Jesus.
Mark starts with Jesus with his first day on the job as and adult as he starts his three year ministry.
Matthew goes back to Abraham, the father of faith. Then comes forward to King David, then to the Babylonian captivity, finally to Jesus' birth and His ministry. Matthew goes way back, but not as far as Luke.
Luke goes back to Adam and brings Jesus' lineage forward to his birth, his childhood, his temptations in the wilderness, and then the ministry begins. Going back to Adam is going way back, but not as far back as John goes.
John starts at the beginning, before there is anything at all, then goes on to the creation, the first light, the first life, and declares Jesus was there way back then. Here is how John writes about this:

"In the beginning was the Word, and the Word was with God, and the Word was God. He was with God in the beginning.

Through him all things were made; without him nothing was made that has been made. In him was life, and that life was the light of men. The light shines in the darkness, but the darkness has not understood it." (John 1:1-5 NIV84)

John helps us see Jesus coming and His purpose clearly in the first chapter of his gospel.

THE BIG PICTURE

John says:

- before there was anywhere, anytime, anyone, before light or darkness, there was JESUS.
- in the beginning even before creation JESUS already was there, even though 'there' did not exist yet.
- at the creation where everything was made out of nothing, it was JESUS making everything.
- JESUS is the reason there is life and light.

John goes all the way back. John wants the reader to know, for sure, who is in charge from the very beginning. This is no small matter that John speaks of an event that is so far back that even evolutionists do not even have a way to tell us about this far back. This is so far back that Sherman and Peabody could not go back this far. We are talking WAY BACK. Yet, when we get back this far who do we find there? Jesus! Wow, that is impressive. Jesus is the one who starts the beginning, so later there can be creation. That thought can hurt a brain to think about it.

THE MESSENGER OF TRUTH

The next thing John, the disciple, tells us about is John, the Baptist.

"There came a man who was sent from God; his name was John. He came as a witness to testify concerning that light,

so that through him all men might believe. He himself was not the light; he came only as a witness to the light." (John 1:6-8 NIV84)

What a contrast this is to Jesus, who is light and life. Here is John, who is just a man. He is not the light but has been selected to tell everyone he can who the real light is. This is the basics of the lives of believers. They are called to point all the way back to the one who has been in charge of everything since before anything even existed.

HIDING FROM JESUS

How has the world responded to the creator?
He was in the world, and though the world was made through him, the world did not recognize him. He came to that which was his own, but his own did not receive him. Yet to all who received him, to those who believed in his name, he gave the right to become children of God– children born not of natural descent, nor of human decision or a husband's will, but born of God. (John 1:10-13 NIV84)

The world did not RECOGNIZE Him and even the religious who said they were watching for Him to come did not RECEIVE Him. They rejected the creator. They refused to believe that Jesus was in charge. Yet, there were some who received Him. They believed Jesus was the one. He was the creator, the one who gave them His birthright as if it was their own. They become children of God, not by their lineage but by their listening and responding to the creator.

JESUS

There is a television program called 'Undercover Boss.' I have to tell you, I have never watched it myself, but have seen the commercials for it. A business owner puts on the uniform of the people who work for him and then tries to do their job while blending in with the rest of his workers. Now, I have always wondered what the other workers must be thinking when some old guy shows up to flip burgers, and he has a film crew with him. That has to be a dead giveaway. He is no ordinary or regular worker. John says *The Word became flesh and made his dwelling among us. We have seen his glory, the glory of the One and Only, who came from the Father, full of grace and truth.* (John 1:14 NIV84)

He was not undercover or hiding, but many did not recognize or submit to His authority. Instead of a camera crew drawing attention to Him, He was surrounded by the sick, demon possessed, and miracles were always happening. He was here among us, the creator from before the beginning, living in the flesh so we could see Him.

WHAT JOHN SAID ABOUT JESUS

Then John brings this all together.

John testifies concerning Him. He cries out, saying, "*This was he of whom I said, 'He who comes after me has surpassed me because he was before me.' " From the fullness of his grace we have all received one blessing after another. For the law was given through Moses; grace and truth came through Jesus Christ. No one has ever seen God, but God the One and Only, who is at the Father's side, has made him known.*" (John 1:15-18 NIV84)

Even though Jesus got there after John, Jesus was first. Remember Jesus was from before the beginning. This is how we know every blessing comes as a result of his gift of grace.

Moses was back there a ways and gave us the Law. The purpose of the Law is so we can know what sin really is. Jesus gives us grace to overcome the penalty of sin. Then, just to be sure we understand the importance of Jesus, we learn that, if we see Jesus, we see the Father. If we know Jesus we know the Father.

WHAT WE KNOW FOR SURE

When we look at the birth of Jesus we learn He is and always has been in charge. What we know:

- Jesus goes back further than anyone else.
- Jesus sends individuals like John to testify about the light.
- Jesus is either rejected or received by each individual. There is no middle ground in this matter.
- Jesus is not hiding from us even though some of us are hiding from Him.
- Jesus is the answer to the problem of sin.

John wants everyone who reads his account to know from the start that Jesus is in charge. We learn that Jesus was there before the beginning, before creation of anything He was there. Jesus had a plan that covered everything. That included how to deal with sin. If He could create it all, then there is nothing he can't do. He has a plan to allow those who have rejected him to change their minds and receive Him as their creator.

So here is the beginning of the story of Jesus. It is set with the definite imperatives that are the tone for the rest of His life, and the rest of eternity. Will you reject or will you receive Him? Will you allow Him to be in charge of your life?

Review Chapter 22

Can you identify the following People, Places or dates and tell how they are important to this week's lesson?

1. Caesar Augustus
2. Mary
3. Gabriel
4. Joseph
5. Jesus
6. Magi
7. Herod
8. Anna & Simeon
9. Bethlehem
10. Jerusalem

Page numbers are from The Story (TS)

1. Though Jesus is not mentioned by name, we learn much about Him from the beginning of the book of John. What key facts do we learn about Jesus right away, even before we see His Birth? (TS 309-310) John 1.1-15

2. What do we learn about Mary as she talks to the angel Gabriel? (TS 310) Why are these facts important?

3. How was Joseph convinced to marry Mary? (TS 312)

4. How are the following places important in the life of Mary, Joseph, and Jesus? Nazareth, Bethlehem, Jerusalem.

5. How do the shepherds help confirm the birth of Jesus in Bethlehem? (TS 312-313)

6. Name three ways that the Magi showed that they were following God's directions in looking for Jesus. (TS 313-314)

7. How does Joseph protect Mary and Jesus? Give two examples. (TS 311-312, 314-315)

8. Each year Joseph and Mary walked to Jerusalem from Nazareth. The trip was about 68 miles. Why did they go to Jerusalem each year, and what does this tell us about how they brought Jesus up? (TS 315)

9. Why did the 12-year-old Jesus stay behind in Jerusalem? (TS 316) How does this help us understand His personal mission?

10. What one thing in this chapter did you learn that can help you on your personal faith journey?

Avoiding Temptation
The Story Unfolds - Chapter 23

Why you don't want to go fishing with the Devil.

There are two old sayings I want you to think about for a minute. The first one says, 'the Devil is in the details.' The second one says, 'If you fail to prepare you are preparing to fail.' Now these are both true in our ordinary lives, but when it comes to our spiritual lives they are doubly true. You may ignore the details, but the devil doesn't. You may fail to prepare, but the devil is always preparing for you. When the opportunity comes along he wants to be ready.

If you knew there was a fight coming that you could not avoid, would you make preparations to win the fight? There are a lot of Christian believers who hold on to the thought that we are going to make it through this life without having to fight, or at least stand up for the truth of what we believe. Tied to this are the problems some have in tying their Christian, spiritual, and religious lives with anything outside of the church. It is like there are two realities in the lives of many believers. The first one is when they go to church, and the other one is the rest of the time.

WOULD YOU LIKE

Let me ask you three questions. Would you like to be stronger and healthier? This question is about preparation and commitment. Would you like to be smarter and live longer? This is about the fear of the Lord and hating evil. Would you like to be superior and have wealth? This is about vows and promises. You will understand these before the end of this chapter.

UNDERSTANDING TEMPTATION

"Each one is tempted when, by his own evil desire, he is dragged away and enticed. Then, after desire has

conceived, it gives birth to sin; and sin, when it is full-grown, gives birth to death." James 1.14-15

Let me illustrate this for you. Imagine there is a little fish swimming in a lake. He has heard the stories of the fish who eats the worm and is dragged out of the lake, never to be seen again. He has been warned by his parents to swim away if he ever sees a worm just floating in the water. Then one day it happens. The little fish is just out swimming around and there is a worm floating in the water. The little fish backs away and starts to leave, but you know, one small look won't hurt. After all the small fish is not touching the worm, only looking at the worm cannot be bad for you. As the little fish looks at the nice juicy worm just hanging there, the fish begins to imagine how good it would taste. Then, thinking, just one small nibble won't hurt, the little fish takes a small nibble. Not really a bite, but just enough to taste it. Everything is all right. The stories were wrong. So the little fish takes a bigger bite, and everything is all right. Then the little fish can contain it no longer, and takes one last big bite to swallow the big juicy worm. It was so good... SUDDENLY, there is the pain, the terrible realization that everything is wrong, that everything he has been warned about is true. The little fish fights for life trying to break free, but there is this line coming from the worm out of the little fish's mouth right to the surface of the lake and the little fish is being pulled toward thc top of the lake. Fighting with all its strength the little fish cannot get away. It is slowly pulled from the lake gasping for 'water.' I have to stop here. What happens next is too gruesome to tell, but death is the result of the little fish stopping to look at the fat juicy worm.

There are eight steps from temptation to death. With the small fish, it was a physical death. In the life of a believer it is often a spiritual death because of decisions made in the physical world.

- STEP 1: The Bible says '<u>each one is tempted</u>.' This means they are baited or put to the test. Being tempted is not sin. Jesus was tempted and he never sinned. We all face various temptations. How we respond is very important.

- STEP 2: It is our 'own desire' that we have to keep our eyes open for. The enemy is going to put stuff in front of you that you want or long for. That is lust. You could not be tempted by a fat juicy worm, but the enemy has a book on you and keeps track.
- STEP 3: A person is 'dragged away' by their own desire. We are drawn toward the bait by our own desire. It is a personal tug-of-war we are willing to lose.
- STEP 4: We are not pushed or forced. We are 'enticed' or lured, and it is usually something we want or are curious about. It is remarkable how free will is the basis for sinning. We have to make the choice to swim toward the bait.
- STEP 5: After the desire has 'conceived' it is not 'if' but 'when.' That may sound like we have lost our free will but the word 'conceived' means 'to become pregnant.' So it means that a person is pregnant with sin. This is why the next step is so logical.
- STEP 6: It then 'gives birth to sin.' This is what happens when you are pregnant; it is not if, but when. So I guess men can get pregnant, at least when it comes to sin.
- STEP 7: Sin becomes 'full-grown,' and takes on a life of its own, taking over the person. Much like the little fish, they may even want to get away, but sin is now in full control.
- STEP 8: Sin 'gives birth to death.' This has both physical and spiritual implications. Physically, it leads to habits and activities that are not healthy and leads a person further away from God. Spiritually, it means the person is separated from God and spiritually dead.

That is a pretty depressing set of circumstances. Even without any details, it makes for a dark commentary on life. So what can we do to keep this from happening? The answer lies in the life of Jesus.

THE DEVIL BAITS JESUS

"Jesus was led by the Spirit into the desert to be tempted by the devil. After fasting forty days and forty nights, he was hungry. The tempter came to him and said, "If you are the Son of God, tell these stones to become bread." Matthew 4.1-3

The other side of temptation is that someone has to bait the hook for you to swallow. The devil is the one who wants us to prove how strong we are, and that we can make our own decisions. He always wants us to question the authority of God and to stand on our own. If he can get us to do that, it is only a matter of time till he wins. "*If you are the Son of God*" was the devil putting something in front of Jesus that would test his grit. Could Jesus have turned the stones into bread? Yes, He was, after all, the Son of God. That is why the devil used this against Jesus. Just because you can, does not mean you should.

MANNA AND THE BODY

Jesus had not eaten for forty days. He was hungry. His body needed nourishment. Why not use that against Him? Why work overtime if he could get Jesus to sin and all it would cost the devil was a rock and some time. Jesus' response was given as He recognized what was happening. Instead of focusing on the physical He focused on God. "It is written: '*Man does not live on bread alone, but on every word that comes from the mouth of God.*" Matthew 4.4 The spiritual trumps the physical for the believer. That does not just happen. It is part of a disciplined life. It is about preparation and paying attention to the details. Jesus quotes the Word of God as his authority to reject temptation.

Are you stronger than God? Jesus was God and He was not about to get into a debate with the devil. He stuck to the facts and did not lose his focus. So, how can you be stronger? It is all about preparation. Jesus had spent time learning the Word of God. At the moment of temptation He did not ask for the devil to wait while he broke out his smart phone to look up a scripture that might help. Jesus was prepared. He was ready before he was tempted. He had already accepted the boundaries set up by God and was not going to violate them.

How can this help me be healthier? It is about commitment to the plan. If you have spent time in the word, then you have been studying the master plan. It has set limits that define the right path. You have to stay committed to the program no matter what comes your way. Jesus did not expect that He would be so hungry He would like to eat a rock, but it happened. In the end, rejecting satisfying his hunger, made Him healthier because He was still in the plan of God.

MORALS AND THE MIND

"Then the devil took him to the holy city and had him stand on the highest point of the temple. "If you are the Son of God," he said, "Throw yourself down. For it is written: "'He will command his angels concerning you, and they will lift you up in their hands, so that you will not strike your foot against a stone." Matthew 4.5-6

Are you smarter than God? That may sound like a ridiculous question, but it isn't. There are plenty of people who have deceived themselves into believing some strange and outlandish things based on God's word. You can believe anything you want if you accept only the parts of God's word you like, or that will benefit you.

Here is the devil using part of the Word of God to try and get Jesus to sin. To use the Word like that is sinning, and it only leads to a selfish approach to scripture. He went after Jesus again with the "*If you are the Son of God*" line. That would not work on me anymore than turning rocks into hot onion bread. It was a temptation the devil used to try and get Jesus to doubt and then to prove who He really was. The devil wanted Jesus to focus on a small scripture and to challenge God to keep His word. Yet again, Jesus was ready.

"*It is also written: 'Do not put the Lord your God to the test.*" Matthew 4.7 Jesus knew to test God was to do wrong. It is believing there are no consequences to our actions. A little fish eats a worm containing a hook and God does not reach down and set the little fish free. Jesus jumps off the top of the temple, and it does not mean he won't go splat at the bottom. Only the lies of the devil could build such a story.

We, as believers, are called on to properly discern the Word of God, and not to try and use it for our own personal gain. When a person tests God, they are trying to transfer the obligations for their sins and actions to God. God will not take responsibility for your sins, but he will deal with you if you decide to sin. You are not smarter than God.

So how do you get smarter? The Bible says the fear of the Lord is to hate evil. Proverbs 8.13 NASB If we put this into practice what we get in return is fantastic. By rejecting, and literally learning to hate evil, we can discover the benefits and get smarter. "*The fear of the LORD is the beginning of knowledge.*" Proverbs 1.7 "*The fear of the LORD is the beginning of wisdom, and knowledge of the Holy One is understanding.*" Proverbs 9.10 Jesus was smarter than the devil. Jesus demonstrated knowledge of the Word and wisdom in applying it to His life when He responded to the devil's twisting of scriptures. It even gets better when we discover that, rejecting evil from our lives, makes us healthier. "*The fear of the LORD is a fountain of life, turning a man from the snares of death.*" Proverbs 14.27 You are not smarter than God, but knowing God's word can make you smarter and healthier.

MONEY AND THE SPIRIT

"*Again, the devil took him to a very high mountain and showed him all the kingdoms of the world and their splendor. "All this I will give you," he said, "if you will bow down and worship me."* Matthew 4.8-9

The devil wants you to believe that you are superior to God. He tried to get Jesus to sell out by placing someone else in God's place.

God has been very clear about how He wants His followers to act. In the Ten Commandments there are two commandments that apply to help us understand this. The first one is the second commandment. "*You shall not make for yourself an idol.*" Exodus 20.4 The other one is the seventh commandment. "*You shall not commit adultery.*" Exodus 20.14 What is remarkable is that most people don't understand that these are about the same basic principle. Idolatry and adultery are basically the same things. They are both about replacing one love with another. They are about giving the love you have promised one, to someone else.

When a spouse cheats and has an affair, he/she is giving to someone else what is not his/her's to give away. They have already given it to their spouse. It is putting someone else in the place that has been reserved and confirmed through marriage. That is what idolatry is. It is giving your love and attention to someone or something other than God. It is spiritually submitting yourself and being unfaithful to God. This is what the devil was trying to get Jesus to do. Everything for next to nothing is how it was presented to Jesus by the enemy of his soul. Jesus knew this and that brought the proper response.

"*Away from me, Satan! For it is written: 'Worship the Lord your God, and serve him only.*" Matthew 4.10

There is a lot more than meets the eye. Jesus knew that the Word of God is the sword of the Spirit. Ephesians 6.17 He also knew it was the only weapon God has given us in our spiritual battle. Jesus said that the person was to do two things in relationship with God to stay on track. First they were to worship the Lord. This is no small statement. The word worship carries with it the concept of a vow for life much like a marriage vow. It is a vow, a pledge, an obligation, a guarantee, a dedication, a pledge of loyalty and allegiance; it is promising faithfulness to God. Worship is about spending time with the one we say we love. When a couple gets married, they are promising that their love belongs to no one else. Worship is our renewing our vows to God.

Jesus said we also are to '*serve him only.*' That means you are going to keep your promise. You are not going to spend time with any other god or spend time listening to the offers of the devil.

The devil approached Jesus with the promise of earthly wealth. Jesus knew the danger and warned us, "*Do not store up for yourselves treasures on earth, where moth and rust destroy, and where thieves break in and steal. But store up for yourselves treasures in heaven, where moth and rust do not destroy, and where thieves do not break in and steal. For where your treasure is, there your heart will be also.*" Matthew 6.19-21

Money and wealth or earthly possessions have a place in the life of the believer but they are not the reason we are here. They are tools to be used. The devil wants them to be the replacement for God in our lives. If we give in to that temptation, we have committed spiritual adultery by making money our idol, replacing our relationship with God.

There was a great article titled "Living frugally and being happy the Amish way" by Gregory Karp in the Chicago Tribune.[10] In the article he outlined six ways the Amish approach money in their lives.

Six money tips from the Amish

1. **Use it up, wear it out, make do or do without**. The Amish have a "reluctance to replace anything before it's fully used."[11] This is far different from

our throwaway society. How many of us have closets and garages and storage units full of stuff that is in perfect working order that we replaced because we could?

2. **Don't work for a dead horse.** "The idea is you don't want to buy a horse on long-term credit because you could be working to pay it off long after the horse is dead. The Amish are fond of this philosophy, attributed to P.T. Barnum of circus fame."[12] The Amish avoid debt as much as they can.
3. **More is caught than taught.** The Amish believe that children learn most about money from watching their parents. The parents help their children practice the proper use of money from an early age, even having them set up saving accounts as children.
4. **Simpler often translates to cheaper.** The Amish see life as simpler, and enjoy the small things because of it. They do not overindulge, and even an ice cream cone can be a great enjoyment. They do not focus on items like flat-screen televisions or new cars, but instead focus on a simpler and less stressful life.
5. **You don't have to buy something new to buy something good.** The Amish avoid paying full price for most items. They love a deal and like garage sales, thrift stores and estate sales. It is not that they cannot afford it. They just believe it is wrong to be wasteful with their spending. Most of what they have is not intended to impress, but to get the job done.
6. **Getting value.** There are the times when the Amish will pay far more than we think an item is worth, but it is for a reason. If they need a hammer it might cost them $100 but it is the best, and they expect it to last a lifetime.

Money is not to be worshiped but is a tool. Jesus knew that all the riches of the world were not worth being separated from God. Jesus had learned His lessons well.

He had stored up the Word of God for just such a day as this, and He was ready. "*When the devil had finished all this tempting, he left him until an opportune time.*" Luke 4.13 He would be back, and Jesus would be ready.

Those three questions are important to our wellbeing and spiritual growth.

Would you like to be stronger and healthier? You have to take the time to make the preparations and commitment needed to answer the devil when he comes.

Would you like to be smarter and live longer? Then you need to reject all evil from your life. This will lead to wisdom, understanding, and knowledge that are directly beneficial to you.

Would you like to be superior and have wealth? Then you need to be faithful in your vows to God. You need to remember that wealth is a tool given us and not something to be worshiped or made the goal of our lives.

Every morning the devil gets up and baits the hook. He drops it into the world and just waits to see who will take a nibble. He does not work hard, but when the hook is set he pulls with all his might. Jesus knew that the Word of God was a vital part of avoiding giving in to the devil's schemes and temptations. You will be tempted. The key is to swim away and don't look back.

Review Chapter 23

Can you identify the following People, Places or dates and tell how they are important to this week's lesson?

1. Jesus
2. John the Baptist
3. Nicodemus
4. Peter
5. Pharisees & Sadducees
6. Samaritan woman
7. Judea
8. Samaria
9. Galilee
10. Capernaum

Page numbers are from The Story (TS)

1. John the Baptist was six months older than Jesus and his cousin. What did John the Baptist wear, what did he preach, and what did he want people to do to prove they had changed? (TS 321-322)

2. What do we learn about Jesus from John the Baptist? (TS 322-324)

3. Nicodemus was a Pharisee or someone who taught there was life after death. What did he want to know from Jesus? What was Jesus' answer? (TS 326-327)

4. The Samaritan woman's conservation with Jesus allowed Jesus to reveal facts about Himself. What facts did He tell the woman about who He was and what He could do? (TS 327-329)

5. Jesus was always busy. Describe the events that took place on the Sabbath in Capernaum. (TS 329-330)

6. Some friends cut a hole in a roof of the house Jesus is in so they can get their sick friend healed. Jesus has a conversation with a teacher of the law and asks him a question. What is the question and what is the answer? (TS 330-331)

7. Jesus was angry with the religious Jews in a synagogue. Why was He angry, and what did He do in spite of their attitudes? (TS 332)

8. Name the twelve disciples chosen by Jesus. (TS 333)

9. What one thing in this chapter did you learn that can help you on your personal faith journey?

Chained or Changed
The Story Unfolds – Chapter 24

When you face God, who will decide where you will spend eternity? Imagine there are two doors, one marked heaven and one marked hades, or hell. Standing between these doors is God. There is a long line of people approaching God. As each one gets to Him He points to a door, and the person is escorted to the door they are to enter. The question is: why is each person directed to the door? How is this determined? We are told "*man is destined to die once, and after that to face judgment.*" Hebrews 9.27 Jesus was clear, at the judgment, a separation will take place. He said one group would "*go away to eternal punishment, but the righteous to eternal life.*" Matthew 25.45 Yet, this does not tell us why. There are two schools of thought on this matter. One says that God has already decided who will go to heaven and hades. He has made this decision even before we were born. This is called <u>predestination</u>. The second way says that each person decides where they will spend eternity by the way they live, and the choices they make while they are alive. They have <u>free will</u> to accept God's offer of eternal life, or can reject it and get eternal punishment instead. That takes us back to the two doors. If God has predetermined or predestined a person to heaven or hades, then all God is doing at the judgment is directing them to where He chosen for them to go. They have no say in the matter. If God has given the person free will to make their own choices then He is honoring their life decisions when He points to one door or the other. If eternity is predetermined, then there is nothing we can do. If it is not and we can make the choice, then our lives are preparation for the greatest moment ever. The moment is when God directs us to a door that we will walk through to eternity.

Completely cut off from God Luke 8.26-39

Jesus and His disciples cross the lake of Galilee. During the crossing Jesus is so tired He sleeps even while a storm starts to sink the boat He is in. The disciples wake Him up; He calms the storm and then rebukes them for their unbelief. It must have been a quiet trip for the rest of the way. The disciples are whispering questions of who Jesus is. How does He have the power to control storms?

They sailed to the region of the Gerasenes. This was located on the east shore of the lake. This region was dominated by a mix of different groups of people with a few Jews sprinkled in, for good measure. The majority of those living there were pagans. As Jesus stepped out of the boat, a demon-possessed man met Him. This man was naked and running around the lake shore like a wild animal. In the distance was a herd of pigs with workers watching over them. The demon-possessed man ran up to Jesus and began yelling at Him at the top of his voice. "*What do you want with me Jesus, Son of the Most High God? I beg you don't torture me.*" The disciples must have wondered what was going on after the night they had just had. Here was Jesus with a naked man yelling at Him on what, otherwise, would be a tranquil morning by a beautiful lake.

We know nothing of this man's first encounter with evil. The choices that he made that so overpowered him by evil that he no longer had any control of his world. He rips off his clothes, runs around terrorizing the people. Any semblance of normal is gone as he lives by himself this life of torment. The people have tried to help him, or, at least control him. They have chained him, put clothes on him, and guarded him to try and keep him in line. Yet, none of these external solutions have worked. He is completely cut off from God. He is cut off spiritually by the demons who rule his life. He is cut off mentally and out of his mind unable to even think about God. He is cut off physically; a man out of control driven away to live and die alone.

Recently a friend was in my office who told of a problem she had with her doctor and medication. She was suffering from a physical problem and had gone to seek help. Medication was prescribed that was supposed to help. Instead of helping, it only got worse. Finally, in desperation, she changed doctors and sought new help. The second doctor determined that she had been misdiagnosed, and the medication was actually making matters worse. She got new medication for the problem and, within a few weeks was showing remarkable improvement. This is what had happened to the demon possessed man. Those who knew him had prescribed clothes and chains to improve his condition. They had only made matters worse by angering the demons and driving the man further from help. If he had not changed doctors and found Jesus his prognoses was extremely bad.

Understanding The Abyss

The man was possessed, or full of demons. There were so many that they called themselves "Legion." This is no small matter. A Roman Legion was made up of about six thousand (6,000) men. Here is a guy who had so many demons in him that they didn't go by a name but by a number. These demons begged Jesus not to send them into the abyss. This abyss is also known as hades or hell. Jesus called it a place of "*eternal fire prepared for the devil and his angels.*" Matthew 25.41 So this place of eternal fire has an eternal purpose that is eternal punishment. The key person it was prepared for is the Devil, Satan, Beelzebub, the Lord of the Flies[13] himself. This is not a place made up by a bunch of preachers who want to scare people. It is a place established by God and confirmed to exist by Jesus. It was not only prepared for the leader of all evil, it was prepared for his angels and all who follow him, too.

[The word, that is translated angels, is really a word that means messengers. The translation to the word angels was done in the early English Bibles. The Greek word

aggelos was transliterated to angels instead of being translated to the word 'messengers'.]

The messengers of the enemy for whom eternal fire has been prepared, are demons, and anyone else who does not accept Jesus as the son of God. Hades was prepared for Satan, demons, and people who work for him or those who have rejected Jesus. The word eternal is about how long the fires burn and how long judgment lasts.

Changed Completely

Jesus sent the demons out of the man and into the pigs. They rushed down the hillside and drowned. It was then that the nearby pig farmers were interested. They rushed to town to report that the herd of pigs had drowned. They had no idea what had happened to the demon-possessed man. Everyone from the town hurried to the lake to see what had happened. It was big news. Like a car wreck or a fire everyone wanted to see for themselves. This was a major event. Yet, what they found was not what they expected. They must have been greatly surprised to arrive at the lake and see the dead pigs floating in the water and there, in front of Jesus, the man they had dealt with on numerous occasions. These were the people who had chained and clothed him. They had stood guard only to have him break the chains, rip off his clothes, and terrorize the town. He was completely different. The demons were gone, and he was spiritually changed. Now he was under the control, or directions of Jesus. He was dressed and had been physically changed. He was now in his right mind or mentally changed. He was sitting at Jesus' feet. He had been completely changed.

The change had happened from the inside out and was a real change. People often get it backwards. They want to change the outside of someone, hoping it will change the person on the inside. The Pharisees were masters this approach. They knew how to dress, how to act, how to perform but "*inside* [they were] *full of dead men's bones and everything unclean.*" Matthew 23.27 Jesus told them to first clean the inside and then the outside would be clean also. Matthew 23.26 That is what had happened to the demon-possessed man. He was cleaned inside by Jesus and the change had carried over to the outside. Those who had tried to change him with chains were unsuccessful.

How many people approach God thinking they can make external changes, and be accepted or righteous before God? The truth is God looks at the heart first. If it is not changed, it does not matter how well you dress up the outside.

Free Will is Free Will

Every day we make choices about what to eat, where to go, and what to watch. Yesterday, a man told me he had been speeding to get to church on time. That was his choice. It is a choice a lot of believers make. I have known quite a few Christians who received tickets on Sunday speeding to church or to the restaurant afterwards. God does not make us speed. It is a personal choice.

Free will allows a person to accept Jesus or to reject him. "*The people of the region of the Gerasenes asked Jesus to leave them because they were overcome with fear.*" They exercised free will. They were afraid that they could lose more than a herd of pigs. They were afraid that someone who could change a demon-possessed man could change them too. They were afraid of a man who could do what they could not. They wanted to remain in control of their lives and that meant they wanted Jesus to leave. People are not much different today. They see what Jesus can do and it scares them. They don't want to change, they are happy the way things are even if that means not having Jesus in their lives. Everyone has the free will to accept Jesus or to reject him.

Free Will is Obedience

The crowds were begging Jesus to leave. The disciples were getting back in the boats after a short visit. No one wants to stay where they are not welcomed. The formerly demon-possessed man headed toward the boat to go with Jesus, when Jesus stopped him. The man "*begged to go with him, but Jesus sent him away.*" Now the man, who was out of control, had to decide if he would follow the directions of the Son of God, or if he would continue to exercise complete and unfettered free will. This was the free will that had gotten him in trouble to begin with. This was the free will that had led to a life full of a Legion of demons. If he was really going to serve Jesus he had to discover that free will was not doing anything you want but doing everything Jesus wants. Free will is about obedience. Free will is also about following directions. Jesus told the man to "*Return home and tell how much God has done for (*him*).*" Jesus had enough disciples in the boat but he did not have any in that region. The local citizens could ask Jesus to leave but this was the formerly demon-possessed man's home. These people needed him to stay and tell how God had changed him on the inside.

"*So the man went away and told all over town how much Jesus had done for him.*" Living under the guidance and control of Jesus is free will. It is a choice God lets us make. We can be like the townspeople and send Jesus away, or like the man who let Jesus rule his heart and took the message back to the town that had just rejected Jesus.

The Power of Jesus

<u>There is the cleansing power of Jesus</u>. It changed a man from demon-possessed and out-of-control to someone who was willing to follow the directions of the Son of God. This cleansing power is available to everyone. "*For there is no difference between Jew and Gentile—the same Lord is Lord of all and richly blesses all who call on him, for, "Everyone who calls on the name of the Lord will be saved.*" Romans 10.12-13 This cleansing power is the same for everyone. It is how we are richly blessed, and how real joy comes into our lives. It is how we are saved. It is the decision that determines the door we pass through into eternity is

marked, heaven. God has let us choose. When a person approaches God at the end of life, He will honoring the decisions we have made.

<u>There is the changing power of Jesus</u>. It is about complete change. It changes a person spiritually first and foremost. It is the inner change that affects the rest of the person. It places the person in contact with the living God and allows him/her to accept Him, or reject Him. This leads to the mental change as the person's thinking comes into line with the directions of God. This finally changes the person externally or physically. It is not about dressing a certain way. It is how they now act on the outside that reflects who they really are on the inside.

<u>There is the controlling power of Jesus</u>. This is not like the enemy who controls and dominates those he has overpowered. The controlling power of Jesus is His requirement of a life of self-control. It is a life of free will and obedience. It is never about Jesus making us do something. It is about his asking and allowing us to do what He has directed or asked us to do. This is not something we can do on our own. If it were, it would not be so hard, and there would not be so few committed believers. Yet, Jesus does know we want to do it. We just need help. "*But the fruit of the Spirit is love, joy, peace, patience, kindness, goodness, faithfulness, gentleness and self-control.*" Galatians 5.22-23 With everything else God has given us He also helps with a dose of self-control. The lack of self-control is a sign of a person out of touch with God. 2 Timothy 3.3 We must make sure self-control is part of our lives if we are going to exercise free will as a gift, and not a curse of a string of wrong decisions. The controlling power of Jesus is to have self-control and to be obedient to His directions for our lives. The man without demons wants to get in the boat, but being obedient, and exercising self-control, he follows the directions given him by Jesus.

Two Questions to Answer

First, are you CHAINED by the world, or are you CHANGED by Jesus?

Second, are you AFRAID of Jesus, or are you SERVING Jesus?

How you answer these questions will determine what happens when you are next in line and God points to a door you will walk through into eternity. Consider carefully your answer and if you need to make some corrections in your life, you still have time. Like the demon-possessed man, you may need to start at the feet of Jesus to be set free. It is your choice, and God will honor whatever choice you make, eternally.

Review Chapter 24

Can you identify the following People, Places or dates and tell how they are important to this week's lesson?

1. Jesus
2. John the Baptist
3. Daughter of Herodias
4. Herodias
5. Jairus
6. Peter
7. Capernaum
8. Sea of Galilee
9. Gennesaret
10. Parables

Page numbers are from The Story (TS)

1. Why did Jesus teach using parables? (TS 335-336)

2. When the tax collectors challenged Jesus for eating with sinners, how did Jesus respond? (TS 337-339)

3. What is the key teaching from the parable of the Lost Coin, Lost Sheep, and the Lost Son?

4. According to Jesus, who is your neighbor? Explain your answer. (TS 339-340)

5. How was the way Jesus described happy (blessed) people different from the way the world sees people being happy? (TS 340-341)

6. What are the keys to praying that Jesus taught his disciples here? (TS 341)

7. How many different kinds of miracles did Jesus do?

8. The woman who was healed from the bleeding disorder had something in common with the daughter of Jairus whom Jesus also healed. What was it? (TS 344-345)

9. Why was John the Baptist in prison? What finally happened to him? (TS 346-347)

10. What one thing in this chapter did you learn that can help you on your personal faith journey?

Who Is Jesus- Really
The Story Unfolds – Chapter 25

People are confused about who Jesus is. In the world today he is seen in many different ways. He is:

- A good man
- A crazy guy
- A prophet of God
- A teacher of great principles
- A good example to follow
- A bad example
- God's one and only son
- The only way to eternal life
- One of many ways to get to heaven

Even in the church this confusion happens. It is happening in the pulpits of many churches and in the pews of many more. Our goal today is to clear away the confusion and answer the question, "Who is Jesus?"

As Jesus began his ministry he was faced with the ties of the first thirty years of his life. The people in his home town of Nazareth listened and watched *"All spoke well of him and were amazed at the gracious words that came from his lips. "Isn't this JOSEPH'S SON?"* Luke 4.22 On the surface this was true. He had been raised from His birth by Joseph and was seen as his son. Joseph was the guardian that God had selected to watch over and raise Jesus. Much of the world saw Jesus as Joseph's son. Their opinion would change several times over the next three years, and most of the time they would be wrong.

PEOPLE CAN BE CONFUSED

"Jesus and his disciples went on to the villages around Caesarea Philippi. On the way he asked them, "Who do people say I am?"

They replied, "Some say John the Baptist; others say Elijah; and still others, one of the prophets." Mark 8.27-28

Jesus wanted to know what the man-on-the-street opinion poll was saying about Him. The disciples had been listening as they traveled down the road. It was apparent that the average person was confused about who Jesus was. There was no universal opinion. Some thought He was a reincarnation of John the Baptist. This put some of the people in the same category as most Hindus today who believe in reincarnation. Some thought He was Elijah, the Old Testament prophet, who had come back from heaven. Yet, others thought He was another prophet of God. The average person on the street did not know who Jesus really was.

Today, it is much the same with people seeing Jesus in a variety of ways. His name is now even an acceptable curse word for most television shows. Try using the name of Mohammad that way and see what happens.

With Jesus, it was either thumbs up or thumbs down. People had all heard of Him and were willing to share their opinions. "*Among the crowds there was widespread whispering about him. Some said, "He is a good man." Others replied, "No, he deceives the people.*" John 7.12 It is much the same today, people either love Jesus or hate Him and it seems everyone has an opinion about His life.

Some thought of Him as a positive influence in the world. "*As Jesus started on his way, a man ran up to him and fell on his knees before him. "Good teacher," he asked, "what must I do to inherit eternal life*?" Mark 10.17 Here was the young man, who many call the rich young ruler. He wanted Jesus to validate his life. He had constructed a pattern of obeying and following the commandments of Moses. Jesus knew that He had one problem that needed to be dealt with. This young man worshiped money, and it stood between him and God. In fact, it had become his god. It was the one thing he could not give up, even if it meant he would not have eternal life.

There are many today who attend churches looking to have their lives validated without making the necessary changes. They flock to churches that preach a message of happiness and which requires little if any sacrifice or change in the life of a person.

The confusion surrounding Jesus led some to believe He was someone important even if they could not agree on who He really was. As He taught and people listened, they began to form opinions. Each was hearing something different and, "*On hearing his words, some of the people said, "Surely this man is the Prophet." Others said, "He is the Christ.*" John 7.40-41 They did not know for sure and were only guessing.

The Pharisees and other religious leaders came to the conclusion that He was "*demon-possessed*!" John 8.52 They went so far as to say the only way He could drive out demons was if He was one Himself. Jesus told them a house divided will not stand. How many today are trying to make Jesus into something evil. He is portrayed in modern movies, television, books, and by bad preachers as a confused and evil man.

The Jews in Jesus' time were looking for a deliverer. This messiah was seen as a leader who would free them from the Romans and who would restore the nation to its glory, as in the days of David. This messiah or Christ was seen as a revolutionary leader who would fight to free them all from the oppression they lived under. When Jesus asked, "*Who do you say I am*?" Mark 9.29 They had a variety of possible answers; John the Baptist, Elijah, a prophet, a good man, a wise teacher or as "*Peter answered, "You are the Christ.*" Mark 8.30 Knowing what the popular thought of who the Christ was supposed to be, may at most be a definite maybe, to understanding, who Jesus really was.

Even as He traveled to Jerusalem after three years of ministry He was faced with the confusion and had to deal with the popular answer of the day. On the Sunday before His death as He made His way toward the city and His destination and destiny "*The CROWDS that went ahead of him and those that followed shouted,*

> *"Hosanna to the Son of David!"*
> *"Blessed is he who comes in the name of the Lord!"*
> *"Hosanna in the highest!"*
> *When Jesus entered Jerusalem, the whole city was stirred and asked, "Who is this?"*
> *The CROWDS answered, "This is Jesus, the prophet from Nazareth in Galilee."* Matthew 21.9-11

The crowds on the road were crying out, "Hosanna." They were literally saying, "save us, save us now." They were looking for a conquering messiah who would throw the Romans out. They saw Jesus as a descendant of King David. They cried out, "*Hosanna in the highest*!" They were calling on Jesus as a heavenly messenger to set them free from their physical captivity. They knew His lineage was from Nazareth of Galilee. They wanted Him to perform miracles like the prophets of old.

This crowd was a pollster's dream or nightmare. They were calling on Him to save them on Sunday, and on Friday, the same people would gather to demand that He be put to death. Crying, "Hosanna" or 'save us' on Sunday, and crying, 'crucify Him' on Friday. They were not committed to Him on Sunday and were only hoping that He might be someone important. By the end of the week, He had disappointed and not fulfilled their expectations, so they turned on Him.

THE FATHER KNOWS

Even on the mountain with Moses and Elijah present, Peter does not seem to understand who Jesus really is. He is taken in by the two heavenly guests that are talking to Jesus. Moses, the receiver of the Laws of God, and Elijah, the greatest Old Testament prophet, attract the attention and the mouth of Peter. He immediately senses this as a great opportunity, and wants to put up tents for them as a gesture of welcome. It is almost like Peter is saying that it is good thing I am here because I know what to do. "*While he was still speaking, a bright cloud enveloped them, and a voice from the cloud said, "This is MY SON, whom I love; with him I am well pleased. Listen to him!"* Matthew 17.5 God has to interrupt Peter and, in essence, tells him to hush. Peter has missed the key point of the meeting. So God says, "*This is my son, whom I love.*"

Everyone else may be confused and struggling to understand who Jesus is but not God. He knows Jesus is His son and He wants people to listen to Him and to focus their attention on Him. We, like Peter, need to learn to "*listen to him*!"

WHAT JESUS SAID

Moses was meeting with God when it dawned on him that he did not know God's name. That is never a good situation to be in. You are talking to someone and you are trying to remember his/her name. The only thing that can make it worse is when someone walks up and you need to introduce them to the person whose name you cannot remember.

Well, Moses was in an even bigger hole than that. He was talking to God, his God, and he did not know God's name. So Moses swallowed his pride and "*said to God, "Suppose I go to the Israelites and say to them, 'The God of your fathers has sent me to you,' and they ask me, 'What is his name?' Then what shall I tell them?"*

God said to Moses, "I AM WHO I AM. This is what you are to say to the Israelites: 'I AM has sent me to you.'" Exodus 3.13-14

Jesus knew that God was known to all of Israel as "I AM." So when Jesus told the Jews "*before Abraham was born, I AM!*" John 8.58 He was not just saying He was, but He was saying He was God almighty. That is why "*they picked up stones to stone him.*" John 8.59

In fact, Jesus had a habit of using the title of God in describing Himself to those who were around Him. We need to see these from a Jewish frame of mind and know what He is saying about Himself.

* John 6:51: I AM the LIVING BREAD
* John 8:23:; I AM FROM ABOVE
* John 8:12: I AM the LIGHT of the world
* John 10:9: I AM the DOOR
* John 10.11: I AM the GOOD SHEPHERD
* John 10:36: I AM the SON OF GOD
* John11:25: I AM the RESURRECTION and the LIFE
* John 14:6: I AM the WAY, the TRUTH, and the LIFE.
* John 15:1: I AM the TRUE VINE
* John 19:2: I AM the KING of the JEWS."'
* Acts 9:5: I AM JESUS

In each case Jesus was defining Himself as God and telling those listening what He was able to do because of who He was. It is important to note that claiming to be from above and to be the Son of God were both punishable by death in the nation of Israel. Claiming to be God, or the great I AM, could get you stoned to death.

When Paul was struck blind on the Damascus road as he traveled to arrest followers of Jesus, he cried out, "*Who are you LORD?*" Acts 9.5 The reply he heard was "*I AM Jesus.*" Moses had seen Him in the burning bush and had to ask His name. He was told "*I AM*" is my name. Paul was struck blind by His presence and had to ask His name and He was told "*I AM Jesus.*" Paul was a Jewish Pharisee. He had studied the law and the prophets and he knew the name of God. He knew Moses had seen him in the burning bush, and the Hebrew children had seen Him in the fiery furnace. When he heard, "*I AM Jesus,*" he knew he was face to face with the God of Abraham, Isaac, and Jacob.

Imagine the full force of this. The whole statement Jesus made to Paul that day was, "*I am Jesus, whom you are persecuting,... now get up and go into the city, and you will be told what you must do.*" John 9.5-6 Paul found out that Jesus was God. He found out that he had been fighting against the living God and that he was being sent as a blind man to wait and find out what God was going to do with him. The next three days must have been the longest of his life.

A PERSONAL DECLARATION OF FAITH

Lazarus was dead, and his sisters, Mary and Martha, were in mourning. They had sent word to Jesus and had hoped that He would arrive in time to heal Lazarus. Jesus arrived after Lazarus had been dead four days. He had been buried, and the family was trying to deal with the loss of this loved one. Word spread ahead of Jesus that He was coming and Martha rushed out to meet him. "*Martha said to Jesus, "if you had been here, my brother would not have died.*" John 11.21 Jesus promised her Lazarus would rise from the dead. Martha responded "*I know he will rise again in the resurrection at the last day.*" John 11.24 She was thinking about the resurrection of everyone at the end of time. She, like most Jews, had trouble understanding that each person is resurrected to eternal life when they die, and do not have to wait for the end of time.

"*Jesus said to her, "I AM the resurrection and the life. He who believes in me will live, even though he dies; and whoever lives and believes in me will never die. Do you believe this*?" John 11.25-26 Jesus makes sure she knows He is the "*I AM,*" and has power over eternal life. Jesus reminds her that believing in Him is the path to life, and anyone with Him has eternal life. What follows next is vital and is often skipped because of the powerful words of Jesus.

Martha, in all her grief, is not blaming Jesus for her brother's death. Martha is surrounded by a crowd. She has rushed out to meet Him while Mary has stayed at home. Jesus has just said He is God and has the power of eternal life. Jesus has asked Martha if she believes this. Then Martha says:

"Yes, Lord," she told him, "I believe that you are the Christ, the Son of God, who was to come into the world." John 11.27

She calls him "*Lord.*" This word refers to the Almighty and goes back to the Old Testament understanding of the power and might of God. This is the Almighty God who created the world and who flooded it later. This is the God who directed all the patriarchs, prophets, judges and kings of Israel. She continues, "*I believe you are Christ.*" She declares He is the Christ or Messiah, literally the Anointed one of God. She saw Him as the promise that fulfilled all the prophecies of the Old Testament. She cannot stop; you are "*the Son of God, who was to come into the world.*" She is committed and sees Him as directly connected to God. She knows He is here on a mission that only He can fulfill. She has declared more in a few seconds of her grief than anyone else has even come close to. She is not declaring this because of a miracle. Her brother is dead. She is not declaring this to gain favor. Jesus has come to her house to comfort her and her sister. Martha believed in spite of her circumstances. She is a woman of great faith.

The world was confused. Was Jesus Joseph's son? Was Jesus John the Baptist, or Elijah, or just another prophet? Was He a good man, or was He a bad man who was deceiving the world? Was He a good teacher with principles to make life better? Was He the Christ who would set them free from Rome? Was He the Son of David who was to make Israel great again? Was He a demon as some of the Pharisees had said? Or, was He the great I AM? Was He the Son of God? Was He the Lord Almighty?

Martha and Mary knew and were rewarded for it. The thief on the cross, that asked to be remembered, knew and was rewarded for it. Paul found out and was never the same, and was rewarded for it. The question is: Can you answer the question Jesus asked Peter?

But what about you?" Who do you say Jesus Is?

What is your answer?

Review Chapter 25

Can you identify the following People, Places or dates and tell how they are important to this week's lesson?

1. Mary
2. Martha
3. Lazarus
4. Peter
5. Elijah and Moses
6. Caiaphas
7. Thomas
8. Messiah
9. Feast of Tabernacles
10. Satan

Page numbers are from The Story (TS)

1. Who did the people think Jesus might be? Who did his disciples believe He was? (TS 353)

2. Who did God say Jesus was? (TS 354)

3. How did Jesus describe Himself? (TS 357)

4. How long has Jesus existed? Why did His answer to this question make the Jews angry? (TS 358)

5. What did Jesus find when He arrived at the home of Lazarus, Mary, and Martha? (TS 358-360)

6. What did Martha believe Jesus would do for those who had died? (TS 359)

7. How did the chief priest, Caiaphas, prophesize about the plans God had for His son, Jesus? (TS 361)

8. According to Jesus, how hard is it for a rich man to get into heaven? How did Jesus say it was even possible for him to get there? (TS 362)

9. When Jesus entered the temple, what did He do? Why did He do it? (TS 364)

10. Many Jewish leaders believed in Jesus, but what stopped them from being public with their belief in Him? (TS 365)

11. What one thing in this chapter did you learn that can help you on your personal faith journey?

Words from the Cross
The Story Unfolds - Chapter 26

What is the most important thing Jesus said? Everything He said was important, but we can learn a lot about Him from the last seven things He said from the cross. While suffering, He spoke from his heart. It is interesting to consider what people say when they are facing death.

Queen Elizabeth I of England died in 1603. She was quoted as having said, "All my possessions for a moment of time." She was not ready to let go of this world and was willing to give up everything she had just to have a little more time. Leonardo da Vinci died in 1519 and was supposed to have said, "I have offended God and mankind because my work did not reach the quality it should have." I cannot imagine what he would have done if he had reached the standard he had set for himself. Then there is the television producer and game show host, Merv Griffin whose tombstone reads, "I will not be right back after the message." He died with a sense of humor and with the knowledge that when it was over, it was over. Then there is the tombstone that says, "Please deactivate my Facebook page because I don't need it anymore." The saddest one says, "Here lies an atheist, all dressed up and no place to go."

From the cross Jesus spoke seven times, and each time it carried a message that we can apply to our lives today.

FIRST, He said: "*Father, forgive them, for they do not know what they are doing.*" (Luke 23.34)

This is His declaration of FORGIVENESS.

Jesus was aware that everyone "*sinned and fell short of the glory of God.*" (Romans 3.23) From the beginning of time He knew that, without His sacrifice, there was no hope. His first word from the cross was about His main purpose in coming to earth. Without Jesus' sacrifice "*men are without excuse."* (Romans 1.20) It was through *"his own blood, having obtained eternal redemption"* (Hebrews 9.12) for humanity He cried out to remind them what they had received.

SECOND, He said: *"I tell you the truth, today you will be with me in Paradise."* (Luke 23.34)

This is His declaration of SALVATION

There were two thieves who were crucified with Jesus. One mocked Him, and the other asked Jesus to allow Him to enter the kingdom. To the one who accepted Jesus as His savior Jesus promised he would leave this world and, that day, be with Jesus in Paradise. We learn in 2 Corinthians 12.2-4 that Paradise is the third heaven where God has His throne. This is where the thief, who has just gotten saved, will spend eternity.

Salvation is not a single action, but a process that takes you from where you are, to heaven's door at the end of your life. Imagine that you are on a boat at sea and it sinks. Now you need saving, so someone sends an S.O.S. The next thing you know the Coast Guard is overhead in a helicopter with a rescue basket to pluck you out of the water. You are now being saved. If, at any time along the way, you decide to jump out of the helicopter you will no longer be in the process of being saved. You have chosen to stop being saved. You may think this is a stupid illustration. Who would stop getting saved? Well, it happens all the time. They start their relationship with Jesus, and then get side-tracked by the world. It is equivalent to a person jumping out of the Coast Guard helicopter.

Salvation is available to *"everyone who calls on the name of the Lord."* (Romans 10.13) Once a person has accepted Jesus as their personal savior, they can *"rejoice and be glad, because great is your reward in heaven."* (Matthew 5.12) This leads to the knowledge that *"he will reward each person according to what he has done."* Matthew 16.27

THIRD He said, "*Dear woman, here is your son,"..."Here is your mother.*" (John 19.26-27)

This is the declaration of FAMILY.

When a person accepts Jesus as their personal savior they become part of the family of God. "*Both the one who makes men holy and those who are made holy are of the same family. So Jesus is not ashamed to call them brothers.*" (Hebrews 2.11) We are united into the family because of the change that Jesus makes for us. As part of the family of God "*we have opportunity, let us do good to all people, especially to those who belong to the family of believers.*" (Galatians 6.10)

As part of this spiritual and eternal family we are to take care of each other. I have three brothers. We grew up together, fought, played, and did all sorts of things together. I did not get to choose my family or my brothers. I was born into the family and, as the family grew, I was just expected to accept the new members because they were family. My spiritual family works pretty much the same way. It is more unique than my biological family. People choose to be part of the spiritual family and to spend eternity with each other.

Jesus believed in family. He wanted to make sure His mother was taken care of so He appointed John to watch out for her. Jesus believed in the traditional family and family values. He never endorsed, approved or even insinuated anything different.

FOURTH He said, "*Eloi, Eloi, lama sabachthani,"..."My God, my God, why have you forsaken me*?" Mark 15.34

This is the declaration of DESPAIR

He had fought with Himself as He prayed in the garden to do His father's will. Yet now on the cross, separated from

God by the sins of humanity, He was totally alone. A person without Christ is a person without hope. (Ephesians 2.12) The individual is living a life of despair.

This despair is not limited to individuals. It can also be felt by a church. Jesus warned a church, in the book of Revelation, that they had "*forsaken [*their*] first love.*" (Revelation 2.5) They had turned away from following Jesus. Whether as a church or individually it is almost always the same things that separate them from Jesus. It may be "*the worries of this life, the deceitfulness of wealth and the desires for other things come in and choke the word, making [*life*] unfruitful.*" Mark 4.19 People or churches who allow this to happen eventually discover that they have replaced the greatness of God with what grows old and cold. This separation, or despair, is a spiritual loneliness that eats away and cannot be satisfied by anything this world has to offer.

FIFTH He said, "*I am thirsty.*" (John 19.28)

This is the declaration of HUMANITY.

Jesus is all human and all God. Here, His humanity is highlighted and shows that it was not a supernatural death. He had to battle in prayer to even submit to the cross. Now it is upon Him and He is suffering alone with the weight of all humanity's sins upon him. We know that Jesus "*has been tempted in every way just as we are - yet without sin.*" Hebrews 4.15

"*He himself bore our sins in his body on the tree, so that we might die to sins and live for righteousness; by his wounds you have been healed.*" 1 Peter 2.24

SIXTH He said, "*It is finished.*" John 19.30

This is the declaration of COMPLETENESS.

God always finishes what He starts. Jesus was saying that He was about to triumph, complete, and achieve total success.

The first time we hear God declaring completeness and announce He was finished, was at creation. "*On the seventh day God had finished creating and rested.*" (Genesis 2.1)

The second time God finishes something is on the cross. It is here Jesus declares, "*It is finished.*" (John 19.30) The payment for the sins has now been paid in full.

The third time God declares He has finished will be when He declares, "*It is done. I am the Alpha and the Omega, the beginning and the end.*" (Revelation 21.6) This is how God will bring all of time to a close. This is what will precede the new heaven and the new earth.

We are also called to finish what we start. We need to be able to say what Paul said about the spiritual race we are in. "*However, I consider my life worth nothing to me, if only I may finish the race and complete the task the Lord Jesus has given me - the task of testifying to the gospel of God's grace.*" (Acts 20.24)

SEVENTH He said, "*Father, into your hands I commit my spirit.*" Luke 23.46

This is the declaration of VICTORY

Jesus was not only dying, He was going home to be with the Father. He knew that it was not the end, but it was a change. Paul writes about this change to the church at Corinth. He told them that "*we will be changed.*" 1 Corinthians 15.51 The physical body cannot enter into heaven. The mortal must put on immortality if it is going to enter heaven or hell. The body of Jesus was about to die, but He would receive his eternal body. Jesus saw this change as a positive. This was what Peter was writing about when he said, "*in keeping with his promise we are looking forward to a new heaven and a new earth, the home of righteousness.*" 1 Peter 3.13

"*Where, O death is your victory? Where, O death is your sting?*" 1 Corinthians 15.55-56

Death is not a barrier or punishment to the believer; it is a door to a victory celebration. There are no bad surprises or fears. It is hard to imagine, but it is about everything positive. It is a wonderful thing to have God waiting for you as your Heavenly Father, and Jesus as your Lord and savior. In contrast, it is a terrible thing to have God waiting for you as your judge, and Jesus as a stranger.

The believer should view death as Jesus did. It was a commitment of everything eternal into the hands of a loving Father.

We can see all the humanity of Jesus from the cross. Here dying for our sins, He speaks from His heart words that have changed humanity FOREVER!

Review Chapter 26

Can you identify the following People, Places or dates and tell how they are important to this week's lesson?

1. Simon of Cyrene
2. Malchus
3. Pilate
4. Judas Iscariot
5. Barabbas
6. Caiaphas
7. Gethsemane
8. Mount of Olives
9. Passover
10. Golgotha

Page numbers are from The Story (TS)

1. What were some reasons that Judas may have betrayed Jesus? (TS 365-369)

2. Jesus used the Passover meal to create a different meaning for his followers. What did this meal become after the resurrection of Jesus? (Hint on page TS 369)

3. What do we learn about heaven from the conversation that Jesus had with Thomas? (TS 369-370)

4. How is a person able to get to know God the Father? (TS 370)

5. What three things did Jesus pray for before his death when He was with His disciples? (TS 371)

6. Who had Jesus arrested? (TS 373)

7. What two leaders did Jesus appear before as part of his trial? (TS 374-375)

8. Why did the Jews want Jesus executed? (TS 374) What was the real reason He died on the cross?

9. Why did Pilate finally give in and execute Jesus? (TS 376-377)

10. What events took place when Jesus died? (TS 380)

11. What one thing in this chapter did you learn that can help you on your personal faith journey?

Christ and The Cross The Story Unfolds - Chapter 27

When I listen to some ministers, I wonder if they are wearing special glasses that can only see part of the Word of God. They are preaching just part of the Gospel and leaving out the parts that they disagree with, or which might make their listeners uncomfortable. In Paul's final visit with the elders at the church at Ephesus he says, "*I declare to you today that I am innocent of the blood of all men. For I have not hesitated to proclaim to you the whole will of God.*" Acts 20.26-27 He was not going to hold back or be guilty of preaching to itching ears. He did not care if it made people uncomfortable. He knew their discomfort could lead to repentance and eternal life.

"In 604, Pope Gregory wrote about the "Seven Deadly Sins" which included pride, gluttony, envy, lust, anger, greed, and laziness."[14] These seemed like the worst things you could do. I wonder if there are not even worse things a person can do.

The number in scripture for man is six. It is the day he was created, and is the number of a life that is lived without God. People often want to be religious without being biblical. They want to be called Christians but do not want to be Christ like. Man's view comes up short and is all wrong. It is based on making people feel good about whatever they are doing. There are six elements to this type of religion we can pinpoint.

I mentioned about being called Christians without being Christ like. That is really more important than you might think. "*The disciples were called Christians first at Antioch.*" Acts 11.26 They were living their lives in such a way that people who saw them were reminded of Jesus. They were called Christians or 'Christ like.' That leads to a series of questions. What is a Christian? What is Christianity? What do Christians believe? What do

Christians do? There is a lot of confusion about the answer to these questions. Different church groups are now getting together to vote on what they believe. It appears to not matter to a majority of Christians what scripture says. All they need is 51%, a simple majority and their church can change its position on anything and everything.

This is leading to a crisis in Christianity. The trend seems to be to remove some of the most basic beliefs that are not seen as part of the modern culture. There are six that stand out today which will cripple the church and cause less than the whole will of God to be proclaimed. The choice for the church is clear. Either the church will proclaim the whole gospel of truth, or it will eliminate anything that might make people feel uncomfortable.

In the public schools there is a battle going on between two forces. The first wants to improve schools, teachers, learning and raise scores. They want to require students to meet minimum standards before going on. This may be more difficult when you consider that upwards of 80% of students in one of the largest cities are not grade levels proficient in reading or math.[15] This was a real sour point when the teachers were out on strike for more money.

The second option for the public schools appears to be the one more and more are adopting. Lower the test scores so that more students can pass. This lowering of standards shows up when students cannot read well enough to do basic daily tasks. Students are receiving high school diplomas who cannot read a paper and who have such poor math skills they cannot balance a checkbook. The answer to the problem may seem obvious, but it is easier to lower scores than it is to try and take on such a daunting task as raising the test scores.

This same dilemma is being faced by the church. The first choice is to teach all the scriptures and Biblical standards; to expect families and individuals to meet those standards as they are laid out in the Word of God.

The second choice is to lower the standards. This means removing those standards that are too hard, or that people disagree with. This allows for more freedom in the type of lifestyles people can live. This will make the church more inclusive and could lead to larger crowds on Sunday for the most popular preachers. This lowering of standards has six key ways of being expressed.

CHRIST WITHOUT THE CROSS

This is Christianity without the cross. There is a move to remove the cross from Christianity. The cross for many is symbolic of violence, and is seen as a hindrance to reaching more modern people. If the cross is removed, it means there are fewer obligations to the one who died on it. If Jesus has done so much for us then He should be able to expect much from His followers, but if He is just a good teacher, much less is expected, and lower standards can be set.

Paul would disagree, he "*resolved to know nothing... except Jesus Christ and him crucified.*" 1 Corinthians 2.2 Paul knew that, without the cross, there was no real savior. It was on the cross He died for the sins of humanity. Yet we live in a time when "*many live as enemies of the cross of Christ.*" Philippians 3.18

We live in an upside down world. People love violence. They flock to violent movies; MMA is hugely successful and violent video games rated MA sell out. On July 12, 2012 inside a Colorado theater showing a PG-13 movie full of violence, a young man started shooting. When he was finished, twelve were dead. This shooting shocked the nation, but why? The culture is being fed violence so should we not expect to see more violence as a result?

This upside down world extends into the churches. "The General Assembly of the Presbyterian Church (USA) meeting [in July of 2012] approved a resolution calling for "an end to the practice of corporal punishment in homes, schools, and child care facilities." Fifty-one percent of the church leaders meeting in Pittsburgh voted for the measure, while 47 percent opposed it. The General Assembly also affirmed and expanded the PCUSA's support of abortion. This year the church supports "full access to reproductive health care for both women and men in both private and public health plans."[16] This is code for abortion on demand at any time in the pregnancy.

If that seems strange, consider what they said at their meeting. You cannot spank your child to correct him/her when they are bad because we are opposed to violence but you can abort or murder him/her without a reason before he/she is born.

The cross was a violent way to die. Yet, it seems so appropriate that the Son of God was willing to suffer in this violent and upside down world. Without the cross there is no Christian faith, and no forgiveness of sins.

Paul was clear "*the wages of sin is death.*" Romans 3.23 The cross of Christ is the payment for our sins. Many do not want to recognize the cross because it means they would have to admit that they are sinners. Without the cross, we cannot obtain "*The gift of God* [that] *is eternal life in Christ Jesus our Lord.*" Romans 6.23

SALVATION WITHOUT SANCTIFICATION

This is Christianity without change. The problem is when believers meet to worship; they look a lot like the world. The problem extends into the world where believers cannot be distinguished from the non-believers. Believers are now the same, only different, and that difference is being different in name only. The actions and attitudes of those inside the church are running parallel to those of the non-believers who don't attend church and do not know Jesus as their person savior.

Jesus "*has saved us and called us to a holy life—not because of anything we have done but because of his own purpose and grace.*" 2 Timothy 1.9-10 We should not be ashamed of who we are. The problem is that, instead of repenting or changing their lives directions and becoming what God wants them to be, many people get "SAVED" (using the religious word) and often do not change. They stop and remain the same. They are exactly the same, only now they call themselves, "Christians." Yet, this is absolutely contrary to the teachings of the Word of God. We are called to a "HOLY LIFE." We are called to get "CONTROL" and do what is holy and honorable.

The word HOLY means "to sanctify" or set aside for a special purpose and not to be used for just anything. It means to not allow evil or sinful actions, words, or thoughts to be part of the believer's life.

This separation for a special purpose is called sanctification. "*It is God's will that you should be sanctified... that each of you should learn to control his own body in a way that is holy and honorable.*" 1 Thessalonians 4.3-4

This sanctification requires that the person remain free from sin. When this happens the person is HONORABLE, or they have real value to God. It is "very costly" for God. It cost Him His son on the cross. This means you should see it as something to be taken care of. It has value and needs to be protected and guarded.

Let me illustrate this for you: If I were to take one of my wife's antique quilts that was given to us by her parents and use it as a cleaning rag, I would be in BIG trouble. It is special and is not just another old towel or scrap rag. It is to be taken care of. It is now set aside and has value. If you belong to God you are not to do just anything. You have been set aside for His purpose and you have value to God. He has given you that value by placing His Holy Spirit inside the sanctified believer.

DECISIONS WITHOUT DISCIPLESHIP

This is Christianity without commitment. I personally cannot imagine Christianity without commitment, but that is now the norm instead of the exception. Jesus was very clear about the need to commit as a follower. "*If anyone would come after me, he must deny himself and take up his cross and follow me. For whoever wants to save his soul*[17] *will lose it, but whoever loses his soul for me will find it.*" Matthew 16.24-25

Jesus was traveling with a large group of disciples. He had more than just the twelve we always hear about. Walking down the road He raises the standards and puts them on the spot. He tells them that "*The Spirit gives life; the flesh counts for nothing.*" John 6.62 He says they need to follow Him on the spiritual level, and they have to give him their soul and body. They have to deny themselves. They have to take up crosses. They have to follow Him and commit completely. Most people miss what happens next. It is one of the most dramatic scenes between Jesus and a group of His disciples. He has just raised the standards when it happens. "*From this time many of his disciples turned back and no longer followed him.*" John 6.66 They told Jesus, "no way, I'm out of here. This is too high a price for us to pay. This is too much commitment for me. SEE YA!" So here is Jesus going down the road in one direction and people who were his disciples just a short time before heading in the other direction. They refused to make the commitment and Jesus just lets them leave. It was their choice. Jesus does not call them back and He does not lower the standards.

What does it take to be committed? It takes a cross. It takes a path that He chooses. It takes you making a decision every day to follow Him. That is why Paul said to the Corinthians "*I die every day.*" 1 Corinthians 15.31 He was saying "I make a decision every day that is a complete commitment." I give everything to God every day.

REWARDS WITHOUT RIGHTEOUSNESS

This is Christianity without covenant. A covenant is a contract between you and God. God sets the conditions and the individual chooses to follow the conditions or to opt out. The modern Christian thinks that covenant means they get from God whatever they want. This is as far as their spiritual thinking takes them. God is their resource center, and they have no obligations or responsibility to God. It is all about what they get from God and not what they do for God. This is a system where the person feels they are rewarded just for being a believer. Yet Jesus was very clear that being a disciple is not about how much you get but about sacrifice. "*If anyone would come after me, he must deny himself and take up his cross and follow me.*" Matthew 16.24 Jesus went so far to say anyone "*who does not give up everything he has cannot be* [His] *disciple.*" Luke 14.33

This brings the disciple to the dilemma of how they should demonstrate and live their lives. Jesus instructs "*let your light shine before men, that they may see your good deeds and praise your Father in heaven.*" Matthew 5.16 Righteous acts are those that cause a believer to do God's will and remain innocent of sin. This is about daily living for Jesus.

There is bad righteousness called unrighteousness and there is good righteousness. Righteousness simply means "to do the right thing." There is a right way and a wrong way to do the right thing. "*Be careful not to do your 'acts of righteousness' before men, to be seen by them. If you do, you will have no reward from your Father in heaven.*" Matthew 6.1 Bad righteousness or doing the right thing the wrong way, with the wrong motives will not be rewarded by God. The motive is wrong if the purpose in doing it is to make oneself look good. The audience the person has chosen is wrong. It is other people. It is a deliberate act of self-approval.

Good righteousness, or doing the right thing the right way, with the right motives, will be rewarded by God. The motive is right. It is to make God look good. It is for His approval and not men. The right audience is God. "*For in the gospel a righteousness from God is revealed, a righteousness that is by faith from first to last, just as it is written: "The righteous will live by faith.*" Romans 1.17 (Habakkuk 2.4)

Faith must be first in your life; Faith must be last in your life. Faith is a key to the life of a believer. Now, faith is not what I get from God, but faith is my covenant with God. It is a contract that says, "Whether I live or die God is my God, and I am His servant. Jesus is my Lord and He chooses the path for my life and I will follow it." It is not seeking any earthly reward. It is living for an eternal inheritance. God chooses and I follow. I care more about God's approval than anything else in the world. That is living by faith. It is being in covenant or contract relationship with God.

Finally, righteousness is not without rewards. It is just that God chooses the rewards, and whether we get them here, or in eternity. We must always remember "*without faith it is impossible to please God, because anyone who comes to him must believe that he exists and that he rewards those who earnestly seek him.*" Hebrews 11.6

JESUS WITHOUT JUSTICE

This is Christianity without compliance. I just bought tickets to go back to see my parents in Pennsylvania. The tickets came with an offer for a first class upgrade. But, in order to get the upgrade, I had to have already been part of a rewards program. I could have cashed in my points only if I had them. I could have called them up and complained, but I never signed up and never earned the points needed to upgrade. The rules applied and they do not bend them for anyone. Either you qualified for the rewards or you don't. We all understand that.

Yet, when it comes to God, many think His rules and the qualifications He has set will be overlooked when it comes time to upgrade. Yet the rules are very clear. You have to upgrade to heaven status before leaving this life or you will NEVER, EVER quality for heaven status.

Pastor, I don't want to hear this. It is too negative. No, it is not negative. It is information you need. No one who sits in my church and hears me preach or reads my books is going to stand in front of God and say, "Well, you see God,

Pastor Bob never told me about the eternal choices. He did not tell me I had to deal with this before I got here. He did not tell me about the difference between eternal life and eternal punishment. He did not tell me about honor and immortality and your wrath and anger." If you don't upgrade and get in compliance you will find that God will not bend the rules for you. Either you qualify for eternal life or you don't.

This is not my opinion. It is what Jesus said. Matthew 25 is a chapter many people skip or skim over when reading the New Testament, but it is a vital chapter if you are going to understand how God deals with people at the end of their lives. Jesus is very clear. Speaking about the judgment he says, "*Then they (*referring to the wicked*) will go away to eternal punishment, but the righteous to eternal life.*" Matthew 25.40 There is a separation at the end of life. Jesus used lots of word pictures to describe it. Sheep and goats that he says are separated and judged by the way they lived their lives. The sheep are His way of representing the righteous and the goats representing the unrighteous.

Paul echoes this theme when he writes, "*to those who by persistence in doing good seek glory, honor and immortality, he will give eternal life. But for those who are self-seeking and who reject the truth and follow evil, there will be wrath and anger.*" Romans 2.7-8

Jesus is the judge when it comes to the end of a person's life. "*Not everyone who says to me, 'Lord, Lord,' will enter the kingdom of heaven, but only he who does the will of my Father who is in heaven.*" Matthew 7.21 There are many who are using the name of Jesus but are not living as He has directed. They may even be preaching, and healing, and fighting against evil, but they are not in compliance with His standards. "*Then I will tell them plainly, 'I never knew you. Away from me, you evildoers!'*" Matthew 7.23 They will be shocked but they should know they were warned. All they had to do was read and come into compliance with His will for their lives. Their deeds without compliance were acts of self-righteousness that have no value in heaven.

If you have not signed up for a first class upgrade with Jesus when you die, you will really not like the traveling or the final destination that comes with coach in God's plan.

First class gets a great banquet (Matthew 22.1-14) when they arrive. Coach cannot even get a drop of water for the tip of their tongue when they get where they are going. (Luke 16.24-26) I did not make that up; you can look it up for yourself, but never say you were not warned.

RELIGION WITHOUT RESURRECTION

This is Christianity without credibility. If I were to ask you what is the most important fact holding all the Old and New Testament together? Would you know? Everything God did from the fall to restore fellowship with His creation is based upon one simple, and yet astonishing fact. The Law of Moses, all the writings of the prophets, everything God did to establish Israel, every event was all leading to one moment. Some would say it was the death of Jesus to pay for the sins of humanity, but anyone can die. That event was only important because of what followed three days later. It was the resurrection. Without the resurrection there is no Christianity, because He would not be Christ. Christ means "the anointed one." Someone so special he is called Lord, Messiah, and Christ. Someone so different it took God thousands of years to prepare for His arrival. Someone so important when He died it broke the heart of God the father.

His resurrection is all we are as believers. "*If Christ has not been raised, our preaching is useless and so is your faith.*" 1 Corinthians 15.14 It is the foundation of everything He came to do and everything we believe. "*In his great mercy [*God*] has given us new birth into a living hope through the resurrection of Jesus Christ from the dead, and into an inheritance that can never perish, spoil or fade.*" 1 Peter 1.3-4 Eternity depends upon the fact that He rose from the dead.

There are those who say that the resurrection is not important to the faith of believers. The problem with we face is the scripture tell us exactly the opposite.

If you want religion without the resurrection there are plenty of them around. They span the spectrum of possibilities. Yet, we, as believers, serve the risen Lord. I remind you what He said about Himself.

* John 6:51: I AM the LIVING BREAD
* John 8:23:; I AM FROM ABOVE
* John 8:12: I AM the LIGHT of the world
* John 10:9: I AM the DOOR
* John 10.11: I AM the GOOD SHEPHERD
* John 10:36: I AM the SON OF GOD
* John11:25: I AM the RESURRECTION and the LIFE
* John 14:6: I AM the WAY, the TRUTH, and the LIFE.
* John 15:1: I AM the TRUE VINE
* John 19:2: I AM the KING of the JEWS."'
* Acts 9:5: I AM JESUS

This is the resurrected Jesus. He is the foundation of all we believe, and He is the one we all will stand before at the end of our lives. He is the reason we live. If He is not risen, then He is not Christ. If He is not Christ, than there is no real hope, and we are as Paul said, without the resurrection, "*to be pitied more than all men.*" 1 Corinthians 15.19

CHRISTIANITY IS

There are six elements, that I believe, separate Christianity from all other belief systems. These six help us know Him and stand with confidence each day as believers.

Christianity is Christ paying the cost on the cross. It was not cheap or without sacrifice that God reached out to reunite with humanity. This is "*Jesus Christ, who gave himself for us to redeem us from all wickedness and to purify for himself a people that are his very own, eager to do what is good."* Titus 2.13-14 He paid the full price for each and every one of us. This is the message of a Savior who died on the cross to pay the cost.

Christianity is Salvation that leads to change. "*But you were washed, you were sanctified, you were justified in the name of the Lord Jesus Christ and by the Spirit of our God.*" 1 Corinthians 6.11 You, as a believer, have been set aside by God for his chosen purpose. He has changed you. You, the sinner, have become a child of God. You have learned to be obedient, so you were baptized. You have been sanctified, or set aside, from the sinful world, to do God's will. You are justified or declared innocent of your sins. You have been made innocent because of the blood of Jesus. You have been changed.

Christianity is decisions that include commitment. Those who are following Jesus will be recognized by their fruit. Matthew 7.16 It means being a disciple of Jesus is turning away from the world of sinful desires, and discovering the will of God for your life.

Christianity is rewards because of the covenant. This means the righteous will live by faith and not by sight. They will not focus on the physical but on the eternal. They will see beyond the horizon and know that the rewards they will receive will last forever. They are in covenant with God. They know He has promised and will deliver to those who live righteous lives. This is a life of making the right and godly decision over and over.

Christianity is Jesus and compliance to His standards. Jesus is a just God. He rewards those who have obeyed Him and served Him in humility and obedience. It also means if He is just, He will punish those who have rejected His covenant and have not accepted His contract of salvation. Those who do not upgrade cannot expect anything less than a just God who has set standards and will enforce them. Those who do upgrade cannot expect anything less than a loving God who took their place on the cross and made it possible for an upgrade to heaven class.

Christianity is religion that is credible. It is religion based on the resurrection and not on the plans and hopes of people who are trying to impress God with their good works, temples, and ceremonies. It is about the Lord who is king over the Kingdom of Heaven. He is resurrected as the savior. He is resurrected and risen and all authority in heaven and on earth has been given to Him by God the Father. Matthew 28.17

When we think about Christ and the cross we cannot stop there. We must look at how He has changed us. We must submit to his decisions for our lives. We must remember He sets the conditions for the covenant and we are called in this contract to live righteous lives in compliance with His will. We must, and I mean we must, believe, teach and hold fast to the resurrection. We must proclaim the whole Gospel no matter how uncomfortable it makes people. Lowering standards, to include more, is a good way to get excluded from eternity yourself. It is a daunting task, but we are called as Christians to follow our Lord and Savior.

As Paul closed the end of his letter to the Corinthian church he wrote these words. "*If anyone does not love the Lord, he is to be accursed. Maranatha.*" 1 Corinthians 16.22 NASB At first that seems harsh, but it is a declaration that this is not our home, and we are here and currently separated from our Lord and King. People have the right to make personal decisions and, if they choose to reject Jesus, that is their choice, and justice is all they can expect. Only by turning to Jesus can anyone expect mercy and God's gracious eternal invitation to upgrade to heaven class. Maranatha means, "O Lord Come!" It affirms the resurrection that is the hope of every believer. He is King, Lord, Savior and will come for us who, as believers remain true. Maranatha, Lord Jesus, Maranatha!

Review Chapter 27

Can you identify the following People, Places or dates and tell how they are important to this week's lesson?

1. Jesus
2. Joseph of Arimathea
3. Mary Magdalene
4. Thomas
5. Cleopas
6. Peter
7. Emmaus road
8. Nathanael
9. Nicodemus
10. Resurrection

Page numbers are from The Story (TS)

1. What day was Jesus crucified? _______ What day did he resurrect from the dead_________? Why was this period of time so important?

2. What two people came to Pilate to get permission to bury Jesus? Where was he buried? (TS 381)

3. Why did the Pharisees insist that guards be put at the tomb of Jesus even though he was dead? (TS 382)

4. Who came to the tomb on the first morning after the Sabbath? (TS 382-384)

5. What happened to the two disciples on the road to Emmaus? (TS 384-385)

6. Which disciple missed Jesus and did not believe He had risen from the dead? ____________ What would he accept as proof that Jesus was alive? (TS 386)

7. What miracle did Jesus do for the disciples by the lake after He had risen from the dead? (TS 387)

8. How many disciples were on the mountain with Jesus? ________ Did they fully understand what was happening? ________ How do you know this? (TS 388)

9. Is everything Jesus did written down in the scriptures? _____ How do we know this?

10. What one thing in this chapter did you learn that can help you on your personal faith journey?

Earnestly Praying
The Story Unfolds - Chapter 28

How should you pray when you aren't sure God is going to answer? Sometimes I find it hard to pray. That may not be something you expect a pastor to say but it is true. I don't like praying out loud. Now, I do it and have for over forty years now, but, even after all the time and prayers I have said out loud I still prefer not to do it. Sometimes I have doubts God is going to answer. Other times I just don't know how to pray or what to ask God for. I don't like it when it appears my prayers are not answered. I don't want to look bad in front of non-believers. Then, there are the times when the matter at hand is not vital or important to me, and that makes it harder to pray. This burst of honesty is nothing new. I have attended special prayer schools and read everything E. M. Bounds ever wrote. I have sought God for long periods and find public prayer is still not my cup of tea. I have listened as others prayed out loud and seem so poetic, fluid, and natural. Then again I realize I am not alone in struggling with prayer. There were those in the Bible who also had problems.

Before I look at them, let me pose some simple questions to you. Do you believe God will answer all or any of your prayers? When you pray are you expecting God to answer, or are you just praying because you are supposed to? Should you pray if you are not sure that God is going to answer? That brings me to the last question I need to ask. Is faith necessary for us to have our prayers answered? We know that "*without faith it is impossible to please God.*" Hebrews 11.6 That would lead us to believe that faith is necessary.

Jesus, along with Peter, James and John, came down off the mount of transfiguration and were met by a confused crowd of arguing people. A man brought his son for the other disciples to heal, and they were unable to cast out the unclean spirit that tormented the boy. Jesus reprimanded His disciples for their lack of faith. This would lead us to believe complete assurance and faith is necessary. Yet, the father of the boy is put on the spot by Jesus. Finally, in desperation, the boy's father tells Jesus, "*I do believe; help me overcome my unbelief*!" Mark 9.24 He has faith but it is not complete or absolute faith. Later, the disciples wanted to know why they had failed. Jesus told them, "*This kind can come out only by prayer.* " Mark 9.29 It was a matter of faith and a matter of praying. Yet everyone came up short and no prayers were said. The father needed more faith yet, the little bit he had would do. The disciples needed a better prayer life, and still Jesus was willing to heal the boy.

The scriptures are full of examples of prayer. In acts 12 there is an instance when the church was called to prayer. It was brought about by circumstances that caused them to unite earnestly in prayer.

BAD things can happen to Christians.

King Herod was persecuting the church. As he grew bolder he had James, the brother of John, put to death. This made the Jews happy so Herod arrested Peter and had him held in prison. We should not be surprised that this was happening. Jesus had warned the disciples "*If they persecuted me, they will persecute you also.*" John 15.20 This continues even today. There are massacres of Christians in Egypt, Algeria, Nigeria, China, and Kenya. You can follow what is happening on websites like persecution.org and see this is a spreading hatred. Yet, even as the

Muslim world seems to be spreading and destroying churches, killing pastors, and hunting down the members of these churches to throw them in jail, Jerry Trousdale, director of the international ministries for City Team International, writes in his new book Miraculous Movement, hundreds of thousands of Muslims are falling in love with Jesus. He reports that, over the last six years, at least 200,000 Muslims including sheiks, imams, Muslim leaders, and ordinary devotees are turning to faith in Jesus Christ. From the moment they convert they are under a death sentence by the Muslims they used to know. Yet, these new believers know they should "*not be afraid of those who kill the body but cannot kill the soul.*" Matthew 10.14 Bad things happen to believers; even Peter got himself arrested and faced a death sentence.

What is EARNEST prayer?

"*So Peter was kept in prison, but the church was earnestly praying to God for him.*" I wonder if any of those praying had doubts. They had prayed for James, and he was killed by Herod. How did they know what they were to ask God for? Should they pray for Peter's release, or should they pray he did not suffer much? When you are standing at the bedside of a very sick person what is the right way to pray? Then again, they may have been wondering if their prayers should have been for self-protection. After Peter, they were next on Herod's list. Earnest prayer may not be what you think it is, and I am sure it was not what they thought it was.

Answered prayer comes when we LEAST expect it and comes as LIGHT shining in the darkness.

The next morning was to be Peter's big day in court. He was chained between two guards with two more guards at the door. He and the guards fell asleep. I don't know how that was possible. Even though I find it hard to pray in public, I guarantee I would not find it hard to pray if it was my last night on earth. There, in that dark cell, an angel appeared, kicked Peter in the side and told him to get up. The guards kept on sleeping even as the chains fell off Peter, and he followed the angel out of the prison. Peter did not expect the angel or he would have been awake and ready to go. Many times God answers our prayers in ways and at times we do not expect.

Many times we do not RECOGNIZE answered prayer when it is happening.

Peter "*had no idea that what the angel was doing was really happening.*" We are often so close to what is happening that we do not see the answer as it is happening. God is moving heaven and earth to get everything lined up for us, and we often miss it because we are not in tune with Him as we should be. It was after he was free and the angel had disappeared that Peter said, "*Now I know without a doubt that the Lord sent his angel and rescued me from Herod's clutches.*" We often can look back and see what God has done in our lives but when it is happening, it is hidden from us.

How do you RESPOND to answered prayer?

Peter cut through the backstreets and went to the door leading to where the Christians had gathered to pray for him. The first clue they were not expecting Peter came when he reached for the handle and the door was locked. They were expecting soldiers, not Peter. Peter knocked and Rhoda, a servant girl, came to the door. She put her ear to the door and asked who was there. Peter spoke and "*she recognized Peter's voice.*" Then, instead of opening the door, she "*ran back without opening it.*" She burst into the prayer meeting full of frightened people yelling, "*Peter is at the door*!"

She was "*overjoyed*" to the point of leaving Peter standing in the dark by himself. How often do we accept God's answer and fail to enjoy it? We should be like Rhoda in our joy. We must also remember to let the answer in.

They responded from their heads and without faith.

"*Peter is at the door*!" must have blasted though the prayer meeting. "*You're out of your mind*," was the response she got. A rational person knows this is not possible. Think, girl, think, Peter is in prison. Tomorrow he is going to die. They may have been praying for Peter, but it is obvious that they were not expecting an answer. They were going through the motions, but no one at that prayer meeting thought Peter would ever walk out of that prison alive. They were having a prayer meeting where it is recorded they were "*earnestly praying*." Yet these prayers were not expected to produce results. So here they are with Rhoda insisting Peter is at the door and the members of the prayer meeting scolding her and Peter is outside.

God's answers may very well SURPRISE you.

Peter just kept on knocking. He must have wondered what was taking so long. Finally, they went to the door to see who was really there. "*When they opened the door and saw him, they were astonished*." They had prayed for James and he was dead. Now they had prayed for Peter and they must have expected him to die too. Astonished is a mild way of saying they never, ever expected to see Peter alive again. Yet they had been praying earnestly. They had doubts, but they kept on praying. They did not know how to really pray, but they still prayed. They were going through the motions, and God still heard and answered.

A Call to Prayer

"*So Peter was kept in prison, but the church was earnestly praying to God for him.*" So how should you pray when you aren't sure God is going to answer? You pray earnestly. You do the best you can because that is better than not praying. You take the matter to God even when you see no possible way for God to answer; well, no humanly way possible, so you just pray.

Preparing for EARNEST Prayer

If you are going to pray, you need a list. On the list you put the things you doubt God will answer, but you put them on the list. Items that confuse you, and you don't know if they should be on the list; put them on the list too. Items you are embarrassed to mention. These can include sinful matters in your life. (You can use code that only you and God know, but they need them to be on the list.) Those non-essential items you think God does not care about, put them on the list. Next to each item, place a little box. Then it is time to pray. How should you pray? Pray earnestly. Take the items on the list to God and pray. Then, on the next day, do it again. Pray earnestly, and pray waiting to be astonished. When God answers a prayer request check it off. That is what the box is for. The list is for your benefit, and the box is for God to show you what He is doing. You may not think God is going to answer, and you may want to skip the boxes, but that is like refusing to answer the door because you know it cannot be Peter.

A Personal Prayer Challenge

Now to do this once and quit will not get you anywhere. Why not make it a personal prayer challenge that lasts for four weeks. Imagine what God can do in four weeks if every day you earnestly prayed. Pray even when you doubt. Pray even when you do not know how to pray. Pray even when it is not important to you. Pray when someone gives you a prayer need that is not vital to you but you still should pray. Pray earnestly and wait to be astonished by God. It will change your prayer life forever.

Review Chapter 28

Can you identify the following People, Places or dates and tell how they are important to this week's lesson?

1. Pentecost
2. Saul
3. Ananias
4. Stephen
5. Mark
6. Caiaphas
7. King Herod
8. Cornelius
9. Rhoda
10. Theophilus

Page numbers are from The Story (TS)

1. Why were the disciples told to wait in Jerusalem? (TS 389)

2. What significant events took place in Jerusalem during Pentecost? (TS 389-392)

3. How did Peter and John help the lame man? What did we learn about the financial status of these great men of God? (TS 392-393)

4. How did the early believers help each other as they waited for the return of Jesus? (TS 395)

5. How were the disciples treated by the Jewish leadership in the temple? (TS 395-396) How did the disciples respond to this treatment?

6. Why was Stephen stoned to death? (TS 398-399)

7. When the church came under attack, what happened to the believers? The Apostles? How did this affect the church? (TS 399)

8. Saul went from hating Christian believers to being one himself. How did this happen? (TS 399-401)

9. How did God persuade Peter to take the good news about Jesus to the non-Jewish gentiles? (TS 401-403)

10. What one thing in this chapter did you learn that can help you on your personal faith journey?

5 Life-Changing KEYS
The Story Unfolds – Chapter 29

Paul left Titus on the small island of Crete to supervise the churches. Paul was clear in his letter to him about this. *"The reason I left you in Crete was that you might straighten out what was left unfinished and appoint elders in every town, as I directed you."* Titus 1.5 The small letter of Titus is filled with directions for leadership in the church, the way believers should live together and how they should live as witnesses for Christ Jesus among a world of non-believers. At the end of his letter in his final remarks are five key directives that could help every believer. Hidden in these final instructions is a daily guide to a richer Christian experience.

"As soon as I send Artemas or Tychicus to you, do your best to come to me at Nicopolis, because I have decided to winter there. Do everything you can to help Zenas the lawyer and Apollos on their way and see that they have everything they need. Our people must learn to devote themselves to doing what is good, in order that they may provide for daily necessities and not live unproductive lives.

Everyone with me sends you greetings. Greet those who love us in the faith.

Grace be with you all." Titus 3.12-15

DO YOUR BEST

"As soon as I send Artemas or Tychicus to you, <u>do your best</u> to come to me at Nicopolis, because I have decided to winter there." Paul has put into words what every parent wants for their children. They want them to do their best. In this case it was to do his best to visit him. Paul was out of prison but he knew it was a possibility that he could be rearrested at any time. He wanted to see Titus one more time.

You need to remember you are not alone in the Christian life. If everyone did their best then, together, the impact will be much greater. Paul has sent Artemas and Tychius to visit Titus. Tychicus was a constant companion of Paul. Paul said about Tychius, "*He is a dear brother, a faithful minister and a fellow servant in the Lord.*" Colossians 4.7 He is mentioned a total of five times in the New Testament[18] and is often overlooked. The key here is that everyone is needed and everyone is important to make the work of the Lord possible. Paul was not able to go to Crete but he knew two men who could go for him and deliver the important letter. He knew that they would do their best and trusted them with this valuable mission.

In the church we are all called to do our best. It does not matter if it is the minister in the pulpit or the lady serving the cookies at the time of refreshment. Everyone needs to do their best. As a believer you are part of a much larger and vital mission that is planned and organized by the Holy Spirit. It is vital that you not see your responsibility as small or unimportant but as part of the total plan of God.

I was given a clock after the death of my brother. When I got it home, it did not work. I looked and looked. There were hundreds of parts. Every one of them seemed to be fine, but the clock would not work. Then I found the problem. One small pin was broken loose, and it had stopped the whole clock from doing what it was designed to do. It could not keep time. Sometimes we see ourselves as unimportant or not a vital part of the local ministry, but the opposite is true. Each person is part of the whole. If you are not doing your part it can cause the whole thing not to work as it was designed. The clock I got did not tell time, but it was still right two times a day. If we do not do our part there will be the occasional times when everything lines up, but it does not mean everything is as it should be. As believers we should make it our goal to do our best at whatever we are called to do.

"If we walk in the light, as he is in the light, we have fellowship with one another, and the blood of Jesus, his Son, purifies us from all sin." 1 John 1.7 When Christian believers work together, each doing their part, we will discover that we have strength together we do not have by ourselves. This strength comes from our fellowship as believers. The word fellowship means to participate or to share together. When we do our best and do our part, we are strengthening the fellowship. This brings others closer to the precious cleansing blood of Jesus.

It is vital that you remember that you are not alone. That is the reason you can do your best. You do not have to do it all. Everyone is needed, and everyone is important.

DO EVERYTHING YOU CAN

"Do everything you can to help Zenas the lawyer and Apollos on their way and see that they have everything they need." Paul tells Titus to do everything he can. He knows that Titus is limited and may not be able to do everything, but that should not stop him from doing what he can do. We need to remember that all believers are given gifts by the Holy Spirit. Each one is designed to accomplish a different purpose or task in the church. *"There are different kinds of gifts, but the same Spirit. There are different kinds of service, but the same Lord. There are different kinds of working, but the same God works all of them in all men."* 1 Corinthians 12.4-6

One of the toughest parts of working in the church is dealing with spiritual gift envy. You may not have heard of it, but it is real. It is the feeling a person gets when he/she sees how others are being used in the church and wishes they had the gifts or ability to do the same thing. There was a preacher who told the story of the toe that wanted the gift of sight. The toe went to God over and over in prayer seeking the gift of sight. Every time God would tell the toe it was not what was needed and would offer the toe other spiritual gifts. Finally the toe bugged God so long that God gave the toe the gift of sight and the toe spent the rest of his life looking at the inside of a sock. If you are to do everything you can then it needs to be within the gifts God's Holy Spirit has chosen for you. Everyone has gifts from God, and everyone can give or participate in the ministry and the mission of the church. You need to focus on what you can do and not on what you cannot or are not gifted to do. You can do much more than you think you can.

"*We have different gifts, according to the grace given* us." Romans 12.6 There are the gifts given us by God and the talents we are born with that need to be developed. A study shows that it takes 10,000 hours to develop a talent and completely master it.[19] This means to be used by God you need to learn to do your best and do everything you can. This also means it will not happen overnight. Even the gifts given us by the Holy Spirit must be developed. A key to doing everything you can is you must avoid making excuses, and use your gifts and talents for God and His kingdom.

DO WHAT IS GOOD

"Our people must learn to devote themselves to doing what is good, in order that they may provide for daily necessities and not live unproductive lives."

I had a close friend who has now gone to be with the Lord. He was the luckiest person at finding things I have ever known. We would go golfing and he would always return with more golf balls than he left with. He would just find them. Other people had given up and left them, but my friend would find them. One day, after playing a round of golf, I came home with one golf ball to my name, and my friend had a whole bag of newly found ones. We stopped by his house. There in his closet were two boxes full of golf balls. These were not small shoe boxes. These boxes were like giant waist high boxes that filled the bottom of his closet. He dumped the ones he had found in and just laughed. I could not help but ask him what he was going to do with them. His response was classic for him. "When I retire and cannot afford to buy golf balls I will always have some." He once found a diamond necklace and earrings in a ditch filled with water. He just looked down, saw them, slipped off his shoes, and waded in. The people with him thought he was crazy till he came out with the haul. (Yes, he contacted the police and no one claimed the find, so it ended up being his.) What was the key to his finding so much stuff? He was always looking for something to find. He was lucky that way.

I heard a good definition of luck. It is when opportunity meets preparation. If you are not ready when opportunity comes along, you cannot take advantage of it. This applies to doing good. You need to practice doing good all the time. Then, when you need it the most, it will be a habit. This leads to having your daily needs taken care of and discovering that you have a productive life. You need to plan and prepare to do good. It needs to become a way of life.

"*You have been set free from sin and have become slaves to righteousness.*" Romans 6.18 Many people miss what it means to live a righteous life. It is doing what is good over and over and always being prepared to do good no matter the circumstances. The word righteous means "to remain innocent" or "free from sin". To become a slave of righteousness means it becomes the only thing you can do. Righteousness has taken control of your life and become your master. If we want to live productive lives with our daily needs taken care of, we need to do what is good or live righteous lives.

I asked my friend, who found things, how he did it. He told me when he was in grade school he once found a quarter. He was very poor and a quarter was a great find. From that day on he focused on looking for quarters and, in the process, learned how to find all kinds of things. He was good at it. Several times we would be looking for golf balls, and he would find them right in front of me. I would be looking right at it and still not see the ball.

We have all found righteousness and a freedom from sin. In order to be successful we need to improve our luck. We need to prepare daily for the opportunity to do what is good.

"*This service that you perform is not only supplying the needs of God's people but is also overflowing in many expressions of thanks to God.*" 2 Corinthians 9.12 Doing good is a shared responsibility. Together we are stronger and will have our needs taken care of. This leads to productive lives that allow each of us to help others. The only way we will truly have productive lives is to prepare for ministry opportunities. Everyone has needs, and if we work together, we can find ways to minister and help each other. Many prayers are not answered because the ones God has chosen to bring the answer have not learned how to do good as a daily practice. As believers we are not looking for quarters or golf balls. We are looking for the opportunity to do good in the name of Jesus and as slaves of righteousness.

MAKE THE CONNECTIONS

"*Everyone with me sends you greetings. Greet those who love us in the faith.*" It is vital that believers have other believers as their closest friends.

We are called to work and team up with Christian believers. "*Don't team up with those who are unbelievers. How can righteousness be a partner with wickedness? How can light live with darkness? What harmony can there be between Christ and the devil?*" 2 Corinthians 6.14.15a This is not saying we should not know and have non-Christian friends but it is clearly saying they are not to be the ones we rely on or who we partner with. Paul is telling Titus to remember that the bond that holds believers together is far stronger and more important than the ones that hold others together. Jesus was clear that our relationship with him comes before the one we have with our earthly family. ""*Anyone who loves his father or mother more than me is not worthy of me; anyone who loves his son or daughter more than me is not worthy of me.*" Matthew 10.37

Paul extends this closeness to other believers. It is the faith in Jesus that binds us together as a family of believers in love. This faith is designed to last forever because we will be in this family for eternity.

"*Therefore, as we have opportunity, let us do good to all people, especially to those who belong to the family of believers.*" Galatians 6.9 We are witnesses to the whole world, but we have a strong responsibility to believers of the family of God. Our fellow Christians deserve our special attention. We need to connect with them and allow that connection to strengthen our faith. If we, as believers, discover the fellowship and commitment to other believers, it would strengthen our churches, our families, and our faith. Putting the family of God first will produce tremendous rewards.

THE KEY INGREDIENT

"*Grace be with you all.*" Grace is often described as unmerited favor or an undeserved gift, but somehow that falls short of the mark of what grace is. The word grace is used over 100 times in the New Testament. It comes from the same word we get charisma from. It is that special quality that stands out and which somehow you are aware of but can't quite describe. Look at these examples of some of the ways grace is mentioned in the New Testament.

- "*The grace of our Lord Jesus be with* you." Romans 16:20
- "*The grace of our Lord Jesus be with you.*" 1 Corinthians 16:23
- "*May the grace of the Lord Jesus Christ, and the love of God, and the fellowship of the Holy Spirit be with you all.*" 2 Corinthians 13:14
- "*The grace of our Lord Jesus Christ be with your spirit, brothers. Amen.*" Galatians 6:18

- *"Grace to all who love our Lord Jesus Christ with an undying love."* Ephesians 6:24
- *"The grace of our Lord Jesus Christ be with your spirit. Amen."* Philippians 4:23
- *"Grace be with you all."* Colossians 4:18
- *"The grace of our Lord Jesus Christ be with you." 1 Thessalonians* 5:28
- *"The grace of our Lord Jesus Christ be with you all."* 2 Thessalonians 3:18
- *"Grace be with you."* 1 Timothy 5:21
- *"Grace be with you."* 2 Timothy 4:22
- *"The grace of the Lord Jesus Christ be with your spirit."* Philemon 25
- *"Grace be with you all."* Hebrews 13:25

The early believers understood and communicated grace to each other. They expected it to be part of their lives. It was more than a blessing. Grace is always associated with Jesus whether it is stated or not. Grace was part of the letters the early believers sent to each other.

Peter concludes his second letter this way: "*But grow in the grace and knowledge of the Lord Jesus Christ...*" 2 Peter 3:18 Grace is a quality that can be increased. It is tied so closely to Jesus He says knowing more about Him will increase your personal grace factor.

The final phrase in the entire Bible is about grace. "*The grace of the Lord Jesus be with God's people. Amen.*" Revelation 22:21 Yet, it is a verse without the word grace in it that best describes what grace is. "*The Word became flesh and made his dwelling among us.*" John 1.14 Jesus in your life is having grace. Without Jesus there is no grace. "*For it is by grace you have been saved, through faith—and this not from yourselves, it is the gift of God.*" Ephesians 2.8

Grace in the life of a believer is Jesus Christ in the present. Look at the list above again. The phrase is repeated over and over. "*The grace of our Lord Jesus Christ be with you." 1 Thessalonians* 5:28 Even when it is not stated it is understood. Grace and Jesus go together. It saves us, it empowers us, and it is a vital part of the believer's life. You cannot make it without grace because without grace, you are without Christ. It is His gift to the believer to be with them in the present. Jesus provided everything we need for eternal life. It is this gift we cannot live without. Everyone is offered grace, and everyone who believes in Jesus receives grace.

TODAY I WILL

Paul closes the letter to Titus with directions that we can apply to our lives.

Every day we need to:

- Do our best: You are not alone, and everyone is needed if we are going to be successful for God.
- Do everything we can: Avoid making excuses, and use your gifts and talents.
- Do what is good: Prepare for the opportunities God is sending your way.
- Make the connections: Make sure you have strong Christian friends. They need you, and you need them.
- Share the grace: Practice the presence of Jesus in the now. Make sure you share Jesus and you will share His grace.

These five life changing keys will make you a stronger believer and prepare you to serve our Lord.

"The grace of our Lord Jesus Christ be with you."

Review Chapter 29

Can you identify the following People, Places or dates and tell how they are important to this week's lesson?

1. Paul
2. Luke
3. Aquila & Priscilla
4. Timothy
5. Apollos
6. Lydia
7. John Mark
8. Demetrius
9. Corinth
10. Thessalonica

Page numbers are from The Story (TS)

1. Where did Paul usually go when he first went to a city and wanted to share about Jesus? Why did he choose this site? (TS 409-410)

2. In Philippi they had to find a different way to reach the city. How did this happen? (TS 412-413)

3. In Corinth who did he work with? What do we learn about Paul's occupation? What key fact changed in Paul's mission? (TS 415)

4. Name some reasons that Paul was always having problems with the people in the various towns. (TS 410)

5. What happened to the Jews who were not believers in Jesus, but they still tried to drive out unclean spirits? (TS 421-422)

6. What problem was separating the believers at Corinth? What did Paul say the solution was? (TS 424-425)

7. What matters did Paul think were of first importance to Christian believers? (TS 427)

8. Why is the resurrection so important to Christian believers? (TS 428)

9. What are the acts of the flesh? What is the fruit of the Spirit? How are they different? (TS 431)

10. What one thing in this chapter did you learn that can help you on your personal faith journey?

Life's Margins
The Story Unfolds - Chapter 30

While in prison for his faith, Paul wrote a series of letters, or epistles, to various churches. In these letters he gave directions to help the churches and individuals live productive Christian lives. Paul never used the words, "life margins,"[20] but he was referring to the principle represented by them.

The first thing a person needs to know about life margins is they are not the time you fill with watching television, claiming to be relaxing and recharging from a hard day's work. Life margins are a part of lives that are designed to protect the most important part of life and relationships.

MARGINS

When you read a page it is surrounded by blank areas called margins. On a six by nine page with a one-half inch margin, the margins take up 20% of the page. That means one fifth of the page is blank space. The margin is there to make the page readable. If the words went all the way to the edge of the page it would be extremely difficult to read. You might think that more space for words and less margins would be good for the reader, but the opposite is true. The eye needs the blank space to help as it scans back and forth across the page. If a page is too full it becomes impossible to read. The lack of margins destroys the ability to read because the page is too cluttered or too full.

GOD MARGINS

"*By the seventh day God completed His work which He had done, and He rested on the seventh day from all His work which He had done. Then God blessed the seventh day and sanctified it, because in it He rested from all His work which God had created and made.*" Genesis 2.2-3

When God created everything there was to create He built a 14% margin of rest into the process. So here is God with a margin in His creation. It was so important to Him that He waited to create humans until they could experience this margin, or rest, right at the beginning. Think about it, they showed up for work, and the first day on the job in the garden was a day of rest.

Here is the margin God built into the process right from the beginning. This buffer or margin may appear to be empty space, wasted time, but it really is the healthy space put there by God. Without it we will get sick, and the pressure will build, and we will crash. It is the blank space where you can meet God and revive. In the Old Testament the punishment for violating the buffer set by God was DEATH. That may seem harsh, but how many men and women die early from the stress of overwork? How many families are ruined because of the wrong focus of the job? How many divorces occur when the spouse has removed the buffer and ended up having an adulterous relationship? Life margins were designed by God because He knew, without them, humanity would fail. Life margins are the buffer, cushion, barrier, shield, safeguard, defense and protection God has put into every life and family to keep them from crashing. Remember, to be able to read a page, you need the blank margins, and, if you want a successful life, you need the life margins designed by God

UNDERSTANDING THE MARGINS

For a person to maintain the needed margins in his/her life he/she must make sure that he/she does not let the margins shrink in size. This happens when a person thinks he/she can cheat on the amount of space needed to maintain a healthy margin. A page needs at least a 20% margin and most will be closer to 35% to 40%. God put a minimum margin of 14% into his plan from the beginning. We need to remember that is the minimum. There will be times when a larger life margin will benefit the person. The problem is when we are under pressure and should increase our margins we often decrease them and increase the pressure we are under.

Paul was a master at seeing life in proper perspective. He wrote to churches and friends to help them keep their lives on track. Though he never used the words "life margins" he knew what they were and knew how to keep them clear of the things that did not belong there. He knew that they should always have at least the 14% minimum that God used from the beginning. This was not about a day of the week for Paul as much as it was about the proper relationship with God and our fellow believers.

LIFE MARGINS

"*Be very careful, then, how you live—not as unwise but as wise.*" Ephesians 5.15 If we are going to have a successful life then we need to protect the margins of life. To do this, we need to make some critical choices which are both positive and negative. In giving directions to early believers Paul helps us keep the margins the right size.

BE VERY CAREFUL is Paul's way of saying you need to keep watching or be observant if you are going to protect your life margins. People who ignore the margins often do not see that they are shrinking. Work comes home in the form of emails, notes, phone calls, or an unfinished project. It will only happen once, but it becomes the norm instead of the exception. There is less time for the family. There is no time for Bible study or prayer. You skip church to catch up, and suddenly, you are not attending church at all. That is why you must be very careful. "*We must pay more careful attention, therefore, to what we have heard, so that we do not drift away.*" Hebrews 2.1 It is so easy to lose sight of what is important because of something that is pressing and running over into the life margins. You have to be very careful. You have to pay more careful attention to the margins of your life.

HOW YOU LIVE is about how you conduct yourself. It is the daily choices that determine your life's direction and ultimately the outcome. How you respond to the call of good and evil has a lot to do with our life margins. They both summon us daily and determine which one is going to hold sway over who we are, and who we will become. Cheating on the margins in your life will always come back to bite you in the end.

NOT AS UNWISE tells us we need to avoid being lazy. Another word for lazy is unrighteousness. That is the decision to make wrong choices. When confronted with the possibilities of life we need to remember that just because we can do something does not mean we should. Just because it appears no one is watching does not mean we will not have to pay for our choices. Life margins are the spaces where we are able to stop and reflect on what is happening in our lives.

BUT AS WISE is the direction we must take if we are going to be successful believers. This is about righteousness or being a skilled and disciplined believer. It takes discipline to maintain the life margins. Here is where it gets real difficult because, even when things are not going right in our lives, we must make the right choices and we must maintain our life margins.

The life margin can be defined in many ways. Here are a few that may help you keep your life margins in proper perspective and keep them from shrinking away.

TIME MARGINS

"*...making the most of every opportunity, because the days are evil.*" Ephesians 5.16 Time is a constant in the lives of every person in the world. No one has more time than anyone else. We all get the same twenty-four hours for each and every day. There are time management books that show us how to squeeze more into every day. I have read a couple of them and they seem to be aimed at the margins. Filling every minute of every day and not "wasting" any time. They fill the mind non-stop and leave no free space for anything. They fill the margins with activities.

Paul writes to make the most of every opportunity. Every opportunity is about time, and what we are going to do with it. He is telling us we need to fill our lives with as much of the good of God as we can, and to avoid the evil that surrounds us. If time is the constant we cannot change then the opportunities are the choices we get to make about what we will do with our time.

Paul warned that the days are evil or toilsome. We could be totally consumed by all the bad in the world. One of the tricks of the enemy is to say we do not have enough time, so what should we cut out that is not necessary? Of course, his suggestion is that we first cut out God. That will improve the amount of time we have by 20%. But the enemy does not work well with life margins. He discovered long ago that life margins lead to God. The enemy of our souls wants us to cut God out and to fill the margins with evil. Oh he does not call it evil, he calls it recreation or fun or relaxation or getting ahead or a thousand other excuses to remove the margins from a person's life.

Vince Lombardi, the football coach, is famous for his time quote, "We didn't lose the game; we just ran out of time." Well, we will all run out of time someday, and then what? It will depend on the choices we have made with our time.

MONEY MARGINS

Jesus had as much to say about money as anything else. He understood its power over people. He saw it as a tool but knew that many turned it into a god. He warned people about the problems of money. In one of His parables, he speaks about money. "*Suppose one of you wants to build a tower. Will he not first sit down and estimate the cost to see if he has enough money to complete it?*" Luke 14.28

Now, it may be hard to grasp this, but just like time, money margins are the same for everyone. It does not matter if you are a widow or wealthy beyond compare. Money margins apply to everyone. Let me illustrate it for you. If you have $100 and you spend $80, then you have a margin of $20 or 20%. If you have $100 and spend $100, then you have a margin of zero. If you have $100 and spend $120 then you have big problems because you have replaced your margin with stress, overload, debt, irritability, fights, and worry.

The number of people today who have no margins built into their finances is remarkable. The first thing to go, in many lives under such circumstances, is the tithe, or giving to the church. They have cheated by replacing the margins with credit, or trying to borrow against the margins of the future. But when the future arrives, and there are no money margins, then the problem grows.

In my ministry I have known only two millionaires. They both gave to the church, but neither one tithed or gave anywhere near a tithe. During the same time I have known scores of widows. I have watched them tithe off of their meager incomes, supporting missions, and sacrificing for kingdom work. The widows never went hungry, but they knew and maintained their money margins. The difference between the widows and the wealthy is their margins and priorities. One of the millionaires told me he could not afford to tithe to the church; If a widow is able to tithe why not a millionaire? Cheating on money margins with God is a form of temptation that can lead a person into thinking they can make excuses about giving and God will understand. That might work if it were not for the widows who are maintaining the proper money margins.

ENERGY MARGINS

Jesus also knew about energy margins. "*Or suppose a king is about to go to war against another king. Will he not first sit down and consider whether he is able with ten thousand men to oppose the one coming against him with twenty thousand?*" Luke 14.31

Jesus was always working on his energy margins. He knew that there was only so much of Him. He would try and slip away to rest and spend some quiet time with His disciples. He would send them on ahead and catch up later so He could spend time with God. Even Jesus, as a man, could not do everything. That may be why he often told people He had healed and helped that they were not to tell anyone else.

A king who did not evaluate His energy margins could find himself losing a war and his head. A person today who does not evaluate and protect his energy margins can find themselves on the road to burnout. This often leads to lying, cheating and, in time, failure. Many people today are running on empty. They are getting less and less sleep as they drive further and further to work. They are bringing their work home with them because there is not enough time at work.

Then, when they have time off, they do not use it wisely to recharge and spend time with people who really need them. Instead of recharging their energy batteries, they try to catch up and start the next week already behind. Remember, it was God who rested and built a 14% margin into creation. It is why Jesus worked so hard at slipping away to recharge.

Recharging is not necessarily being alone, but it definitely is not about work. You can recharge with loved ones. You can recharge at church. You can recharge by changing your focus, and by separating yourself from the creation/work process.

MARRIAGE MARGINS

The husband and wife, man and woman, relationship is sacred. God made Adam and then made "*a helper suitable for him.*" Genesis 2.18 This relationship between man and woman is sacred. Eve was designed to help Adam and the word "suitable" has two key meanings we need to consider here. First, it comes from a root word that means "to be conspicuous." She was supposed to stand out and to be different. God did a good job there. The original model has not changed in that, men and women are certainly different. The second meaning deals with the concept of being opposite or against. This helps us see that she was not designed to be a slave but a helper with a complete set of opinions of her own. God put her here to balance Adam out.

Though Paul was not married, he knew far more about marriage than most people give him credit for. There is a key teaching that most people read and think they know what it means but they usually get it wrong. The men get it wrong and the women get it wrong.

"However, each one of you also must love his wife as he loves himself, and the wife must respect her husband." Ephesians 5.33

Before I break it down, the one thing you need to know is that women read it wrong, and men read it wrong or, should I say they read the wrong parts.

MARRIAGE MARGINS FOR HUSBANDS

Most men know what the second half of this verse says, or at least they think they know what it says. They think it means that she is to submit to him, and that he is the boss. Well, we will get to what it means when I share about wives' marriage margins, but here is the key for men. It is none of your business what it says to your wife. Look at the verse again. The second half is written to women, but it is the part men love to quote. Why, it was not written to you. You, as a married man, should be paying attention to the first half, the part where it directly tells married men what to do.

It says each husband is to love his wife as he loves himself. The directive here is for the husband to provide for his wife what she needs the most, love. This means that the man who somehow is less emotional, needs to be reminded what his wife needs from him. He needs to work at it to get it right. Paul knew what love really was. In fact, he listed the things a person should do for the person they love. If husbands want to learn how to love their wives, here is how to do it. In first Corinthians 13 Paul defines love. Here is a checklist you can use to work on loving your wife.

- Love is patient,
- Love is kind.
- Love does not envy,
- Love does not boast,
- Love is not proud.
- Love is not rude,
- Love is not self-seeking,
- Love is not easily angered,
- Love keeps no record of wrongs.
- Love does not delight in evil but rejoices with the truth.
- Love always protects,
- Love always trusts,
- Love always hopes,
- Love always perseveres.
- Love never fails. 1 Corinthians 13.4-8a

Here is how I share it with husbands in counseling. They should put their names in the list in place of the word love. Any place it does not fit, that is a place they need to work on. There are no excuses for not doing this for your wife. It is imperative *"Husbands, love your wives and do not be harsh with them."* Colossians 3.19 The key is not being the first perfect husband on the planet. The key is working to make your marriage the best you can. Paul was even more explicit when he said *"Husbands, love your wives, just as Christ loved the church and gave himself up for her."* Ephesians 5.25 This verse puts it out there. I have worked with too many husbands who think, since they have married the little woman, that should be enough. How much did Christ love the church? He loved it enough to die for her. If a husband wants to protect the margins in his marriage, he needs to protect the relationship he has with his wife, and the only way to do that is to love her. You are to be kind to you wife. You are to sacrifice for her; you are to put her first.

So, to all the women who want to point these needs out to their husbands, stop right now. The part written to him is for him and not for you. It is his responsibility and not yours. Besides that, you have your own responsibilities to hold up if you are going to protect your marriage margins.

MARRIAGE MARGINS FOR WIVES

Paul was clear that the responsibilities were different. "*The wife must respect her husband.*" The word respect is a modern translation of the word, and does not help us understand what Paul wanted the women he was writing this to understand. The verse should literally say, 'the wife must FEAR her husband.' This is more difficult to understand, but it is vital for the marriage. We will need to go to the Old Testament to lay a foundation to help us with this.

The Old Testament says "*Fear the LORD your God, serve him only.*" Deuteronomy 6.13 There are rewards for doing this. They include:

- The fear of the LORD is the beginning of wisdom Psalm 111.10
- The fear of the LORD is the beginning of knowledge, Proverbs 1.7
- The fear of the LORD adds length to life, Proverbs 10.27
- The fear of the LORD is a fountain of life, Proverbs 14.27
- He will be the sure foundation for your times, a rich store of salvation and wisdom and knowledge; the fear of the LORD is the key to this treasure. Isaiah 33.6
- Then the church throughout Judea, Galilee and Samaria enjoyed a time of peace. It was strengthened; and encouraged by the Holy Spirit, it grew in numbers, living in the fear of the Lord. Acts 9.31

The benefits of fearing God are obvious, but what does it mean to fear God? Am I supposed to live my life worried about Him squashing me like a bug? Am I to be worried if He is in a bad mood I will find myself turned into a frog? We need to remember that one of the four keys to interpreting scripture is, 'Scripture interprets Scripture.' That means God has put answers in His word so we can understand what He is saying. It is like a puzzle with a secret code. So what does it mean to 'Fear the Lord?'

Proverbs says, "To fear the LORD is to hate evil." Proverbs 8.13a That means when you hate evil you have wisdom and understanding. When you hate evil it will lead to a longer life. When you hate evil it strengthens a church and causes it to grow. So, when God told the people, "*Fear the LORD your God, serve him only,*" Deuteronomy 6.13 He was saying if they were going to serve Him, they had to hate evil. It was not to be part of their lives because it would mess up the relationship.

Now, back to wives. Paul knew this was the meaning of fear in a relationship. It was not about trembling. It was about keeping evil or sinfulness out of the relationship. The responsibility of the wife is to watch out for evil and make sure it stays out of the marriage. She needs to do this for her husband. The wife must fear her husband. This means she must keep all evil away from their marriage. Husbands should be receptive to their wives when they get one of those feelings about something. If the wife is in prayer, then God is working with her to protect the marriage.

MARRIAGE MARGINS REVIEW

A husband is not the boss of his wife, he is to love her. This is about sacrificing and protecting her and the relationship. A wife is not a slave, but is to guard their relationship against evil getting into the marriage.

Why were different instructions given to each of them? Men need to work at love. They think it is an understood quality. They often feel that it does not need to be repeated or said too often. 'Hey, she knows I love her,' is a phrase of a clueless man, who is not watching over his marriage margins. The wife who does not protect the marriage from evil influences is not facing the reality of this very wicked world and is not meeting her responsibilities in the relationship.

Women know how to love, but they need to be reminded to deal with evil. Men know all about evil but need to be reminded to love. If they both do their part the marriage will grow stronger, and the margins will be safe.

CHECKING THE MARGINS

"By the seventh day God had finished the work he had been doing; so on the seventh day he rested from all his work. And God blessed the seventh day and made it holy, because on it he rested from all the work of creating that he had done." Genesis 2.2-3

The word rested means God ceased or stopped creating. It is something we often miss. We don't stop or cease but find new ways to keep going seven days a week. So God built a minimum margin of 14% into the plan. Have you checked your margins recently?

How is your time margin? Is God a priority, or is He secondary when you can get to Him. How is your money margin? Is money so tight that you are borrowing against next year? Is tithing, or supporting the church, something you don't like to hear about because you have no money margins that include God? What about your energy margins? Are you serving or selfish? Are you running on empty and using your recharging time to catch up instead of preparing for the coming week by recharging your personal batteries? What about your marriage margins? Are they a priority or are they understood that everything is good. Ignore it long enough and you won't have to worry about it. Husbands, love your wives. They are counting on you. Wives, protect your husbands from evil. They are counting on you.

RESETTING THE MARGINS

People often think they can just push the margins back where they should be, and everything will be all right. You did not move the margins in one day, and it will take more than one day to get them back where they need to be. A 5% margin needs to become a 6% margin. Then it needs to become a 7% and then an 8%. You will have to work at this but, as the margins grow, so do the things that really matter. Without margins, a book is all but impossible to read. Without proper margins, life is all but impossible.

"Be very careful, then, how you live—not as unwise but as wise, making the most of every opportunity, because the days are evil." Ephesians 5.15-16

Review Chapter 30

Can you identify the following People, Places or dates and tell how they are important to this week's lesson?

1. Agabus

2. Timothy

3. Julius

4. Felix

5. Festus

6. Herod Agrippa II

7. Philip

8. Malta

9. Rome

10. Fair Haven

Page numbers are from The Story (TS)

1. Why did Paul want to get to Jerusalem in such a hurry? (TS 439)

2. Who was Agabus, and what information did he bring to Paul? (Ts 440)

3. Why was Paul arrested? (TS 441)

4. What do we learn about Paul's background? (TS 442)

5. Why did Paul say he was on trial and how did it help him cause confusion in the Sanhedrin? (TS 444-445)

6. Why was Paul going to Rome? What did he expect to happen there? (TS 446-447)

7. What happened to the ship Paul was on that convinced the Centurion that Paul got directions from God? How did this help save their lives? (TS448-450)

8. What miracles happened on the island after Paul was shipwrecked there? (TS 450)

9. How long was Paul in prison in Rome? What did he do while held there? (TS 452)

10. What two letters did Paul write while he was a prisoner in Rome that are now part of our Bibles? (TS 452 & 456)

11. What one thing in this chapter did you learn that can help you on your personal faith journey?

The Answer To The Three Questions
The Story Unfolds – Chapter 31

Genesis, creation along with Adam and Eve, seems so long ago when you remember when you started this study through The Story. Some have read it for the first time. Others have discovered there is a lot they had forgotten. We have seen great acts of faith and the lives of those who have failed to measure up to God's standards. We have watched people come to God and others reject Him completely. The Bible is not about perfect people who never make mistakes. It is about real people who make mistakes and get help from a loving God. It has heroes and villains. It has people who have names you cannot even pronounce. There are great men like Abraham, Elisha, David, Peter, James, John and Paul. There are terrible men like Ahab, Herod, Judas and Demas who deserted Paul for the world. There are great women like, Sarah, Rebekah, Rehab, Ester, Naomi, Deborah, Martha, Mary, and Pricilla. The list is long. There are vicious women like Jezebel. They are capable of murder, adultery, slavery, deceit. We have seen the worst of humanity and the best of humanity.

We have witnessed creation from God's point of view and the fall from first person accounts of Adam and Eve as they spoke to God about their first encounter with evil. There is the downward spiral of humanity till God selects eight individuals to start over with after the great flood. There is a long journey starting with Abraham and Sarah, Isaac and Rebekah, and Jacob with Leah and Rachel. This is followed by Joseph's trip to Egypt and his family's eventual enslavement to Pharaoh. We see Moses stand against Pharaoh and lead the Exodus through the Red Sea, forty years of wandering in the wilderness. There was Joshua and the great victory at Jericho. There are the Judges, Kings, Prophets, Babylonians, Assyrians, Meads and Persians all taking them slaves. We witnessed the rebuilding of the temple and then the 400 years of silence. There is the angelic announcement of the

promised Messiah. We saw the life, death, and resurrection of Jesus. Next came the dramatic birth of the church and its spread throughout the known world. Here, at the end of the Word of God, is the promise of the new heaven and new earth. Here is where we must finally answer the three questions we first asked in Genesis.

JOHN ON PATMOS

Here is the aged apostle of Christ Jesus. He has been exiled to the small island of Patmos by the Roman Emperor Domitian. He is the last of the original twelve disciples who formed the inner circle with Christ. He has already written his gospel memoirs, along with 1st, 2nd & 3rd John. This aged saint has been sent here to die far from the churches he loves and had fought for the greater part of his life. He is among a shrinking number of those who had actually seen Jesus alive after the resurrection. His faith is strong.

It is here on the small Greek island in the Aegean Sea that Jesus again speaks and shows Himself to John. It was a Sunday morning, the Lord's day, when John heard a loud voice behind him. He turned and was greeted by a great sight of seven lampstands and, in the middle of them, was the Son of Man, Jesus, speaking to him. John is given seven clear messages to deliver to seven churches from the Lord. After that, he is given a great vision of the struggle between good and evil. Again and again evil attacks and again and again evil is defeated until finally, there is a vision of the victory and the end of evil.

THE BRIDE AND HER HUSBAND

I have done my share of weddings during the last four decades. There have been brides and grooms of all sizes and different personalities. Families that took the wedding so seriously I thought they would die if anything went wrong, and some that used the weddings to play longstanding family tricks. One family had a stash of rubber floppy animals that came out for every wedding.

They were not sure how it got started, but sometime, someone had placed one in a bunch of flowers, and it just grew from there. They would wait till the very last possible moment and then suddenly, try and put them on everything in sight. There had to be close to one hundred of them. I had heard about it during counseling, so I was not caught off guard when we entered and the place was a cross between an expensive flower shop and a toy store.

There is one moment in every wedding I look forward to and know that, no matter what else is taking place, it will be the highlight of the wedding. The groom is in place with his groomsmen at the front of the church. The bridesmaids have all come in and the music stops. I ask everyone to rise and then, there, in the doorway at the back of the church, is the bride in her gown. She is on the arm of her father who will walk her down the aisle and present her to the groom.

Paul had a vision that I think of every time I see that bride standing in the church doorway.

> *"Then I saw a new heaven and a new earth, for the first heaven and the first earth had passed away, and there was no longer any sea. I saw the Holy City, the new Jerusalem, coming down out of heaven from God, prepared as a bride beautifully dressed for her husband."* Revelation 21.1-2

There is the passing of the old and the beginning of the new. There is the vastness of a new heaven that stretches beyond anything God has done before. The new earth is linked to the eternal and is part of this new heaven. The picture of the Holy City represents the church as she is gathered together to come before God. It has always been God's plan to "*present to Himself the church in all her glory, having no spot or wrinkle or any such thing; but that she would be holy and blameless.*" Ephesians 5.27 Spots come from being sloppy, and wrinkles from being lazy. Those who are God's chosen are neither sloppy nor lazy. They have lived holy, pure, blameless lives.

The doors of heaven are opened. There is God and the church ready to enter. The old world is gone, dealt with, replaced by a new heaven and earth. This is about the final overcoming and defeat of sin. Those entering with God are the final harvest of all those who have defeated sin, with the help of their God and savior.

The vision continues with twelve angels at the twelve gates of heaven. "*On the gates were written the names of the twelve tribes of Israel.*" Rev. 21.12 God has included the faithful from the Old Testament and the Old Covenant. These are those who looked forward to Christ coming and releasing them from their sins. "*There were three gates on the east, three on the north, three on the south and three on the west.*" Rev. 21.13 The saved will come from every direction and from every nation. God has made sure they can find their way in. "*The wall of the city had twelve foundations, and on them were the names of the twelve apostles of the Lamb.*" Rev. 21.14 Jesus has laid this whole victory and the new upon those who were faithful after He left. The twelve apostles represent the original twelve from the day of Pentecost and all those who have been faithful since then. Everything is built on the Lamb of God, the Savior, Messiah, Christ, Lord, Jesus!

The final temple is there, but it is not what most expect to find. It is not a building. "I *did not see a temple in the city, because the Lord God Almighty and the Lamb are its temple.*" Rev. 21.22 This is heaven. It is a place without sin or sinners. It is a place for those who have made a reservation through the blood and resurrection of Jesus. They have their reservations, and, at death, exchange physical bodies for spiritual, eternal ones. Yet, what has it taken for them to walk into this new heaven and new earth?

THE THREE QUESTIONS

Back in the garden Eve and Adam sinned by eating of the forbidden fruit. "*Then the man and his wife heard the sound of the LORD God as he was walking in the garden in the cool of the day, and they hid from the LORD God among the trees of the garden.*" Genesis 3.8 God asked three questions of them that mattered a lot to Him then, and still have to be answered if we are going to get to be part of the new heaven and new earth. We looked at them in the first chapter and will look at them one more time here. You need to be able to answer these. I hope you know the right answers after spending the time on the journey through The Story.

QUESTION #1 – Where are you?

Adam and Eve were hiding because they had sinned. It may not have been called sin then, but that is what it was. The Lord God called out, "*Where are you?*" The question was not because God did not know, it was because they needed to realize the position they were in. Then Adam answered "*I heard you in the garden, and I was afraid because I was naked: so I hid.*" He was already aware of the separation that sin had caused. He had removed himself from God. His actions had broken the bond between him and the living God.

God wanted to know where he was. God also wants to know where you are in your relationship to Him. Adam and Eve were hiding from God. You might think that sounds stupid, but it is no more stupid than people today thinking God cannot see what their lives are like. God is not asking you so He will know; He is asking so you will know you are separated from Him and hiding. It is His way of letting you give yourself a personal evaluation of where you are in life.

So what is your plan to get back into a real relationship with God? Many people think they can get their lives ready to meet God. They think when they are good enough they will be ready and then, they will join up with God. That makes about as much sense as Adam and Eve thinking a few leaves discreetly placed would make everything better. Your spiritual life plan needs to include a new relationship with His Son, Jesus.

The question, "Where are you?" can be either a positive or a negative question. If you are trying to hide from God you are in a whole lot of trouble and need to make a course correction. If you are in a current relationship with God that includes His Son and the Holy Spirit, it is a positive.

QUESTION #2 – Who are you listening to?

There they were in their new fig leaf outfits having a conversation with God. They told Him they had put on the clothes to cover their nakedness. God wanted to know who told them they were naked. In essence God was asking them, "*Who are you listening to*?" They had not learned this on their own, and God had not told them. They had gotten into all this trouble because they were listening to the wrong individual.

Each person needs to answer that same question. Are you listening on the physical level where you cannot see or know the final results of your actions? Here is where temptation rules, and we think we can do anything we want to do. But, we need to remember that, in our relationship with God, He is the adult, and we are the children. He sets the boundaries in life for our protection. He knows what the outcome of making the wrong decision will be. Adam and Eve were told by God not to eat from one tree. They should have listened to Him. Instead, they sought a second opinion and then temptation kicked in. Are you in touch with the living God? Do you spend time with Him in prayer, in His word and with other believers learning, or are you enthralled by the world and all it has to offer?

The alternative is to listen to God and move toward a spiritual relationship with Him through a new birth with His Son, Jesus, and a spirit filled life. If you listen to God He will direct your life and will keep you from making wrong decisions. Here is where a life of faith begins. You as the child, and God, as the adult, directing your life toward maturity till you are finally able to make the right decisions by reflex. Faith says it does not matter if I live or die, you are my God, and I will follow your directions because I am your child. It allows you to trust God because you know He can see the final outcome and knows what is best for you and His kingdom.

QUESTION #3 – What Have you done?

God wanted to know if they had eaten of the tree He had told them not to eat from. This was not for His benefit. It was the first step toward restoring a relationship with God. Confession is part of our restoring a relationship with God. Until we are willing to admit we are sinners and separated from God there is nothing more to be said. They made excuses and found that those who do not repent will pay the price.

What is in your life that needs to be dealt with? The first step is to admit it should not be part of your life and then you need to allow God to help you to make the necessary changes.

The other half of the question is what have you done that you need to keep on doing? The act of doing the right thing over and over is called righteous living or righteousness. This is possible because of a restored relationship with God through His Son. This will lead to a life of obedience and finally becoming a mature Christian believer. You need to form strong spiritual habits that lead you away from temptation and sin and toward a deeper relationship with God.

ARE YOU PREPARED TO CROSS OVER?

God asks three question of every person in one way or another.

1. Where are YOU?
2. Who are YOU listening to?
3. What have YOU done?

These are all personal questions we need to be able to answer. The story is about people. Many of them ended up in the wrong place because they listened to the wrong individuals. Many of them lived lives outside of God's plan. These people failed the test of life and ended up outside of the care of a heavenly Father who wanted only the best for them.

The story is also about people who went the right way. They were people who listened to God and God's messengers; people who lived and did what God approved of.

In the end, it all comes down to the 21st chapter of the book of Revelation. It is a chapter full of contrast. For the believer there is "*the city of pure gold.*" While those who live their lives in open rebellion to God "*their place will be in the fiery lake of burning sulfur.*" It is either eternal rewards or eternal punishment. In the end, we know in heaven, "*Nothing impure will ever enter it, nor will anyone who does what is shameful or deceitful, but only those whose names are written in the Lamb's book of life.*" There is an old gospel song that says, "it is a long, long line, I think I'll die a thousand times, when he opens the book he's gonna see a blank space where my name should be. Lord have mercy on me, it's a long, long line." You cannot wait to make the changes. You need to make the necessary changes in your life starting with turning to Jesus as your personal savior. The scripture is clear. "*man is destined to die once, and after that to face judgment.*" Hebrews 9.27

Answer the questions now and get your life back on track or answer them later when standing in front of God and find yourself like Adam and Eve, cast out and lost.

The choice is clearly yours. The results of how you answer the questions and live your life have eternal results and consequences. Either way, the results are forever and cannot be undone. It is now time for your story to unfold and become part of the eternal plan of God.

Review Chapter 31

Can you identify the following People, Places or dates and tell how they are important to this week's lesson?

1. John
2. Isle of Patmos
3. Jesus
4. Seven Churches
5. Revelations
6. The Lamb
7. King of Kings and Lord of Lords
8. Alpha and Omega
9. Heavenly Temple
10. "The grace of the Lord Jesus be with God's People. Amen."

Page numbers are from The Story (TS)

1. Why was John given the Revelations? Who gave them to him? (TS 459)

2. Who was to get the first message from the Revelations, and why would this seem important? (TS 459)

3. In writing to the church at Ephesus what do we learn they had done right? What had they done wrong? (TS461)

4. Identify the following: The one who sits on the throne, the lamb with seven horns and seven eyes. (TS 464)

5. What else do we learn about this lamb here?

6. How does a person know they are to spend eternity in heaven? (TS 467)

7. What is different about his/her life in heaven?

8. How does a person know he/she is separated eternally from God? (TS 467)

9. What is it like for these individuals?

10. What do we learn about a temple in heaven? (TS 468)

11. Why was this message given, and who sent it? (TS 469)

12. What one thing in this chapter did you learn that can help you on your personal faith journey?

Other books and materials available at
bobhighlands.com

The Real Jesus
Journals and Study Guides
Volumes 1-4

The Journey
The Six basic truths that are
the foundation of the Christian Faith

Is This Heaven For Real
A Biblical exposition
of the book Heaven is For Real

Removing the Mask
A Monograph On Developing Open
Communications in Local Church Leadership

END NOTES

[i] The Story, © 2005, 2008, 2011Published by Zondervan, Grand Rapids Michigan.
[2] From The Emperor Who Ate the Bible, © 1991 Scot Morris, Published by Doubleday.
[3] Glenn Beck & Kevin Balfe, *Being George Washington* (New York: Threshold Editions, Mercury Radio Arts, 2011) 217-218.
[4] I used the words Christ Like separately instead of together Christlike as is standard. This is for emphasis and to make clear the meaning of the expression leading up to the disciples and followers of Jesus being called Christians or Christ like.
[5] Charles R. Swindoll, Living on the Ragged EDGE (New York: Guidepost, 1985) This book is an excellent look at the book of Ecclesiastes and the wisdom of Solomon.
[6] Also written by Solomon
[7] Hebrews 6.1-2 list six foundational teaching of the church every believer should know and understand.
[8] http://www.barna.org/barna-update/article/13-culture/111-survey-explores-who-qualifies-as-an-evangelical?q=percentage+evangelicals accessed 6-8-2012
[9] copyright (c) Sony/ATV Music Publishing LLC
[10] http://articles.chicagotribune.com/2011-06-24/news/sc-cons-0623-karpspend-20110624_1_amish-way-amish-community-horse-drawn-buggies Accessed February 12, 2013 The article was taken from the book by Lorilee Craker, author of "Money Secrets of the Amish: Finding True Abundance in Simplicity, Sharing and Saving.
[11] IBID
[12] IBID
[13] Beelzebub is the name Jesus called Satan. (Matthew 12.25-28) Beelzebub means Lord of the Flies.
[14] http://www.sermoncentral.com/pastors-preaching-articles/steve-murrell-seven-deadly-sins-in-the-pulpit-1309.asp (accessed July 18, 2012) I used his opening and the first three key points from his article. Beyond that it is an original message. Thanks Steve, I always enjoy your articles and your messages.
[15]Http://townhall.com/tipsheet/katiepavlich/2012/09/11/as_chicago_teachers_strike_79_percent_of_students_cant_read
[16] http://shepherdsnotes.com/?p=3048 accessed March 27, 2013
[17] Word can be translated life or soul. Soul is used here in both instances to emphasis the spiritual and eternal consequences of these decisions.
[18] Acts 20.4, Ephesians 6.21, Colossians 4.7, 2 Timothy 4.12, Titus 3.12
[19] See Malcolm Gladwell, Outliers The Story of Success (New York: Little Brown and Company, 2008) Chapter three
[20] Inspired by the message "Building Margins and Resources" by Wayne Cordeiro accessed 11-4-2009 at Http://sermoncentral.com/print_friendly.asp?ContributorID=&SermonID=114108

Made in the USA
San Bernardino, CA
11 January 2014